The Paris Cookbook

ALSO BY PATRICIA WELLS

Patricia Wells at Home in Provence

Patricia Wells' Trattoria

Simply French

Bistro Cooking

The Food Lover's Guide to France

The Food Lover's Guide to Paris

The Paris

COOKBOOK

PATRICIA WELLS

HarperCollinsPublishers

FIRST EDITION

Designed by Vertigo Design, NYC
Photographs by Owen Franken

Printed on acid-free paper

LIBRARY OF CONGRESS CATALOGING-IN-PUBLICATION DATA
Wells, Patricia.
The Paris cookbook / Patricia Wells.—1st ed.
    p.   cm.
ISBN 0-06-018469-8
1. Cookery, French. 2. Cookery—France—Paris. I. Title.
TX719 .W428 2001
641.5944—dc21   2001016704

01 02 03 04 05 ❖/RRD 10 9 8 7 6 5

For Julia Child and Joël Robuchon, two people who have had a dramatic influence on my life. With immense gratitude for their example, their inspiration, and their support and encouragement.

Contents

ACKNOWLEDGMENTS

After more than two glorious decades of life in Paris, the greatest acknowledgment goes to the city itself, a place in the world that is born anew with each day, every moment a surprise and an inspiration.

But people are the ones who affect me the most deeply, and I owe thanks to every baker and chef, fruit and vegetable merchant, fishmonger and butcher, pastry chef and simple cook, who has enhanced my life here. Thanks to the known and the unknown.

My life would be much less enriched without having met the chefs and artisans who still serve as my teachers and mentors: Joël Robuchon, Guy Savoy, Jean-Claude Vrinat, Alain Dutournier, baker Lionel Poilâne; those no longer in Paris, such as the dear Pile ou Face trio of Alain Dumergue, Claude Udron, and Philippe Marquet; and those no longer at the stove, such as the famed Antoine Magnin from L'Ami Louis and the indefatigable Adrienne Biasin from Chez la Vieille.

I want to say a special thanks to those who make my life that much easier by eagerly joining me at restaurants known and unknown, beginning with my husband, Walter (who after twenty-one years never says no to yet another meal out), friends Susan and Michael Loomis, Pat Thompson and Jim Bitterman, Rita and Yale Kramer, Devon Fredericks and Eli Zabar, Ina and Jeffrey Garten, Dorie and Michael Greenspan.

In the publishing world, many people have helped this book see the light of day. A special thank-you to Susan Friedland.

INTRODUCTION
A LIFE OF MOVEABLE FEASTS

When I moved to Paris during the first week of January 1980, there was no way to know it would be "for good." My husband and I had both left jobs as journalists at the *New York Times*—Walter as an assistant national editor and I as a food writer—to live in Paris for two years. That week, Walter began his job as the new deputy editor of the *International Herald Tribune* and I began life as a freelance writer.

I was thirty-three years old and had an immense passion for food, and for learning all there was to know about it. And Paris seemed to be the perfect spot for my little sabbatical, the ideal city to use as my testing and tasting ground for what I call my Ph.D. in food.

In those early years, my greatest luxury was time. Walter worked long days, and I was alone all day and late into the evening. So I walked and I wandered this all-embracing city, pressing my nose against pastry shop windows and *boulangeries*, making regular pilgrimages to the famed Androuët cheese shop (then in the 9th arrondissement near the place de Clichy), sampling food from every bistro on my ever-growing list of spots to try, studying the menus posted outside every eating place in town, and weaving my way through the surprising number of restaurants run by young up-and-coming chefs with names like Guy Savoy, Joël Robuchon, and Alain Dutournier.

I remember my first visit to the rue Poncelet outdoor food market in our new neighborhood on the Right Bank. It was a cold, dark afternoon in January when I literally stumbled upon the market as I was exploring the blocks that fanned off from our home on rue Daru. I almost cried with joy when I saw it, marveling at the array of gorgeous, impeccably displayed fruits and vegetables, fish, meats, and poultry. I was shocked to see rabbits on display, hanging by their still-attached furry feet, and an entire bristly wild boar—head, feet, and all—carefully draped over a table outside the butcher's shop. I was awed by all the sounds I heard as vendors hawked and cajoled, teased and shouted. And I could not believe my good fortune.

A combination of innocence and naïveté, energy and enthusiasm, and an intense curiosity for all things culinary and French propelled me through life in those days. Everything, it seemed, was new. And everything was worth commenting upon and reporting. Soon I began my regular restaurant reviews for the *International Herald Tribune* and sent regular dispatches to the *New York Times*, *Travel & Leisure*, and *Food & Wine*.

Two years grew into three, and before we knew it, returning "home" to New York was no longer a topic of conversation. I had begun a new career, had started writing books, and quite literally never looked back.

Paris was now our home. And on Walter's free evenings when we were not dining out, I was learning how to use the huge lineup of fresh ingredients that were all so new to me. There was so much material for great meals: rabbit and game, the immense variety of fish and shellfish, the brilliant selection of meats, the tender young vegetables, juicy fresh fruits, not to mention the tempting selection of cheeses.

Years before, as a novice cook, a favorite pastime had been to try to reproduce dishes I sampled in restaurants. Now, in Paris, I not only had this embarrassingly rich larder, but I also had thousands of cookbooks, a codified cuisine, and a nation full of Frenchmen and -women willing to share each and every recipe.

As part of my restaurant reviewing research, I regularly spent mornings in restaurant kitchens, to see what really went on behind the scenes and to gather knowledge as well cooking tips and recipes.

This, my latest book, really began that first month of

January 1980. For twenty years Paris and its markets, its people, its restaurants, have been my classroom. Wherever I go, it seems, people talk to me about food: in the dentist's chair, at the hairdresser's, in taxis, and of course in markets and at restaurants. I am constantly jotting down tips and *trucs*, recipes and menu ideas on the back of receipts or strips of paper. I never stop learning, and I doubt that food will ever be a topic that does not interest me immensely.

Paris as a city, France as a country, and the world of food as a whole have changed tremendously since those early days. Then, there were perhaps two or three varieties of potatoes in the markets; today there are a dozen or more. Paris markets now offer delicious tomatoes all year round, excellent varieties of strawberries throughout the year, and it seems that the selection of fresh and wild mushrooms, the variety of fish and shellfish, the choice of new and aged cheeses, the shape, color, and style of breads, grow by the day.

Yet, happily, France remains a nation of tradition. And so this cookbook includes many of the most classic and renowned of French dishes: A classic Tarte Tatin from chef Benoît Guichard at Jamin. The late-night bistro favorite, French Onion Soup, from the Left Bank Brasserie Balzar. An outrageously rich and irresistible version of Potatoes Anna from chef David Van Laer. And a classic Hanger Steak from one of my preferred wine bars, Le Mauzac. For dessert, La Maison du Chocolat agreed to share their scrumptious chocolate mousse, and a Left Bank pastry shop, La Bonbonnerie de Buci, provided inspiration for a puckery lemon tart.

Cafés and bistros suggest an entire collection of traditional salads, and here I share Allard's Lamb's Lettuce and Beets, Café Bonaparte's Chicken Salad, and Le Nemrod's

Auvergne-Style Salad. The modern world loves greens too, so I have included such contemporary creations as Le Cap Vernet's Salade à la Maraîchère, as well as Le Bistro Mazarin's Spinach, Bacon, Avocado, and Tomato Salad. Not to mention *the* salad of the 1980s, Joël Robuchon's Salade Pastorale, a veritable festival of greens and fresh herbs.

Paris remains on the cutting edge of modern cuisine, and so it is only fitting that this cookbook offers some popular contemporary fare, such as Noirmoutier Potatoes with Fleur de Sel, Slow-Roasted Salmon with Sorrel Sauce, chef William Ledeuil's Fresh Cod Brandade and his remarkable Cream of Corn Soup from the bistro Les Bookinistes, along with Tante Louise's innovative Caramelized Cauliflower Soup with Foie Gras.

My daily trips to markets around Paris inspired many of the recipes between these pages, such as the Boulevard Raspail Cream of Mushroom Soup from the Sunday morning organic market; a Wednesday morning discovery—a delicious wintertime Guinea Hen with Sauerkraut—from the place Monge market; and one of my favorite recipes in the entire book, The Apple Lady's Apple Cake from the Left Bank market in the shadow of the Eiffel Tower, the row of stands that stretch out along the avenue de Breteuil each Thursday and Saturday morning.

Grand Parisian restaurants continue to offer daily inspiration and learning, in the form of Taillevent's Cream of Watercress Soup with Caviar, Pré Catelan's Four-Hour Roast Pork, Guy Savoy's amazing Lentil Ragout with Truffles, and a vegetable dish inspired by L'Ambroisie's chef-owner Bernard Pacaud, in the form of a perky and simply sublime dish of White Beans with Mustard and Sage.

Fish restaurants offer their share of stimulus, with Le Duc's very simple and satisfying Hot Curried Oysters; the unforgettable Sole Meunière, with tips from Le Dôme's chef Frank Graux; the outgoing Gérard Allemandou's easy and ethereal Sea Scallops with Warm Vinaigrette from his trendy bistro La Cagouille; and the Dôme's bistro favorite, Clams with Fresh Thyme.

Paris restaurants offer an almost endless choice of specialties from all the regions of France, and I have included a sampling of dishes from throughout the country: from the Auvergne, a rich salad of flinty lentils from the Ambassade d'Auvergne; from the Basque region, a spicy-crusted leg of lamb from Jean-Guy Lousteau's bistro Au Bascou; and of course from Alsace, the fortifying, invigorating regional specialty of sausages, meats, and sauerkraut, *choucroute,* from the lively wine bar Alsaco.

The French—and Parisians in particular—never seem to get enough of a sweet thing, and so the dessert chapter is overflowing with some of my favorites, many of them inspired by the fruits of the market. From rue Poncelet's Cherries in Sweet Red Wine, to a Fresh Fig and Almond Gratin, and on to a popular and easy-to-make Ultra-Thin Apple Tart, fresh fruits have their moment in the sun.

This, then, is *my* Paris. You may not be able to spend a day or a week, a month or a year, in this remarkable city, but in opening my kitchen to you I hope that you can stroll through the markets with me, walk from one end of town to the next, share specialties from my favorite cafés, bistros, wine bars, markets, cheese shops, and restaurants, and let Paris live in your soul, in your kitchen, and in your home every day of the year.

The Paris Cookbook

ASPARAGUS VELOUTÉ

MOLARD'S HAM AND GOAT CHEESE WRAPS

TAILLEVENT GOAT CHEESE AND DRIED TOMATO APPETIZER

ARTICHOKES AND GOAT CHEESE CHEZ MICHEL

TOASTY SALTED ALMONDS

DOMAINE SAINT LUC'S CAKE AUX OLIVES

RUE SAINT-DOMINIQUE "CAVIAR"

ARPÈGE EGGS WITH MAPLE SYRUP

APPETIZERS, STARTERS, AND FIRST COURSES
Les Hors d'Oeuvres et les Entrées

LEDOYEN'S QUICK SAUTÉED FOIE GRAS WITH GARLIC AND LEMON PURÉE

LAURENT'S FOIE GRAS WITH SPICY BLACK BEANS

HORS D'OEUVRES VARIÉS: CARROTS, BEETS, AND CELERY ROOT
REMOULADE

JR'S PARMESAN CHIPS

CHUNKY GREEN OLIVE PISTOU-TAPENADE

BLACK OLIVE TAPENADE

MARINATED RED PEPPERS

MARINATED PARIS MUSHROOMS

SCRAMBLED EGGS WITH TRUFFLES

ASPARAGUS VELOUTÉ

Velouté d'Asperges

Parisian restaurants are famous for getting the most out of every ingredient. I confess that in the past, I have been a bit wasteful with asparagus. I love the sweet green tips and the tender portion of this magical vegetable, but when it comes to those often tough and woody stems, I am less charmed. However, in the course of studying what restaurant chefs do to come up with creative new *amuse-bouches*, "surprise starters" or appetizers, I discovered an excellent way to deal with the tougher portion of the asparagus: Whenever I cook asparagus, I cut off the woody ends and freeze them, and when I have enough, I make this smooth, rich, brilliant green soup, which I serve in tiny portions as a first course. Be sure to include a good part of the green portion of the leek—it helps to keep the soup a gorgeous green color. Hot or cold, this surprise starter always attracts raves.

2 tablespoons extra-virgin olive oil

Fine sea salt to taste

1 leek, white portion and most of the green, rinsed and cut into thin rings

About 1 pound green asparagus stems, finely chopped

About 1½ cups Homemade Chicken Stock (page 297)

EQUIPMENT:
A food processor; a food mill.

4 SERVINGS

1. In a large pot, combine the oil, a pinch of sea salt, and the leeks. Cover and sweat (cook over low heat without allowing the vegetable to color) until soft and translucent, about 5 minutes. Add the asparagus, cover, and sweat about 5 minutes more. Add the chicken stock, cover, and simmer over low heat for 15 minutes.

2. Transfer the mixture to the bowl of a food processor, and process to a purée. Pass the soup through the fine blade of a food mill to remove any remaining fibers and create a perfectly smooth, velvety texture. Taste for seasoning. Transfer to small espresso cups and serve hot or cold.

MOLARD'S HAM AND GOAT CHEESE WRAPS

La Bûchette Charcutière de la Fromagerie Molard

Something wonderful happens to young, fresh goat cheese when it is warmed and melted, especially when it is wrapped in a fragrant bundle of smoky bacon. The marriage of the cured meat and the cheese makes two plus two taste like twenty-five, as the sweet lactic flavor of the cheese merges with the smoky richness of the bacon. My favorite version of this now common Parisian appetizer—seen at many cheese shops and outdoor markets—comes from the reputable cheese shop Molard, situated along the lively rue des Martyrs market street in the city's 9th arrondissement. Serve this as an appetizer, with a tossed green salad alongside.

About 1 tablespoon minced fresh herbs, such as chives, chervil, tarragon, or thyme, or a mixture

4 small goat cheese rounds (each about 2 ounces)

8 extra-thin slices smoked bacon, pancetta, or smoked ham (each about $1^{1}/_{2} \times 8$ inches)

4 SERVINGS

1. Sprinkle the herbs on both sides of each goat cheese round, pressing down lightly so they adhere to the cheese.

2. Wrap two slices of bacon, crisscross fashion, around each round of goat cheese. (The goat cheese can be prepared to this stage up to 8 hours in advance. Cover and keep the cheese in a cool spot.)

3. Heat a large nonstick skillet over moderate heat. Add the wrapped cheese and cook until the meat is browned, about 2 minutes per side. Serve immediately.

La Maison du Fromage "Molard"

48, RUE DES MARTYRS
PARIS 9
TELEPHONE: 01 45 26 84 88
MÉTRO: NOTRE-DAME DE LORETTE

I always associate goat cheese with the flinty flavor of a white Sancerre, for that's where—in the Loire Valley—I tasted my first goat cheese many years ago. Whatever you choose, make sure it is chilled, dry, and white.

TAILLEVENT GOAT CHEESE AND DRIED TOMATO APPETIZER

L'Amuse-Gueule de Taillevent

In October 1999, Michel Del Burgo took over the kitchens of the famed Taillevent. This simple appetizer—what is called an *amuse-gueule*, or palate teaser—was the first creation I sampled from his hands. When I dipped my demitasse spoon into this ethereal, pungent mixture, I knew that Del Burgo was on a successful path. This has become a favorite for entertaining since it is quick, easy, and can be prepared in advance. It is delicious both hot and at room temperature.

In the bowl of a food processor, combine the goat cheese, chives, and 1 teaspoon oil. Process to blend. Add additional oil if the mixture is too firm. Spoon the mixture into 8 porcelain egg cups. Then spoon a thin layer of Sun-Dried Tomato Paste over the cheese. (The egg cups can be prepared up to 2 hours in advance and stored, covered, at room temperature.) Serve at room temperature. Or to serve warm, place the egg cups beneath a preheated broiler and grill until the tomato paste sizzles, about 1 minute.

Champagne, always champagne.

5 ounces fresh goat cheese

2 tablespoons finely minced fresh chives

About 1 teaspoon extra-virgin olive oil

About 2 tablespoons Sun-Dried Tomato Paste (page 299)

EQUIPMENT:
8 porcelain egg cups or miniature ramekins; a food processor.

8 SERVINGS

Taillevent

15, RUE LAMMENAIS
PARIS 8
TELEPHONE: 01 44 95 15 01
FAX: 01 42 25 95 18
MÉTRO: CHARLES DE
GAULLE—ETOILE OR GEORGE V

ARTICHOKES AND GOAT CHEESE CHEZ MICHEL

Fondant d'Artichaut au Fromage de Chèvre Chez Michel

I sampled this appealing first course the first time I visited the reincarnated Chez Michel in the 1980s. The dish combines all the foods I love: artichokes, goat cheese, salad greens, and basil, all pulled together with my home-made vinaigrette.

1. Preheat the broiler.

2. In the bowl of a food processor, combine the goat cheese and oil and process until smooth. Spread the cheese mixture into the hollows of the artichoke bottoms, smoothing it out with a spatula. Arrange the artichoke bottoms side by side on a baking sheet. Place the baking sheet on an oven rack about 3 inches from the heat. Broil until the cheese is golden brown and bubbly, 2 to 3 minutes.

3. Meanwhile, toss the *mesclun* with the basil chiffonnade. Toss the salad with the vinaigrette. Arrange the salad on 4 large salad plates, place two grilled artichoke bottoms alongside each portion, and serve.

With this I sampled the Mâcon-Villages Mâcon-Clessé, a well-made white Burgundy from winemaker Jean Thévenet's Domaine de Bongrand. It is a remarkably big and fragrant white, and one that pairs well with goat cheese and artichokes.

3 ounces soft goat cheese

2 tablespoons extra-virgin olive oil

8 frozen artichoke bottoms, thawed

8 cups (about 4 ounces loosely packed *mesclun* (see page 45)

20 fresh basil leaves, cut into a chiffonnade

Classic Vinaigrette (page 278) to taste

EQUIPMENT:
A food processor.

4 SERVINGS

Chez Michel

10, RUE BELZUNCE
PARIS 10
TELEPHONE: 01 44 53 06 20
FAX: 01 44 53 61 31
MÉTRO: Poissonnière or
GARE DU NORD

TOASTY SALTED ALMONDS

Amandes Salées Poêlées

I love almonds, and I am always looking for ways to introduce a new almond appetizer into my repertoire. This is a "back of the box" recipe from a package of French Vanihé brand almonds. The whole almonds are toasted in a skillet while you spray them with a fine shower of brine. The salt spray creates a delicate white film on the almonds. That salty tang on the tongue wakes up the palate and puts our appetite in gear.

1 teaspoon fine sea salt
1 cup whole unblanched
    almonds

EQUIPMENT:
A perfume atomizer or
    small garden mister.

1 CUP

1. Fill a perfume atomizer or a small garden mister with 4 tablespoons water and the sea salt. Shake to dissolve the salt.

2. Place the almonds in a dry skillet over moderate heat. Cook, stirring or shaking the pan frequently to prevent burning, spraying from time to time, until the almonds are toasted, covered with a delicate white film, and beginning to release their fragrance, about 4 minutes total. Transfer the nuts to a baking sheet to cool. Serve at room temperature. (The almonds can be stored, covered, in a cool dry place for up to 2 weeks.)

Any aperitif wine is ideal here: Champagne, a fino (dry) sherry, a Riesling, or a Chenin Blanc.

DOMAINE SAINT LUC'S CAKE AUX OLIVES

Cake aux Olives Domaine Saint Luc

Eliane Cornillon is one of the best home cooks I know. When in Provence we often share a meal at the lively *ferme auberge* (a working farm that takes in guests and serves a family meal each evening to them) of her and her husband, Ludovic, sipping away at Ludovic Cornillon's fine wines. We are lucky enough to find his wines at many restaurants, as well as wine shops, in Paris. This moist and fragrant light olive cake always receives raves, and I thank Eliane for sharing it with me. At home I serve this either as an appetizer, sliced and then cut into cubes, or as a first course, plated and served with fresh tomato sauce alongside. While black olives are traditional in the French olive cake, you can used pitted green olives or a combination.

1. Butter a 6-cup loaf pan (preferably nonstick), and set it aside.

2. In a large bowl, combine the flour, baking powder, and salt, and stir to blend. Slowly add the eggs, whisking to incorporate. Whisk in the milk, cheese, olives, and oil. Set aside for 2 hours to allow the flour to absorb the liquids (making for a lighter cake).

4 tablespoons all-purpose flour

2 teaspoons baking powder

½ teaspoon salt

4 large eggs, lightly beaten

1 cup whole milk

3 ounces (1 cup) freshly grated Parmigiano-Reggiano or Swiss Gruyère cheese

1 scant cup black Nyons olives, pitted and halved lengthwise

1 tablespoon extra-virgin olive oil

About 1 cup homemade Tomato Sauce (page 300; optional)

EQUIPMENT:
A 6-cup rectangular loaf pan, preferably nonstick.

8 SERVINGS

3. Preheat the oven to 425 degrees F.

4. Stir the batter to blend once again. Pour the batter into the prepared loaf pan. Place in the center of the oven and bake until firm and golden, about 30 minutes. Serve at room temperature, sliced and cut into cubes. Or to serve as a first course, slice and serve with fresh tomato sauce.

This cake can easily be paired with a fragrant white wine, or with one of the more powerful Côtes du Rhône, such as Ludovic Cornillon's Domaine St. Luc Coteaux du Tricastan.

You can find Ludovic Cornillon's wines at

Cave Miard

9, RUE DES QUATRE-VENTS
PARIS 6
TELEPHONE: 01 43 54 99 30
FAX: 01 44 07 27 73
MÉTRO: ODÉON

RUE SAINT-DOMINIQUE "CAVIAR"

"Caviar" Rue Saint-Dominique

On my first visit to Christian Constant's Left Bank restaurant, Le Violin d'Ingres, on the rue Saint-Dominique, the waiter arrived with crusty rolls accompanied by a generous pat of butter sprinkled with this vibrant salt, pepper, and spice mixture—which I've now dubbed Rue Saint-Dominique "Caviar." What a delightful way to change the way one looks at "buttered bread." This simple blend of coarsely ground black pepper, white pepper, and allspice combined with the precious *fleur de sel* makes for a palate-opening accent that is particularly delicious spread on tangy sourdough bread. I keep a batch of this in a separate pepper mill, and guests never fail to ask, "What's in it?"

2 tablespoons black
   peppercorns (preferably
   Indian Tellicherry)
2 tablespoons white
   peppercorns
2 tablespoons allspice
   berries
Unsalted butter, at room
   temperature
Fleur de sel (see page 102)
   or fine sea salt to taste

½ CUP

Combine the peppercorns and allspice berries in a pepper mill. At serving time, place several pats of butter on a small plate. Coarsely grind the spice mix over the butter. Sprinkle with a touch of *fleur de sel,* and serve.

Le Violin d'Ingres

135, RUE SAINT-DOMINIQUE
PARIS 7
TELEPHONE: 01 45 55 15 05
FAX: 01 45 55 48 42
MÉTRO: ECOLE MILITAIRE

ARPÈGE EGGS WITH MAPLE SYRUP

Le Chaudfroid d'Oeufs au Sirop d'Erable d'Arpège

Ninety percent of the time, my first impressions remain unchanged for life. The first time I sampled Alain Passard's food at Arpège, in the very early 1980s, I was not terribly impressed. Save for his brilliant chocolate puff pastry, which I had sampled at his previous restaurant in the Paris suburbs, I just couldn't figure out what all the fuss was about. But palates I respected urged me on, and I persisted. After about half a dozen visits to Arpège, in Paris's 7th arrondissement, I became a convert, and today I remain one of Passard's staunchest advocates. One dish that won me over immediately was this adorable palate pleaser that appeared out of nowhere at the beginning of a meal, a surprising mixture of egg, cream, maple syrup, and sherry vinegar all served in the shell—an appetizer that properly awakens your palate with a jolt of surprise and a clap of acclamation. I knew that Passard's wife was Canadian, so it was no surprise to find maple syrup on his menu. But it's his unusual use of this very special sweetener that sets it apart: With the richness of the egg and the sweetness of the maple syrup, set off by the slightly acidic cream, this is a true *amuse-bouche*. When preparing this, be sure to have a few extra eggs on hand, for there is always a chance that one shell will crack. This recipe is a little tricky at first, but once you get the knack, you will make it over and over again.

4 tablespoons heavy cream

About ¾ teaspoon sherry vinegar, or to taste

Sea salt to taste

6 very fresh eggs, at room temperature

2 teaspoons finely minced fresh chives

Freshly ground black pepper to taste

About 2 teaspoons maple syrup

EQUIPMENT:

An egg cutter or a very sharp knife; 6 porcelain egg cups.

6 SERVINGS

1. Place a bowl in the freezer for at least 30 minutes. In the chilled bowl, whisk the cream until soft peaks form. Season with the sherry vinegar and sea salt. Set aside.

2. Place an egg in your hand, tapered end up. Using an egg cutter or a very sharp knife, carefully slice off about the top third of the eggshell. Carefully pour the egg white out of the shell into a small bowl, holding back the yolk with the flat side of a knife. (Reserve the white for another use.) With a damp paper towel, wipe the bottom of the shell. Place the shell in a porcelain egg cup. (If you return the eggs to the egg carton, they are likely to stick and will be impossible to remove later.) Repeat with the remaining eggs.

3. Select a large, shallow skillet that is large enough to hold the eggshells in a single layer. Add water to about 2 inches in depth. Bring just to a simmer.

Although this dish can easily stand alone without an accompanying wine, it is perfect with a glass of champagne, or with whatever white wine you will be enjoying with your first course.

WHAT'S AN EGG CUTTER?

AN EGG CUTTER IS A SMALL UTENSIL, made sometimes of metal and sometimes of metal and plastic, that can be used to cleanly cut off the top third of an egg. The utensil can be found in most well-equipped kitchenware shops.

4. Carefully lift the eggshells from the egg cups and place them in the simmering water (the eggshells should just bob on top of the water). Cook just until the yolk begins to set around the edges, about 3 minutes. Using your fingertips, carefully remove the eggshells from the water and return them to the egg cups.

5. Sprinkle each cooked egg yolk with minced chives. Season with sea salt and pepper. Then carefully spoon the whipped cream over the yolk up to the rim of each egg cup. Drizzle with maple syrup, and serve immediately.

Arpège

84, RUE DE VARENNE
PARIS 7
TELEPHONE: 01 45 51 47 33
FAX: 01 44 18 98 39
MÉTRO: VARENNE

Chef Alain Passard of Arpège

LEDOYEN'S QUICK SAUTÉED FOIE GRAS WITH GARLIC AND LEMON PURÉE

Le Foie Gras Poêlée, Purée d'Ail et de Citron de Ledoyen

When I spend time in restaurant kitchens, I like to sleuth about, sticking my nose in pots and asking questions. How else is one to learn? When passing a morning with chef Christian Le Squer at Ledoyen one spring day, I inquired about the whole cloves of garlic simmering away on the stove. Le Squer explained that the garlic was cooked in milk until tender, then peeled and puréed with cubes of lemon. The purée serves as a lively, refreshing condiment for slices of seared fresh foie gras. I also love to use the puckery, pungent creation as a condiment for roasted meats and poultry.

1. Prepare the garlic and lemon purée: Place the garlic in a small saucepan. Cover with about 2 cups of the milk. Bring just to a simmer over moderate heat. Pour the garlic and milk into a fine-mesh sieve, and discard the milk. Return the garlic to the pan, cover with the remaining 2 cups milk, and simmer, uncovered, over low heat until the garlic is soft and a small knife inserted into a clove meets no resistance, about 20 minutes. Let the garlic cool in the milk. Gently press the garlic cloves between your fingers, releasing them from their skin. Transfer the garlic cloves to the bowl of a food processor, and purée. Add the diced lemon and pulse

THE GARLIC AND LEMON PURÉE

4 plump, fresh heads garlic, separated into cloves but skin intact

1 quart whole milk

1 lemon, preferably organic, rinsed, sliced, and cut into a small dice

Fine sea salt to taste

THE FOIE GRAS

1 fresh duck foie gras (1 to 1½ pounds)

Fleur de sel (see page 102) or fine sea salt to taste

Coarsely ground white pepper to taste

2 tablespoons finely minced fresh chives

EQUIPMENT:

A food processor.

4 TO 6 SERVINGS

just to blend. Add salt to taste. (The purée can be stored, covered and refrigerated, for up to 2 days.)

2. Prepare the foie gras: Note that a duck liver consists of two lobes, one small and one large. With the tip of a small, sharp knife, carefully remove any traces of green from the surface of the foie gras. With your hands, separate the larger lobe from the smaller lobe by pulling them apart gently. With the tip of a small, sharp knife, remove the thin, transparent skin surrounding each piece of duck liver. With the tip of the knife remove and discard the thin red blood vessel that runs lengthwise through the inside of each lobe. With a sharp knife, slice the foie gras diagonally into scallops about ¾ inch thick. Cover with plastic wrap and refrigerate until serving time.

3. Heat a large nonstick skillet until it is very hot. Add the foie gras and sear for 30 seconds on each side, turning the pieces carefully with tongs. Transfer the cooked foie gras to a platter covered with paper towels, and allow to drain. Sprinkle with *fleur de sel*, white pepper, and the chives. Transfer to warmed salad plates.

4. Place a small spoonful of the Garlic and Lemon Purée alongside the foie gras, and serve.

Fresh foie gras can be ordered from D'Artagnan, Inc., 399–419 Saint Paul Avenue, Jersey City, New Jersey 07306; telephone (201) 792-0748. Ask for "Moulard Duck foie gras A Prime." The foie gras arrives vacuum-packed in heavy plastic, and before cooking has about a 10-day shelf life.

Certainly the most traditional wine with foie gras is Sauternes, but don't limit it to the sweet, famed Bordeaux. Try a Riesling or a Gewürztraminer, a wine with its own lemony tang.

Ledoyen

CARRÉ DES CHAMPS-ELYSÉES
PARIS 8
TELEPHONE: 01 53 05 10 01
FAX: 01 47 42 55 01
MÉTRO: CHAMPS ELYSÉES–
CLÉMENCEAU

APPETIZERS, STARTERS, AND FIRST COURSES

LAURENT'S FOIE GRAS WITH
SPICY BLACK BEANS

Foie Gras aux Haricots Noirs Pimentés de Laurent

I first sampled this elegant dish of spicy black beans and foie gras at the grand Parisian restaurant Laurent, where chef Philippe Braun manages to surprise us with dishes, such as this one, that totally stray from the French tradition. Here, the spice serves as a perfect foil for the richness of foie gras. Note the double smokiness of flavors and aromas, from both the smoked bacon and the smoky hot red pepper. When chef Braun is not into surprising us, his repertoire might include the most sublime and simple of French fare, such as a thick and meaty veal chop teamed up with green asparagus from Provence and spring morel mushrooms. There are few restaurants as romantic as Laurent, whether you are indoors listening to the soothing music coming from the baby grand piano or, in good weather, seated at one of the precious tables set at the edge of the gardens of the Champs Elysées.

1. Prepare the foie gras: Note that a duck liver consists of two lobes, one small and one large. With the tip of a small, sharp knife, carefully remove any traces of green from the surface of the foie gras. With your hands, separate the larger lobe from the smaller lobe by pulling them apart gently. With the tip of a small, sharp knife, remove the thin, transparent skin surrounding each piece of duck

THE FOIE GRAS

1 fresh duck foie gras (1 to 1½ pounds)

1 teaspoon coarsely ground black pepper

2 tablespoons finely minced fresh chives

1 teaspoon *fleur de sel* (see page 102) or fine sea salt

THE BLACK BEANS

1 pound dried black beans

1½ quarts Homemade Chicken Stock (page 297), plus additional as necessary

2 ounces smoked bacon, in a single slice

3 plump, fresh cloves garlic, peeled, halved, and green germ removed

1 onion, peeled and halved

liver. With the tip of the knife remove and discard the thin red blood vessel that runs lengthwise through the inside of each lobe. With a sharp knife, slice the foie gras diagonally into a total of four scallops, each about 4 ounces. Cover with plastic wrap and refrigerate until serving time.

2. Preheat the oven to 350 degrees F.

3. Prepare the black beans: Bring 1½ quarts of water to a boil in large ovenproof saucepan or casserole. When the water boils, add the black beans and cook just until the water returns to a boil, 1 to 2 minutes. Remove the pan from the heat and drain the beans, discarding the water. Return the beans to the pan. Cover with the stock. Add the bacon, garlic, onion, tomato, bell pepper, hot pepper, coarse sea salt, and bouquet garni. Cover and place in the center of the oven. Bake until the beans are tender, 2½ to 3 hours. (The cooking time will depend upon the freshness of the beans. Younger beans cook more quickly than older beans.)

4. Once the beans are cooked, transfer about 2 ladlefuls of the beans and several tablespoons of the cooking liquid to a small saucepan. Cover and keep warm.

5. Remove the bacon, onion, hot pepper, and bouquet garni from the large pan of beans, and discard. Leave the bell pepper and the garlic with the beans. Transfer the beans and remaining cooking liquid to the bowl of a food processor and purée. (The purée should be fairly liquid, not a thick paste. If necessary, thin it with additional chicken stock.) Place a food mill fitted with a medium grid on top of a large saucepan. Pass the purée through the

1 tomato, cored, peeled, seeded, and chopped

1 red bell pepper, trimmed and cut into fine cubes

1 small smoked hot pepper, such as a chipolte adobado, or to taste

2 teaspoons coarse sea salt

1 bouquet garni: several sprigs fresh or dried thyme, several ribs celery, and several sprigs fresh parsley, tied securely with cotton string

6 tablespoons heavy cream

10 tablespoons unsalted butter, softened

EQUIPMENT:
A food mill; a food processor or a handheld immersion blender.

4 SERVINGS

mill into the saucepan. Stir in the cream and 6 table-spoons of the butter. Taste for seasoning. Process the mixture in a food processor or with a handheld immersion blender until emulsified and smooth. Keep warm.

6. Add the remaining 4 tablespoons butter to the whole beans in the small saucepan. Keep warm.

7. Heat a large nonstick skillet until it is very hot. Add the foie gras and sear for 30 seconds on each side, turning the pieces carefully with tongs. Transfer the cooked foie gras to a platter covered with paper towels, and allow to drain. Sprinkle with the black pepper, chives, and *fleur de sel.*

8. Pour a ladleful of the puréed bean mixture into each of four warmed shallow soup bowls. Spoon the whole beans on top. Place the foie gras on top of the whole beans, and serve immediately.

Fresh foie gras can be ordered from D'Artagnan, Inc., 399–419 Saint Paul Avenue, Jersey City, New Jersey 07306; telephone (201) 792-0748. Ask for "Moulard Duck foie gras A Prime." The foie gras arrives vacuum-packed in heavy plastic, and before cooking has about a 10-day shelf life.

Laurent's sommelier Patrick Lair suggests two very different wines to accompany this racy dish: either a Tokay Pinot Gris from Trimbach, vintage 1995, or Pierre Gaillard's Côte Rôtie "Rose Pourpre" 1996.

Laurent

41, AVENUE GABRIEL
PARIS 8
TELEPHONE: 01 42 25 00 39
FAX: 01 45 62 45 21
MÉTRO: CHAMPS ELYSÉES–
CLÉMENCEAU

HORS D'OEUVRES VARIÉS

Walk past just about any Paris café and you will find Hors d'Oeuvre Variés on just about every menu, with varying compositions. Technically, the word "hors d'oeuvre" translates as "outside the menu." It should be something that whets the appetite and is not too rich. Hors d'oeuvre can be cold or warm, made up of vegetables or seafood, charcuterie, or, as here, a mixture of raw and cooked vegetables, including beets, carrots, and celery root.

CARROTS

Carottes

Carrots and cumin are a marriage made in heaven. Here the cool sweetness of the carrots mingles with the fragrant warmth of the cumin seed, creating an appealing, mouth-filling salad. To benefit from cumin's fragrance and flavor, grind the seeds in a spice mill at the very last moment.

In a large bowl, combine the carrots and shallots. In a small bowl, combine the sugar, salt, cumin, and pepper. Add this to the carrots and toss to blend. Add the lemon juice and toss again. Set aside, uncovered, to marinate for 1 hour. Sprinkle with parsley and serve at room temperature. (The salad should be served the day it is made, or the flavors will fade.)

6 carrots, peeled and
   grated
2 shallots, peeled and
   finely chopped
2 tablespoons sugar
½ teaspoon salt
½ teaspoon freshly
   ground cumin seed
Freshly ground black
   pepper to taste
3 tablespoons freshly
   squeezed lemon juice
Several tablespoons finely
   minced fresh parsley
   leaves

4 SERVINGS

BEETS

Betteraves

In France, beets are generally sold cooked, a practice begun during World War II, when beet growers cooked their crops in giant cauldrons in the field in order to cook in bulk and save precious fuel for both the farmer and the French housewife. This turned out to be a great sales technique: Fuel was expensive, and housewives were certainly more likely to buy cooked beets over the raw version. Pickled beets make a colorful addition to any vegetable platter; serve them also as a first-course salad or as an accompaniment to cooked beef.

1 pound beets, cooked, peeled, and diced
½ cup champagne vinegar (or substitute cider vinegar or white wine vinegar)
½ cup water
½ cup sugar
1 teaspoon fine sea salt
Freshly ground black pepper to taste

4 SERVINGS

1. Place the cooled cooked beets in a medium-size bowl. Set aside.

2. In a small saucepan, combine the vinegar, water, sugar, and sea salt; bring to a boil over high heat. Cook for 2 minutes, stirring to dissolve the sugar. Pour the vinegar mixture over the beets and let cool, uncovered, to room temperature.

3. Cover and refrigerate for at least 12 hours, stirring once or twice during that time. (The salad can be stored for up to 1 week, securely covered and refrigerated.)

4. Drain thoroughly and season with freshly ground black pepper at serving time.

I LIKE STEAMED BEETS THE BEST

HERE'S AN EASY METHOD: Bring 1 quart of water to a simmer in the bottom of a vegetable steamer. Place the beets on the steaming rack. Place the rack over the simmering water, cover, and steam until the beets can be pierced with a paring knife, about 20 minutes for baby beets, up to 1 hour for larger beets. (You may have to add water from time to time to keep the steamer from running dry.) Drain, and let cool just long enough so you can handle them. Most of the peel will just slip off, but stubborn patches can be peeled off with a paring knife. Cut off the root end, and dice.

A toast at Bistro le Rubis

CELERY ROOT REMOULADE

Céleri Rémoulade

The French manage to find many clever uses for celery root, generally an underutilized vegetable in the United States. My favorite method is to grate it fine and toss it with a mustard-puckery homemade mayonnaise.

1 pound celery root
About 1 cup Mustard
Mayonnaise (page 283)

6 TO 8 SERVINGS

Cut the celery root into quarters and peel it. With the grating blade of a food processor or the finest blade of a hand grater, grate the celery root. Place it in a bowl, add the mayonnaise, and toss to coat evenly. Taste for seasoning. (The salad may be prepared several hours in advance. Cover securely and refrigerate.) Serve chilled or at room temperature.

JR'S PARMESAN CHIPS

Tuiles au Parmesan JR

As consultant, Joël Robuchon has created a marvelously modern table at the elegant Restaurant de l'Astor in the Right Bank Hotel Astor. When the restaurant first opened in 1997, this Parmesan chip was a popular appetizer on the menu. The addition of verdant fresh herbs makes for lively color as well as flavor.

1. Preheat the oven to 400 degrees F.

2. Place a baking sheet in the freezer for at least 30 minutes.

3. Place the cheese in a small bowl.

4. Place a cold nonstick baking sheet on your work surface. With the cookie cutter acting as a form, use your fingers to sprinkle 1 tablespoon of the cheese into a 2-inch round. Take care to spread the cheese out as thin as possible so the chips will bake evenly. Leave enough space—1 inch—between the rounds for the cheese to spread out as it cooks. Sprinkle each round with one or two sprigs of the herbs.

5. Place the baking sheet in the center of the oven and bake just until the chips are firm, 2 to 3 minutes. Watch carefully—if the chips brown, they will turn bitter. Remove the sheet from the oven and immediately transfer the chips to a cool surface to cool. Serve immediately.

About 1½ cups (4 ounces) freshly grated Parmigiano-Reggiano cheese

Assorted sprigs of fresh herbs: chervil, tarragon, parsley, dill, fennel fronds, and/or thyme leaves

EQUIPMENT:
A 2-inch round metal cookie cutter.

25 TO 30 CHIPS

Champagne, always champagne. Make mine Veuve-Clicquot.

Astor

11, RUE ASTORG
PARIS 8
TELEPHONE: 01 53 05 05 20
FAX: 01 53 05 05 30
MÉTRO: SAINT-AUGUSTIN

CHUNKY GREEN OLIVE PISTOU-TAPENADE

Tapenade aux Olives Vertes et Pistou

This olive pistou-tapenade is laced with garlic and pungent with basil. It was inspired by the delectable green olives of my good friend and olive merchant Jean-Louis Martin, from Provence. I prepare this as soon as the first crop of *olives cassées de Les Baux* arrives in the markets in late September. The olives have the pungent flavor of the wild fennel with which they are cured, and are as fragrant as the Provençal hills. Serve this on toast.

In the bowl of a food processor, combine the olives, basil, and garlic. Process to a chunky purée. Add enough olive oil to form a chunky tapenade. Transfer to a small bowl and smooth out the top with a spatula. The tapenade can be stored, covered and refrigerated, for up to one week.

1 cup green olives, pitted
½ cup fresh basil leaves
4 plump, fresh cloves garlic, peeled, halved, green germ removed
2 tablespoons extra-virgin olive oil

EQUIPMENT:
A food processor.

1 CUP

An excellent source for good-quality olives is

Oliviers & Co.

28, RUE DE BUCI
PARIS 6
TELEPHONE: 01 44 07 15 43
MÉTRO: SAINT-GERMAIN DES PRÉS OR ODÉON

BLACK OLIVE TAPENADE

Tapenade aux Olives Noires

This classic spread combines all the glorious flavors of Provence: the tang of home-cured black olives, the saltiness of the tiny anchovies, the briny flavor of the capers, the vibrant sharpness of garlic, the heady scent of thyme, and the unifying quality of a haunting olive oil.

1. In a small, shallow bowl, combine the anchovies and milk. Set aside for 15 minutes to rid the anchovies of their salt and to soften and plump them. Drain.

2. In the bowl of a food processor, combine the drained anchovies, olives, capers, mustard, garlic, and thyme. Process to form a thick paste.

3. With the processor running, add the oil a steady stream until it is thoroughly incorporated into the mixture. Season with pepper. Taste for seasoning, and serve. (The tapenade can be stored, covered and refrigerated, for up to one week.)

10 anchovy fillets, packed in salt

4 tablespoons milk

2 cups best-quality French brine-cured black olives, pitted

1 tablespoon capers, drained

1 teaspoon French Dijon mustard

1 plump, fresh clove garlic, peeled, green germ removed, and minced

1/4 teaspoon fresh thyme leaves

6 tablespoons extra-virgin olive oil

Freshly ground black pepper to taste

EQUIPMENT:

A food processor.

1 1/2 CUPS

APPETIZERS, STARTERS, AND FIRST COURSES

MARINATED RED PEPPERS

Poivrons Rouges Marinés

Paris market stalls are filled with giant red peppers all year long, with winter varieties coming from Spain and Israel, and summer ones from Provence and the southwest of France. I love anything pickled, and these are among my favorites. Serve them as part of an antipasto platter with sausages and ham, use them in sandwiches, or scatter them over a pizza. Eat and enjoy!

1. In a shallow nonreactive pan, combine the oil, vinegar, sea salt, and sugar. Bring to a boil over high heat. Add the pepper strips and stir constantly over high heat for exactly 2 minutes. Remove from the heat and allow the peppers to cool in the liquid.

2. Transfer the peppers and liquid to a sterilized jar and cover securely. Refrigerate. Once the jar is opened, be sure the peppers remain immersed in the liquid to prevent them from spoiling. (The peppers can be stored, covered and refrigerated, for up to one week.)

2 cups extra-virgin olive oil (or substitute grapeseed or canola oil)
1 cup best-quality white wine vinegar
1 tablespoon sea salt
2 tablespoons sugar
4 red bell peppers, rinsed, trimmed, and cut lengthwise into thin strips

EQUIPMENT:
A 1-quart canning jar, sterilized.

1 QUART

MARINATED PARIS MUSHROOMS

Champignons de Paris Marinés

Plain old "button" mushrooms, which the French call *champignons de Paris*, tend to get ignored in this world of exotic wild and domesticated mushrooms. During Napoleon's reign the mushrooms were cultivated in the quarried-out rock of Paris's 15th arrondissement—thus the name "Paris mushroom." Today they are more likely to be found growing north of Paris or in the Loire Valley. This is a quick and easy way of preserving their goodness. Serve the marinated mushrooms as part of an antipasto platter with sausages, olives, and ham, use them in sandwiches, or scatter them on top of a pizza.

2 cups best-quality white wine vinegar

1 cup dry white wine

2 tablespoons sea salt

6 bay leaves

Several sprigs fresh rosemary

1 pound button mushrooms, cleaned, trimmed, and thinly sliced

About 1 cup extra-virgin olive oil (or substitute grapeseed or canola oil)

EQUIPMENT:

A 1-pint canning jar, sterilized.

1 PINT

1. In a shallow nonreactive saucepan, combine the vinegar, wine, sea salt, bay leaves, and the rosemary. Bring to a simmer over moderate heat and simmer for 10 minutes to burn the alcohol from the wine and to infuse the liquid with the herbs. Then add the mushrooms and simmer 10 minutes more. Drain the mushrooms in a fine-mesh sieve. Set aside to cool.

2. Transfer the mushrooms, bay leaves, and rosemary to a sterilized pint jar, and cover with the oil. Cover securely. Refrigerate without opening for about 1 week. Once the jar is opened, be sure the mushrooms remain immersed in oil to prevent them from spoiling. (The mushrooms can be stored, covered and refrigerated, for up to one week.)

SCRAMBLED EGGS WITH TRUFFLES

Brouillade de Truffes

This is not only my favorite way to prepare eggs but also one of the finest ways to experience a fresh truffle. Straining the eggs makes for an ethereally fine mixture. Cooking them in a double boiler is more time-consuming than cooking them directly in a skillet, but well worth the effort. The results are so incredible you will say, "I can't believe I made these." Take the time to store the truffles and the eggs together for at least 4 hours and up to 2 days. The eggs will be "inoculated" with the truffle's magic aroma. Before preparing the scrambled eggs, be sure to preheat your dinner plates or prepare clean eggshells for serving the eggs.

1. At least 6 hours (and as much as 2 days) before preparing the eggs, carefully arrange the truffles and eggs in a sterilized canning jar so that the eggs surround the truffles. Seal and refrigerate.

2. Remove the jar of eggs and truffles from the refrigerator about 2 hours before preparing the eggs. Just before preparing the eggs, slice one of the truffles into paper-thin slices with a truffle slicer or an extra-sharp knife. Finely mince the remaining truffle. Break the eggs into a bowl and beat lightly with a fork. Set a wide-mesh sieve over a bowl, and pour the eggs through the sieve. Stir the minced truffles into the strained eggs, and season with sea salt.

2 fresh truffles (each about 2 ounces), scrubbed

6 ultra-fresh farm eggs

Fine sea salt

4 tablespoons unsalted butter, cut into small pieces

Freshly ground white pepper

2 tablespoons *crème fraîche*

2 slices Brioche (page 60), toasted

1 tablespoon Truffle Butter (page 286)

EQUIPMENT:

A 1-quart canning jar, sterilized; a double boiler.

2 SERVINGS

3. Transfer the eggs to the top of a double boiler set over, but not touching, simmering water. Add 3 tablespoons of the butter. Stir constantly with a wooden spoon until the eggs form a creamy, homogeneous mass. They should cook slowly and evenly. Fluffy just-cooked eggs will take about 10 minutes.

4. Remove the pan from the heat, and carefully stir in the remaining 1 tablespoon butter and the *crème fraîche.* Season with freshly ground white pepper and sea salt, if necessary. With a large spoon, transfer the mixture to two very hot dinner plates. Top with the slices of truffle. (Alternatively, spoon the scrambled eggs into clean eggshells set in egg cups. Top with slices of truffle.) Serve with the toasted brioche spread with Truffle Butter.

While eggs can spoil the flavor of good wines and clash with others, one will rarely miss with a glass of bubbly champagne.

LE CAP VERNET GARDENER'S SALAD

LE BISTROT MAZARIN'S SPINACH, BACON, AVOCADO, AND
TOMATO SALAD

LADURÉE'S ASPARAGUS, ARUGULA, AND PARMESAN SALAD

CAFÉ BONAPARTE CHICKEN SALAD

LE NEMROD'S AUVERGNE-STYLE SALAD

SALADS
Les Salades

CHEZ BENOÎT'S SPRING SALAD

JR'S HERB SALAD

CHARPENTIERS' MESCLUN SALAD WITH ROQUEFORT "VINAIGRETTE"

SALAD OF CURLY ENDIVE, BACON, AND ROQUEFORT

SPRING MADNESS: LAMB'S LETTUCE AND BEETS

WINTER MESCLUN

Wine Bar Jacques Melac

LE CAP VERNET GARDENER'S SALAD

Salade à la Maraîchère Cap Vernet

In the winter months, as often as my schedule permits, I dip into Guy Savoy's brasserie, Cap Vernet, for lunch and an oyster fix, because this restaurant has some of Paris's best and freshest oysters. I always have at least half a dozen of Yvon Madec's iodine-infused *boudeuses* from the far-north Breton port of Prat-au-Coum. The oyster orgy is generally followed by this refreshing salad, which is decorated, teepee-style, with thin strips of moist, nutty Parmigiano-Reggiano cheese. Chef Stéphane Perraud prepares this with a mix of greens to contrast color, texture, and flavor. Just before serving the salad, I like to anoint the cheese with a few drops of balsamic vinegar, almost as a blessing for the feast. A *maraîcher,* by the way, is a market gardener, and the name of the dish comes from the many market gardeners who grow the freshest of greens in the rich soil on the outskirts of Paris.

About 6 cups (5 ounces) loosely packed mixed greens, such as frisée, radicchio, and oak-leaf lettuce, washed, dried, and torn into bite-size pieces

Several tablespoons Classic Vinaigrette (page 278)

Sea salt to taste

Freshly ground white pepper to taste

One 2-ounce chunk of Parmigiano-Reggiano cheese

A few drops of balsamic vinegar

2 SERVINGS AS A MAIN COURSE; 4 SERVINGS AS A FIRST COURSE OR SALAD COURSE

1. In a large salad bowl, combine the greens and toss to mix. Add enough vinaigrette to evenly coat the ingredients, tossing to thoroughly coat the greens with the dressing. Season with sea salt and white pepper.

2. Transfer the salad to large dinner plates.

3. Using a vegetable peeler, shave the Parmesan cheese into long thick strips. Arrange the strips of cheese, teepee-style, on top of the dressed greens. Drizzle with a few drops of balsamic vinegar, and serve.

Cap Vernet

82, AVENUE MARCEAU
PARIS 8
TELEPHONE: 01 47 20 20 40
FAX: 01 47 20 95 36
MÉTRO: CHARLES DE
GAULLE—ETOILE

Guy Savoy

SALADS

35

LE BISTROT MAZARIN'S SPINACH, BACON, AVOCADO, AND TOMATO SALAD

Le Méli-Mélo d'Epinards du Bistrot Mazarin

When I was restoring my office/studio on the rue Jacob in the late 1990s, Bistrot Mazarin was one of my hangouts. During that particularly cold winter, I visited the unheated work site almost daily to meet with masons and plumbers, painters and cabinetmakers. The tradesmen and I would often have lunch at the nearby Bistrot Mazarin, which had moved its outdoor gas heaters indoors to supplement the central heat on icy days. In summer months, the terrace is always lively. This salad appeared as a special one day in May. I can never get enough greens, and this hit the spot as an evening's first course.

1. Place the spinach, avocado, and tomatoes in a large salad bowl. Set aside.

2. Place the bacon in a large skillet and cook, stirring frequently, over medium-high heat just until it begins to give off its fat and starts to brown, 4 to 5 minutes.

3. Using a slotted spoon, scatter the bacon over the salad. Toss to mix well. Add enough vinaigrette to evenly coat the ingredients. Toss again, season with sea salt and pepper to taste, and serve.

4 cups baby spinach leaves, washed, dried, and stemmed

1 ripe avocado, peeled, pitted, and cubed

4 tomatoes, cored, peeled, and each cut into 8 wedges (use only the shell of the tomato, not the inner pulp)

1 cup cubed smoked slab bacon

Several tablespoons Classic Vinaigrette (page 278)

Sea salt to taste

Freshly ground black pepper to taste

2 SERVINGS AS A MAIN COURSE; 4 SERVINGS AS A FIRST OR SALAD COURSE

Bistrot Mazarin

42, RUE MAZARINE
PARIS 6
TELEPHONE: 01 43 29 99 01
MÉTRO: MABILLON

LADURÉE'S ASPARAGUS, ARUGULA, AND PARMESAN SALAD

La Salade de Roquette, Asperges, et Parmesan de Ladurée

I was fortunate enough to spend an entire day at Ladurée with Pierre Hermé, then the famed pâtisserie's pastry chef. We sampled everything, from buttery croissants to the entire line of chocolates. We had to stop for lunch, of course, and this is the spring salad I sampled on that glorious day.

1. Trim off the tough ends of the asparagus spears. With a small knife, cut off the little green buds along the length of the spears. Set the trimmed asparagus aside. (A good French cook will use these trimmings: Discarding any white part, peel the tough green ends of the asparagus spears. Use the peeled ends, and the trimmed-off buds, for soup.)

2. Prepare a large bowl of ice water.

3. Fill a 4-quart pasta pot, fitted with a colander, with 3 quarts water and bring to a boil over high heat. Add the salt and the asparagus spears and cook, uncovered, until crisp-tender, about 5 minutes. (Cooking time will vary according to the size and tenderness of the asparagus.) Immediately remove the colander from the water, allow the water to drain from the asparagus, and plunge the colander into the ice water so the asparagus will cool down as quickly as possible. As soon as the asparagus is cool (no longer than 1 to 2 minutes, or they will become soggy and

16 plump asparagus spears
  (about 1½ pounds)
4 tablespoons salt
1 tablespoon distilled
  vinegar
4 large extra-fresh farm
  eggs
1 tablespoon olive oil
About 8 cups (8 ounces)
  loosely packed fresh
  arugula, rinsed, spun dry,
  and stemmed
Several tablespoons Classic
  Vinaigrette (page 278)
One 2-ounce chunk of
  Parmigiano-Reggiano
  cheese
Freshly ground black
  pepper to taste

EQUIPMENT:
A 4-quart pasta pot fitted
  with a colander.

4 SERVINGS

begin to lose flavor), transfer them to a tea towel and wrap to dry. (The asparagus can be cooked up to 4 hours in advance. Keep them wrapped in the towel. Unless the kitchen is very hot, store at room temperature; the asparagus will reheat more quickly at serving time.)

4. Shortly before serving time, warm four dinner plates.

5. Poach the eggs: In a shallow 10-inch skillet, bring 3 inches of water to a boil over high heat. Add the vinegar. (The vinegar will help the white of the egg cook faster so it does not spread out too much.) Remove the pan from the heat and immediately break the 4 eggs directly into the pan, carefully opening the shells close to the water's surface so the eggs slip into the water in one piece. Immediately cover the pan with a tight-fitting lid to retain the heat and cook the eggs. Do not disturb the pan. After 3 minutes, remove the lid and check the eggs. They are ready when the whites are opaque and the yolks are covered with a thin, translucent layer of white. Rinse the eggs gently under cold running water to rid them of any taste of vinegar.

6. While the eggs are cooking, heat the oil in a large nonstick skillet over high heat. When it is hot but not smoking, add the asparagus, reduce the heat to low, and gently reheat, 2 to 3 minutes.

7. Place the arugula in a large bowl. Drizzle with several tablespoons of Classic Vinaigrette and toss to coat evenly with the dressing. Divide the arugula among 4 warmed dinner plates. Arrange 4 asparagus spears on each of the plates, and cover the asparagus with a poached egg. Shave the cheese over the arugula. Season generously with black pepper, and serve.

Ladurée

75, AVENUE DES CHAMPS-
ELYSÉES
PARIS 8
TELEPHONE: 01 40 75 08 75
MÉTRO: GEORGE V

CAFÉ BONAPARTE CHICKEN SALAD

La Salade Apollinaire du Café Bonaparte

About once a week I get a hankering for this simple, tasty, wholesome, filling salad, a satisfying combination of chicken, greens, hard-cooked eggs, tomatoes, and cucumbers. Late in the morning, just when I begin to have that sinking, falling-down-with-hunger feeling, I give a call to a neighborhood friend and pop the question: "Is this a Bonaparte salad day?" The answer is usually yes, and if we are lucky we secure a table on the terrace in the shadow of the Saint-Germain church, with a front-row seat on all the activity of the heart of Saint-Germain des Prés. Le Bonaparte is what some might consider a second-string café in the neighborhood, lined up right behind the glittery Café Flore and Les Deux Magots, the two stars of the 6th arrondissement. Le Bonaparte's bright red and blue décor always cheers me up, the service is generally friendly and swift, and the clientele is properly international. The salad, by the way, goes by the name Apollinaire because the café faces the short rue Guillaume Apollinaire. One might also call it the Endless Plate of Salad, because no matter how much I eat, it seems as though the ingredients continue to almost grow on the plate. Of course, I always finish every last bite.

Place the chicken in a large salad bowl. Season well with sea salt and black pepper. Add the tomatoes and cucumbers,

2 cups cubed cooked, skinned chicken

Sea salt to taste

Freshly ground black pepper to taste

3 small tomatoes, cored and cut lengthwise into eighths

1 small cucumber, peeled and thinly sliced

1 small head lettuce, washed, dried, and torn into bite-size pieces

Classic Vinaigrette to taste (page 278)

2 large hard-cooked eggs, peeled and quartered lengthwise

2 SERVINGS AS A MAIN COURSE

and season once again. Add the lettuce. Toss the mixture carefully with your hands. Add the vinaigrette, tossing with your hands until all the ingredients are evenly distributed. Taste for seasoning. Divide the salad between two large salad plates, arrange the egg wedges around the salad, and serve.

Le Bonaparte

42, RUE BONAPARTE
PARIS 6
TELEPHONE: 01 43 26 42 81
MÉTRO: SAINT-GERMAIN DES
PRÉS

LE NEMROD'S AUVERGNE-STYLE SALAD

Frisée au Jambon, Cantal, et Noix Le Nemrod

Owners Richard and Michelle Bonal run a great neighborhood café, Le Nemrod, in the heart of the Left Bank. They offer an assortment of cold sandwiches on the sublime Poilâne bread, as well as this hearty salad that combines the best ingredients of the Auvergne region in south central France: silken ham, earthy and lactic Cantal cheese, and fresh walnuts. Toss it with the freshest of curly endive and a great homemade vinaigrette. And don't forget a nice touch of freshly ground black pepper at the end, to tie it all together.

In a large salad bowl, combine the frisée, ham, cheese, and walnuts. Toss to mix well. Add enough vinaigrette to evenly coat the ingredients, and toss to blend. Season with sea salt and black pepper.

Beaujolais, Beaujolais, and more Beaujolais.

3 ounces curly endive (frisée, or chicory), washed, dried, and torn into bite-size pieces (6 cups loosely packed)

1/8 cup matchstick-sliced ham

1/2 cup cubed French Cantal cheese (or substitute an aged cheddar)

1/4 cup walnut halves

Several tablespoons Classic Vinaigrette (page 278)

Sea salt to taste

Freshly ground black pepper to taste

2 SERVINGS AS A MAIN COURSE; 4 SERVINGS AS A FIRST OR SALAD COURSE

Le Nemrod

51, RUE DU CHERCHE-MIDI
PARIS 6
TELEPHONE: 01 45 48 17 05
MÉTRO: SÈVRES-BABYLONE

CHEZ BENOÎT'S SPRING SALAD

Salade de Printemps de Chez Benoît

At least four times a year I make a pilgrimage to this most classic and most beautiful of Paris bistros. Owner Michel Petit manages to keep the menu traditional without getting stale, and each season he adds a new dish that warms the soul. This dish has become a modern favorite in our family. Sometimes I set the salad on a bed of dressed and tossed baby *mesclun* leaves, for a true Salad-as-a-Meal.

1 pound asparagus

4 tablespoons sea salt

8 ounces green beans, rinsed, trimmed, and cut into 1-inch pieces

8 ounces snow peas, rinsed, trimmed, and cut into 1-inch pieces

WALNUT OIL DRESSING

2 tablespoons freshly squeezed lemon juice

Fine sea salt to taste

5 tablespoons walnut oil (or substitute hazelnut oil or extra-virgin olive oil)

Several tablespoons minced fresh chives

Several tablespoons fresh chervil leaves (or substitute fresh tarragon leaves)

1. Trim the asparagus to about 4 inches in length. (Reserve the trimmed ends for another use, such the Asparagus Velouté on page 4.) Cut the asparagus on the diagonal into three or four bite-size pieces. Set aside.

2. Prepare several large bowls of ice water.

3. Fill a large pot with 6 quarts of water and bring to a boil over high heat. Add the 4 tablespoons salt and the green beans, and cook in rapidly boiling water, uncovered, until crisp-tender, 3 to 4 minutes. (The cooking time will vary according to the size and tenderness of the beans.) Immediately remove the colander from the water, allow the water to drain from the beans, and plunge the colander into the ice water so the beans cool down as quickly as possible. As soon as the beans are cool (no longer than 1 to 2 minutes, or they will become soggy and begin to lose

flavor), drain them and wrap them in a thick towel to dry. (The beans can be cooked up to 4 hours in advance. Keep them wrapped in the towel, and refrigerate if desired.)

4. Repeat for the snow peas: Bring the water back to a boil, add the snow peas, and cook, uncovered, until they are crisp-tender, 2 to 3 minutes. (The cooking time will vary according to the size and tenderness of the vegetable.) Immediately remove the colander from the pot and plunge it into the ice water. Let the peas cool for 1 to 2 minutes, then drain and wrap in a thick towel to dry. (The peas can be cooked up to 4 hours in advance. Keep them wrapped in the towel, and refrigerate if desired.)

5. Repeat for the asparagus: Bring the water back to a boil, add the asparagus, and cook, uncovered, until crisp-tender, about 3 minutes. (The cooking time will vary according to the size of the asparagus.) Immediately remove the colander from the pot and plunge it into the ice water. Let the asparagus cool for 1 to 2 minutes, then drain, and wrap in a thick towel to dry. (The asparagus can be cooked up to 2 hours in advance. Keep them wrapped in the towel and hold at room temperature.)

6. Prepare the walnut oil dressing: In a small bowl combine the lemon juice and sea salt. Whisk in the oil and taste for seasoning. Set aside. (Do not dress the salad until the very last moment or the vegetables will turn soggy and will discolor from the acid in the dressing.)

7. To serve, combine all the vegetables in a large, shallow bowl. Sprinkle with the chives and chervil. Drizzle with the dressing and toss very gently to blend. Taste for seasoning and serve.

EQUIPMENT:
A 6-quart pasta pot fitted
   with a colander.

4 SERVINGS AS A FIRST
COURSE; 2 SERVINGS
AS A MAIN COURSE

Benoît

20, RUE SAINT MARTIN
PARIS 4
TELEPHONE: 01 42 72 25 76
FAX: 01 42 72 45 68
MÉTRO: CHÂTELET OR HÔTEL
DE VILLE

SALADS

43

JR'S HERB SALAD

Salade Pastorale aux Herbes JR

It is hard to believe, but it took a chef with the talent of Joël Robuchon to bring the common tossed salad to a place of honor at the three-star table. From the early days of the 1980s when Robuchon tended the stoves at Jamin, this salad—served in tiny portions, with each leaf meticulously cut into tiny pieces—was served with every meal. In wintertime, finely minced fresh truffles were tossed with the vinaigrette for an added touch of flavor and elegance.

1. Prepare the vinaigrette: In a small bowl, combine the salt and vinegars and whisk to blend. Slowly whisk in the oil. Season with white pepper. Taste for seasoning.

2. Carefully wash, trim, and dry the salad greens. Tear them all into small bite-size pieces; you should have ½ cup of each variety of green. Place the greens in a large salad bowl, add the herbs, and toss to blend. Slowly add the vinaigrette, tossing to evenly coat the greens.

3. Arrange the salad in a mound on each of six salad plates. Garnish with the mint and celery leaves. Drizzle with a few drops of vinegar, and serve immediately.

THE VINAIGRETTE

Sea salt to taste

1 tablespoon red wine vinegar

1 tablespoon sherry vinegar

6 tablespoons extra-virgin olive oil

Freshly ground white pepper to taste

THE SALAD

½ cup (1 ounce) frisée (chicory, or curly endive)

½ cup (1 ounce) oak-leaf lettuce

½ cup (1 ounce) curly red-leaf lettuce

½ cup (1 ounce) radicchio

½ cup (1 ounce) romaine lettuce

½ cup (1 ounce) *mesclun*

½ cup (1 ounce) lamb's lettuce

1 ounce arugula

MESCLUN, ALSO KNOWN AS *MESCLUM*, is a Provençal blend of up to ten different salad greens and herbs, each varying in flavor, texture, and color. A mix might include red- and green-tipped oak-leaf lettuce, arugula, romaine, chervil, colorful red radicchio, curly white endive (frisée) as well as Belgian endive, escarole, and bitter dandelion greens. Generally fresh herbs are also added to this mix, including sage, dill, and tarragon. Today *mesclun* has become ubiquitous, and more often than not it is a pale version of its true self—often just two or three greens and a few tangles of herbs. The best versions, like this one, are made of a variety of fresh greens that are cut into bite-size pieces and tossed together at the last moment.

¼ cup fresh marjoram leaves

½ cup chopped fresh chervil leaves

½ cup chopped fresh basil leaves

½ cup fresh flat-leaf parsley leaves

½ cup fresh dill leaves

½ cup chopped fresh tarragon leaves

THE GARNISH

6 small fresh mint leaves

6 small celery leaves

Several drops of red wine vinegar

6 SERVINGS

CHARPENTIERS' MESCLUN SALAD WITH ROQUEFORT "VINAIGRETTE"

Salade de Mesclun, Sauce Roquefort aux Charpentiers

For some 20 years I have been a regular at the family-style bistro Aux Charpentiers, where one finds such simple daily specials as roast chicken or duck, or roasted saddle of lamb. One summer's evening we sat on the restaurant's sidewalk terrace and sampled this very simple first course. Try for a good variety of greens for a modern allure. I created the sauce, motivated by chef-owner Paul Bardeche's own inspiration.

1. Place the greens in a large salad bowl. Set aside.

2. Prepare the Roquefort "vinaigrette": In a small jar, combine the lemon juice, walnut oil, and cheese. Cover tightly and shake to blend. The cheese will remain in crumbled bits.

3. Toss the dressing over the salad, seasoning with sea salt and plenty of freshly ground black pepper. Serve immediately.

4 ounces *mesclun* (see page 45), washed, dried, and torn into bite-size pieces (8 cups loosely packed)

THE ROQUEFORT "VINAIGRETTE"

3 tablespoons freshly squeezed lemon juice

1/2 cup best-quality walnut oil

4 ounces Roquefort cheese, crumbled (about 1 cup)

Fine sea salt to taste

Freshly ground black pepper to taste

4 SERVINGS

Aux Charpentiers

10, RUE MABILLON
PARIS 6
TELEPHONE: 01 43 26 30 05
FAX: 01 46 33 07 98
MÉTRO: MABILLON

SALAD OF CURLY ENDIVE, BACON, AND ROQUEFORT

Frisée aux Lardons et Roquefort

There is no limit to the varieties of salad one finds in Parisian cafés and bistros. This one, with the ever-present curly endive, full of color and crunch, pairs two deliciously salty ingredients, creamy Roquefort cheese and crisp warm bacon.

1. Place the bacon in a large skillet and cook, stirring frequently, over medium-high heat just until it begins to give off its fat and starts to brown, 4 to 5 minutes.

2. Meanwhile, in a large salad bowl, combine the curly endive and cheese. Set aside.

3. When the bacon is cooked, use a slotted spoon to remove it from the pan. Scatter the bacon over the salad, and toss to mix well.

4. Add enough vinaigrette to evenly coat the ingredients. Toss again, season with sea salt and black pepper to taste, and serve.

4 ounces smoked slab bacon, rind removed, cut into cubes (1 cup)

4 ounces curly endive (frisée, or chicory), washed, dried, and torn into bite-size pieces (6 cups loosely packed)

4 ounces Roquefort cheese, crumbled (1 cup)

Several tablespoons Classic Vinaigrette (page 278)

Sea salt to taste

Freshly ground black pepper to taste

2 SERVINGS AS A MAIN COURSE; 4 SERVINGS AS A FIRST OR SALAD COURSE

Although wine is not always served with a salad, a chilled glass of Beaujolais is always in order.

SPRING MADNESS: LAMB'S LETTUCE AND BEETS

Salade de Mâche et Betterave

One of the most welcome signs of spring in Paris is the arrival of the popular classic mix of tender green lamb's lettuce paired with just slightly sweet cooked red beets for a *Salade de Mâche et Betterave*. In vegetable markets, the two are always found side by side, contrasting the crimson red and the brilliant green, shouting out "Buy me—take me home for dinner." The salad is also classic Parisian bistro fare, and is usually on the spring menu at one of my favorite old-time bistros, Chez Allard.

1. Prepare the vinaigrette: In a large salad bowl, combine the vinegar and sea salt. Whisk to blend. Add the oil, whisking to blend. Taste for seasoning.

2. Add the beets to the vinaigrette and toss to thoroughly coat them with the dressing. Set aside for at least 5 minutes and up to 30 minutes.

3. At serving time, add the lamb's lettuce and shallots. Toss gently to thoroughly coat the ingredients with the dressing. Serve on salad plates, being sure to evenly distribute the beets, which tend to fall to the bottom of the bowl.

THE VINAIGRETTE

1 tablespoon best-quality sherry vinegar

Fine sea salt to taste

4 tablespoons extra-virgin olive oil

2 beets (about 1 pound), cooked, peeled, and cubed

About 2 cups (4 ounces) lamb's lettuce, rinsed and dried

1 small shallot, peeled and cut into thin rounds

4 SERVINGS

Allard

1, RUE DE L'EPÉRON
PARIS 6
TELEPHONE: 01 43 26 48 23
MÉTRO: ODÉON

WINTER MESCLUN

Mesclun d'Hiver

One weekday just before Christmas, I strolled into my neighborhood greengrocer's and he proudly announced, "Even Pierre Gagnaire hasn't seen this yet!" Chef Gagnaire and I share the same produce merchant, who held up an alabaster ball of lettuce tinged with a deep ruby red. It was white radicchio, a winter version with the colors exactly the reverse of the common red radicchio. I gathered it up, along with all the baby greens in his display, and for lunch friends and I had a veritable feast.

1. Rinse and dry all the greens and herbs. Be sure that they are all carefully stemmed.

2. Place the greens and herbs in a large bowl and toss with your hands to mix. Drizzle with Classic Vinaigrette, and toss to coat evenly with the dressing. Taste for seasoning. Serve.

Pierre Gagnaire and I shop for produce at

Le Jardin de Courcelles

96, RUE DE COURCELLES
PARIS 17
TELEPHONE: 01 47 63 70 55
MÉTRO: COURCELLES

½ cup (1 ounce) lamb's
  lettuce leaves
½ cup (1 ounce) baby
  spinach leaves, stemmed
½ cup (1 ounce) arugula
  leaves, stemmed
½ cup (1 ounce) dandelion
  greens, stemmed
½ cup (1 ounce) sorrel
  leaves, stemmed (optional)
½ cup (1 ounce) torn red
  radicchio leaves (bite-
  size pieces)
½ cup (1 ounce) torn white
  radicchio leaves (bite-size
  pieces; optional)
6 leaves Belgian endive, cut
  into ribbons (chiffonnade)
¼ cup fresh mint leaves
¼ cup fresh dill leaves
¼ cup fresh tarragon leaves
¼ cup fresh chervil leaves
  (optional)
Several tablespoons Classic
  Vinaigrette (page 278)
Fine sea salt to taste
Freshly ground white pepper
  to taste

6 SERVINGS

Rue Jacob Walnut Bread

Eight-Grain Parisian Bread

Parmesan Bread

BREADS
Les Pains

Rye Water Crackers

Brioche

Socca: Chickpea Flour Crêpes from Nice

RUE JACOB WALNUT BREAD

Pain aux Noix rue Jacob

Some of the finest walnut oil and most deliciously fresh walnuts in France can be found at the minuscule family-run boutique Huilerie Artisanale Leblanc on the rue Jacob. Using their products, I created this walnut bread, bursting with fragrant walnuts and perfumed with the nut's own rich oil. It is one of the most rewarding treats I know. I love to pair the bread with fresh, tangy goat's-milk cheese. The milk in this dough makes for a light, almost cakelike bread, and the triple rise at room temperature allows it to develop a rich flavor. Be sure to use the freshest nuts and oil you can find.

1. In the bowl of a heavy-duty electric mixer fitted with the dough hook, combine the yeast, sugar, and lukewarm milk, and stir to blend. Let stand until foamy, about 5 minutes. Stir in the oil and sea salt.

2. Add the nuts and the 3¾ cups flour all at once, and mix at medium-low speed until most of the flour has been absorbed and the dough forms a ball. Continue to knead at medium-low speed until the dough is soft and satiny but still firm, 4 to 5 minutes. If necessary, add a little more flour to keep the dough from sticking.

3. Transfer the dough to another bowl, cover tightly with plastic wrap, and let rise until doubled in bulk, about 1 hour. Punch the dough down and let it rise again until doubled in bulk, about 1 hour.

1 package (2½ teaspoons) active dry yeast

1 teaspoon sugar

1⅓ cups milk, heated to lukewarm

1 tablespoon walnut oil

2 teaspoons fine sea salt

4 ounces walnuts, coarsely chopped (1 cup)

3¾ cups bread flour or whole-wheat bread flour, or more if needed

1 large egg beaten with 1 tablespoon cold water, for egg wash

EQUIPMENT:

A 1-quart rectangular loaf pan, preferably nonstick; a heavy-duty mixer.

1 LOAF, ABOUT 12 SLICES

4. Punch the dough down again, and form it into a tight rectangle. Place the dough in a nonstick 1-quart rectangular bread pan. Cover with a clean cloth and let rise until doubled in bulk, about 1 hour.

WHAT I LEARNED: When baking any bread that contains milk (as opposed to water), bake at a lower temperature than you would dough prepared with water. The sugar in the milk will make the dough brown more quickly, and the bread could easily burn at a higher temperature. Note that the bread and the crust will be softer and more golden than bread made with water.

5. Preheat the oven to 425 degrees F.

6. Brush the top of the dough with the egg wash. With a razor blade, slash the top of the dough several times, so it can expand evenly during baking. Place the bread pan on the bottom shelf of the oven, and bake until the bread is lightly browned and nicely risen, about 15 minutes. Then reduce the heat to 375 degrees F. Rotate the loaf so that it browns evenly. Bake until the crust is firm and golden brown, and the bread sounds hollow when tapped on the bottom, about 30 minutes. Transfer the bread to a rack to cool. Do not slice the bread for at least 1 hour, for it will continue to bake as it cools.

Huilerie Artisanale Leblanc et Fils

6, RUE JACOB
PARIS 6
TEL: 01 46 34 61 55
MÉTRO: MABILLON

EIGHT-GRAIN PARISIAN BREAD

Pain Parisien aux Huit Céréales

In the past decade, Paris has undergone a major bread revival. On nearly every street corner one finds an incredible variety of breads, many of them studded with all manner of grains, from cornmeal to sesame seeds, flax and poppy seeds, and often the popular French grain *épeautre*, often called "poor man's wheat" because it will grow in even the poorest of soils. Inspired by the wholesome breads of the city, I created this loaf to reflect the modern style.

1. In the bowl of a heavy-duty electric mixer fitted with the dough hook, combine the yeast, sugar, and 1/3 cup of the lukewarm water; stir to blend. Let stand until foamy, about 5 minutes. Then stir in the remaining 1 cup lukewarm water and the sea salt.

2. Add the 3¾ cups flour all at once, and mix at medium speed until most of the flour has been absorbed and the dough forms a ball. Add all the seeds and grains, and continue to knead until the dough is smooth and satiny but still firm, 4 to 5 minutes. If necessary, add a little more flour to keep the dough from sticking. Transfer the dough to a clean, floured work surface, and knead by hand for 1 minute to help distribute the seeds and grains.

3. Place the dough in a clean bowl, cover it securely with plastic wrap, and set it in the refrigerator. Let the dough

1 teaspoon active dry yeast

1 teaspoon sugar

1⅓ cups lukewarm water

2 teaspoons fine sea salt

3¾ cups bread flour, or
   more if needed

2 tablespoons sesame seeds

3 tablespoons polenta
   (cornmeal)

1 tablespoon pumpkin seeds

1 tablespoon oatmeal flakes

1 tablespoon *épeautre* or
   spelt (or substitute wheat
   berries)

1 tablespoon flax seeds

1 tablespoon sunflower
   seeds

1 large egg beaten with 1 tablespoon cold water, for
   egg wash

EQUIPMENT:

A 1-quart rectangular bread
   pan, preferably nonstick;
   a heavy-duty mixer.

1 LOAF, ABOUT 12
SLICES

rise until doubled or tripled in bulk, 8 to 12 hours. (This slow refrigerator rise will make for a more flavorful, well-developed bread.)

4. Remove the dough from the refrigerator and punch it down. Cover the bowl securely with plastic wrap again, and let the dough rise until doubled in bulk, about 1 hour. Punch the dough down once more, and let it rise again until doubled in bulk, about 1 hour.

5. Punch the dough down again, and form it into a tight rectangle. Place the dough in a nonstick 1-quart rectangular bread pan. Cover with a clean cloth and let rise until doubled in bulk, about 1 hour.

6. Preheat the oven to 425 degrees F.

7. Brush the top of the dough with the egg wash. With a razor blade, slash the top of the dough several times, so it can expand evenly during baking. Place the bread pan on the bottom shelf of the oven. Bake until the crust is firm and golden brown and the bread sounds hollow when tapped on the bottom (or until an instant-read thermometer plunged into the center of the bread reads 200 degrees F), about 45 minutes. Transfer the bread to a rack to cool. Do not slice the bread for at least 1 hour, for it will continue to bake as it cools.

PARMESAN BREAD

Pain au Parmesan

Inspired by a Gruyère bread I tasted at one of my favorite bakeries—Boulangerie Onfroy—I developed this rich, full-flavored Parmesan bread. It's delicious toasted and served with a cheese course or as part of a bacon, lettuce, and tomato sandwich. The bread can be made, start to finish, in just under 3 hours.

1 teaspoon active dry yeast

1 teaspoon sugar

1⅓ cups lukewarm water

2 tablespoons extra-virgin olive oil

2 teaspoons fine sea salt

3¾ cups (1 pound) bread flour, or more if needed

3 ounces freshly grated Parmigiano-Reggiano cheese (¾ cup)

1 large egg beaten with 1 tablespoon cold water, for egg wash

EQUIPMENT:

A 1-quart rectangular bread pan, preferably nonstick; a heavy-duty mixer.

1 LOAF, ABOUT 12 SLICES

1. In the bowl of a heavy-duty electric mixer fitted with the dough hook, combine the yeast, sugar, and lukewarm water, and stir to blend. Let stand until foamy, about 5 minutes. Then stir in the oil and the sea salt.

2. Add the 3¾ cups flour and the cheese all at once, and mix at medium speed until most of the flour has been absorbed and the dough forms a ball. Continue to knead until the dough is soft and satiny but still firm, 4 to 5 minutes. If necessary, add a little more flour to keep the dough from sticking. Transfer the dough to a clean, floured work surface and knead by hand for 1 minute. The dough should be smooth and should spring back when indented with your fingertip.

3. Place the dough in a clean bowl, cover the bowl with plastic wrap, and let the dough rise until doubled in bulk, about 1 hour. Punch the dough down and shape it into a tight rectangle. Place the dough in a nonstick 1-quart rec-

tangular bread pan. Cover it with a clean cloth and let it rise until doubled in bulk, about 1 hour.

4. Preheat the oven to 425 degrees F.

5. Brush the top of the dough with the egg wash. With the tips of a pair of scissors, snip the top of the dough all over, about 15 times, to allow it to expand evenly during baking. Place the bread pan on the bottom shelf of the oven. Bake until firm and golden brown, and the bread sounds hollow when tapped on the bottom, or until an instant-read thermometer plunged into the center of the bread reads 200 degrees F, 35 to 40 minutes. Transfer the bread to a rack to cool.

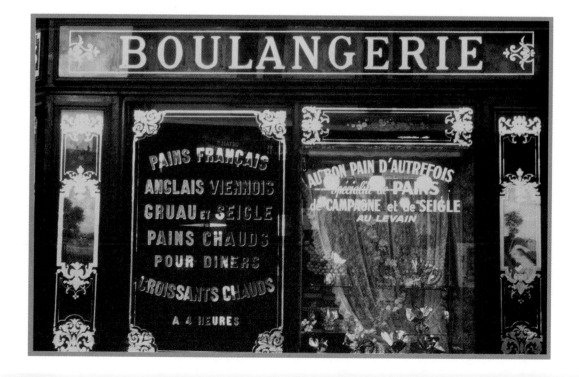

RYE WATER CRACKERS

Biscuits de Seigle

The dense flavor of rye has always appealed, and I love nothing better than crunchy crackers with my cheese. Try these with an assortment of blue cheeses or with a rustic farm cheddar.

1. Preheat the oven to 400 degrees F.

2. Combine the flours and sea salt in the bowl of a food processor. Add the oil and the cold water, and pulse until the mixture comes together. The dough should not form a ball.

3. With a pastry scraper, transfer the dough to a floured work surface. Using the palms of your hands, gently work the mass of dough into a round. Cut it into two pieces. Roll each piece out about 1/8 inch thick. Cut out rounds with a 2¼-inch cookie cutter. Transfer the rounds to nonstick baking sheets. Pierce each round 4 or 5 times with the tines of a fork to create an attractive design. With a garden mister, generously spray the crackers with water. (This will make them even more crisp and will help the salt and seeds adhere.) Sprinkle with the coarse sea salt and caraway seeds.

4. Place the baking sheets in the oven and bake until the crackers are firm in texture and lightly browned around the edges, 20 to 25 minutes. If your oven has a tendency to

1½ cups rye flour

1 cup unbleached all-purpose flour

1 teaspoon fine sea salt

⅓ cup grapeseed or canola oil

½ cup cold water

1 teaspoon coarse sea salt

1 teaspoon caraway or cumin seeds

EQUIPMENT:

A 2¼-inch scalloped cookie cutter; a garden mister; a food processor; nonstick baking sheets.

ABOUT 40 CRACKERS

bake unevenly, rotate the baking sheets from top to bottom and from front to back halfway through the baking period.

5. Remove the crackers from the oven and let them cool on the baking sheets for 1 minute to firm up. Then, using a metal spatula, transfer the crackers to wire racks to cool completely. The crackers can be stored in an airtight container at room temperature for 1 week.

BRIOCHE

Brioche

I have never counted the number of versions of brioche one finds in Paris, but over time I have developed a recipe I love and I'm going to share it with you here. Once you get hooked on making brioche, you are set for life! There is nothing more satisfying than removing a pair of shiny, golden-brown crowns from your oven on a chilly day. You will say to yourself, "I made this?" Although brioche is a traditional breakfast treat in France, usually served toasted with butter and jam, I like to serve it as a rich dinner bread, sliced and toasted and served as a first course with smoked salmon or foie gras.

1. In the bowl of a heavy-duty mixer fitted with the dough hook, combine the warm milk, yeast, and sugar and stir to blend. Let stand until foamy, about 5 minutes. Stir in 1 cup of the flour and the egg, and stir to blend. The sponge will be sticky and fairly dry. Sprinkle with the remaining 1 cup flour to cover the sponge. Set aside to rest, uncovered, for 30 to 40 minutes. The sponge should erupt slightly, cracking the flour.

2. Add the sugar, sea salt, eggs, and 1 cup of the flour to the sponge. With the dough hook, mix at low speed for 1 or 2 minutes, just until the ingredients come together. Still mixing, sprinkle in the remaining ½ cup flour. When the flour is incorporated, increase the mixer speed to

THE SPONGE
⅓ cup whole milk, warmed

1 package (2½ teaspoons) active dry yeast

1 teaspoon sugar

2 cups unbleached all-purpose flour

1 large egg, lightly beaten

THE DOUGH
⅓ cup sugar

1 teaspoon fine sea salt

4 large eggs, lightly beaten

1½ cups unbleached all purpose-flour

12 tablespoons unsalted butter, at room temperature

THE EGG WASH
1 large egg beaten with 1 tablespoon cold water

medium and beat for 15 minutes, scraping down the hook and bowl as needed.

3. To incorporate the butter into the dough, you will need to work it until it is the same consistency as the dough: Place the butter on a flat work surface, and with a dough scraper, smear it bit by bit across the surface. The butter is ready when it is smooth, soft, and still cool.

4. With the mixer on medium-low speed, add the butter, a few tablespoons at a time. When all of the butter has been added, increase the mixer speed to medium-high for 1 minute. Then reduce the speed to medium and beat the dough for 5 minutes. The dough will be soft and sticky.

5. Cover the bowl tightly with plastic wrap, and let the dough rise at room temperature until doubled in bulk, 2 to 2½ hours.

6. Punch the dough down. Cover the bowl tightly with plastic wrap and refrigerate the dough overnight, or for at least 4 to 6 hours, during which time it will continue to rise and may double in size again. (At this point the dough can be frozen: Punch it down, wrap it tightly in plastic wrap, and store it in the freezer. The dough can remain frozen for up to 1 month. Thaw the dough, still wrapped, in the refrigerator overnight and use it directly from the refrigerator.)

7. Butter two rectangular bread pans and set them aside.

8. Divide the dough into 12 equal pieces. Roll each piece of dough tightly into a ball, and place 6 pieces side by side in each of the pans. Cover the pans with a clean cloth, and let the dough rise until doubled in bulk, 1 to 1½ hours.

EQUIPMENT:
Two 1-quart rectangular bread pans, preferably nonstick; a heavy-duty mixer.

2 LOAVES, ABOUT 12 SLICES EACH

9. Preheat the oven to 375 degrees F.

10. Lightly brush the brioche with the egg wash. Working quickly, use the tips of a pair of sharp scissors to snip several crosses along the top of the dough. (This will help the brioche rise evenly as it bakes.) Place the pans in the center of the oven and bake until the loaves are deeply golden and an instant-read thermometer plunged into the center of the bread reads 200 degrees F, 30 to 35 minutes. Remove the pans from the oven and place them on a rack to cool. Turn the loaves out once they have cooled.

NOTE: The brioche is best eaten the day it is baked. It can be stored for a day or two, tightly wrapped. To freeze, wrap it tightly and store for up to 1 month. Thaw the brioche, still wrapped, at room temperature.

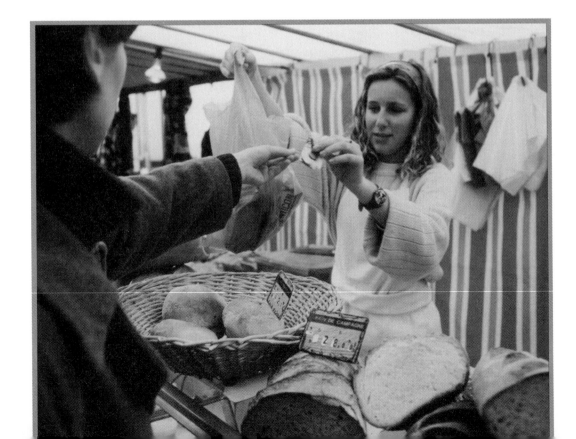

SOCCA: CHICKPEA FLOUR CRÊPES FROM NICE

Socca: Crêpes Niçoises à la Farine de Pois Chiches

On those many gray and rainy days in Paris, I often light the oven and make these delicious crêpes as an appetizer to a warming cold-weather meal. These golden treats, which can be found on the market streets of Nice, are very easy to make at home and I find that they are always a great hit with guests. They can be cut into wedges, rolled up like a crêpe, and eaten out of hand.

1. In a large bowl, combine the flour and water and stir to blend. Stir in the oil and sea salt.

2. Preheat the oven to 450 degrees F.

3. Brush a 12-inch paella or pizza pan with oil, and place it in the oven until the oil sizzles, 3 to 4 minutes. Pour about one fourth of the batter into the hot pan, tipping and swirling it to evenly coat the pan. (The batter should be about ⅛ inch thick.) Place the pan in the center of the oven and bake until the crêpe is firm and is just beginning to brown around the edges, 4 to 5 minutes.

4. Remove from the oven, drizzle with additional oil if desired, and season generously with freshly ground black pepper. Repeat with the remaining batter. Serve immediately, cutting the *socca* into wedges. Guests can roll the slices like a crêpe and eat the *socca* out of hand. Serve with plenty of paper napkins!

2 cups chickpea flour

2 cups water

4 tablespoons extra-virgin olive oil

1 teaspoon fine sea salt

Extra-virgin olive oil, for garnish (optional)

Freshly ground black pepper to taste

EQUIPMENT:
A 12-inch paella pan or pizza pan.

4 12-INCH CRÊPES, ABOUT 16 SERVINGS

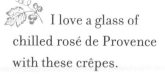 I love a glass of chilled rosé de Provence with these crêpes.

FRESH ALMONDS, ZUCCHINI, CURRY, AND MINT

RICHARD-LENOIR MARKET ZUCCHINI-TOMATO GRATIN

ZUCCHINI STUFFED WITH GOAT CHEESE AND MINT

EGGPLANT, TOMATO, AND PARMESAN GRATIN

SAUTÉED ASPARAGUS WITH SPRING HERBS

ASPARAGUS, MORELS, AND ASPARAGUS CREAM

RICH AND POOR: ASPARAGUS AND BABY LEEKS

VEGETABLES
Les Légumes

GÉRARD MULOT'S GREEN BEANS WITH SNOW PEAS AND CHIVES

GALLOPIN'S GREEN BEAN, MUSHROOM, AND HAZELNUT SALAD

WILD MOREL MUSHROOMS IN CREAM AND BOUILLON

FRÉDÉRIC ANTON'S TWICE-COOKED MUSHROOMS

PIERRE GAGNAIRE'S JERUSALEM ARTICHOKE PURÉE

BENOÎT'S CARROTS WITH CUMIN AND ORANGE

ALAIN PASSARD'S TURNIP GRATIN

FRESH ALMONDS, ZUCCHINI, CURRY, AND MINT

Etuvée de Jeunes Courgettes aux Curry, Menthe, et Amandes Fraîches

During the last days of chef Joël Robuchon's reign on avenue Raymond Poincaré, during the spring of 1996, he served this dish. I make it often, especially when I can find fresh almonds from Provence in the market. Serve this as an accompaniment to roast squab or lamb.

1. In a large bowl, combine the zucchini, almonds, curry powder, sea salt, and white pepper. Toss together, cover securely with plastic wrap, and set aside for 15 minutes for the almonds and zucchini to absorb the seasonings.

2. In a large nonstick skillet, heat the oil over high heat until hot but not smoking. Transfer the almond-zucchini mixture to the pan and cook, shaking the pan frequently, until golden, 3 to 4 minutes. The zucchini should remain crunchy. Add the mint and toss to blend evenly. Taste for seasoning.

3. Mound the warm almond-zucchini mixture in a serving bowl, and serve family-style.

1 pound young zucchini, scrubbed, trimmed (but not peeled), cut into pieces roughly the size of an almond

½ cup fresh shelled almonds (or substitute whole blanched almonds)

2 teaspoons Homemade Curry Powder (page 289), or to taste

Fine sea salt to taste

Freshly ground white pepper to taste

2 tablespoons extra-virgin olive oil

24 fresh mint leaves, cut into a fine chiffonade (fine slivers)

6 SERVINGS

Curry suggests a fragrant wine that will withstand its power: Try a rosé Côtes-du-Provence or a rosé Arbois from the Jura. If accompanied by lamb or pigeon, try a Savingy-lès-Beaune from Burgundy.

RICHARD-LENOIR MARKET ZUCCHINI-TOMATO GRATIN

Gratin de Courgettes aux Tomates Marché Richard-Lenoir

In the summer months, Paris's roving markets are filled with blindingly beautiful fresh fruits and vegetables, many of them grown just on the outskirts of the city. On Sunday mornings I can often be found on the boulevard Richard-Lenoir near the Bastille, shopping for tiny, tender zucchini with the blossoms still attached. The golden blossoms give the dish an almost Asian flavor.

1. Preheat the oven to 450 degrees F.

2. In a 1-quart gratin dish, layer half of the bread crumbs, half of the zucchini, a fine sprinkling of sea salt, half the zucchini blossoms, if using, and half of the tomato sauce. Continue with the remaining bread crumbs, half of the cheese, the remaining zucchini, a fine sprinkling of sea salt, the remaining blossoms, if using, the remaining tomato sauce, and the remaining cheese.

3. Place the dish in the center of the oven and bake until the gratin is bubbling and crisp, 20 to 25 minutes. Serve warm or at room temperature.

⅓ cup fresh bread crumbs
1 pound small fresh zucchini, scrubbed and cut into thin rounds
Fine sea salt to taste
12 zucchini blossoms (optional)
2 cups Tomato Sauce (page 300)
1 cup freshly grated Parmigiano-Reggiano cheese

EQUIPMENT:
A 1-quart gratin dish.

4 SERVINGS

Marché Richard-Lenoir

BOULEVARD RICHARD-LENOIR,
BEGINNING AT RUE AMELOT
PARIS 11
9 A.M. TO NOON, THURSDAY AND
SUNDAY
MÉTRO: BASTILLE OR RICHARD
LENOIR

ZUCCHINI STUFFED WITH GOAT CHEESE AND MINT

Courgettes Farcies au Fromage de Chèvre et à la Menthe

I confess that during the summer months, I am thoroughly addicted to this preparation—tender round zucchini stuffed with goat cheese and mint. Sometimes I serve abundant portions as a vegetarian main course, along with a huge green salad. When I can find the tiny round zucchini in the markets, that's what I use, because they are truly made for stuffing. If they are not available, use the smallest and freshest standard elongated zucchini you can find, cutting them in half lengthwise and proceeding as described.

1. Preheat the oven to 400 degrees F. Prepare a large bowl of ice water.

2. Cut the tops off the zucchini, and reserve. With a small spoon, scoop out the pulp of the zucchini. Chop the pulp. Reserve both the pulp and the zucchini shells.

3. Bring a large pot of water to a boil. Add the zucchini shells and the tops, and blanch until softened but still firm, about 5 minutes. Transfer the zucchini to the bowl of ice water to refresh and firm the vegetable, and to retain its bright green color. Drain.

2 pounds (about 8) small round zucchini

1 small onion, peeled and cut into thin rounds

2 tablespoons extra-virgin olive oil

Sea salt to taste

Curry powder, preferably homemade (page 289), to taste

About 8 ounces fresh goat cheese

Several tablespoons heavy cream or whole milk

4 tablespoons fresh mint leaves, cut into a chiffonade

EQUIPMENT:
A food processor.

8 SERVINGS

4. In a small heavy skillet, combine the onions, oil, and a pinch of sea salt. Sweat the onions, covered, over low heat until soft and cooked through, about 5 minutes. The onions should not brown. Add the zucchini pulp and curry powder, and cook until softened, about 5 more minutes. Set aside.

5. In the bowl of a food processor, combine the goat cheese and 1 tablespoon of the cream. Process to a purée. If necessary, add more cream to form a smooth mixture. Set aside.

6. Place the zucchini side by side in a large baking dish. Spoon the curried onion mixture into the zucchini, filling each one about two-thirds full. Sprinkle with half the mint. Spoon the cheese purée over the curried mixture, filling the zucchini all the way to the top. Sprinkle with the rest of the mint. Place the tops on the zucchini.

7. Place the dish in the center of the oven and bake until the zucchini are soft, about 15 minutes. Serve warm or at room temperature.

EGGPLANT, TOMATO, AND PARMESAN GRATIN

Gratin d'Aubergines, Tomates, et Parmesan

The classic trio of shiny black eggplant, brilliant red tomato sauce, and nutty freshly grated Parmesan cheese remains one of my very favorite combinations. Come August, when Paris empties out and seems more like a village than a big city, and we have delightfully generous hours of daylight, this is a favorite weeknight main-dish dinner, often served with a green salad and a nice, spicy red wine from the Rhône Valley.

1. Preheat the oven to 425 degrees F.

2. Prick the eggplants all over with a two-pronged fork. Place the eggplants directly on the oven rack (to allow air to circulate as they cook). The eggplant will roast rather than steam, giving the vegetable a richer, denser, and slightly smoky flavor. Place a baking sheet on a rack beneath the eggplants to collect any juices. Cook until the eggplants are soft and collapsed, about 25 minutes.

3. Remove the eggplants from the oven, but leave the oven on. Trim off the stem end. Cut each eggplant in half lengthwise, without cutting through the bottom skin. Open like a book, and flatten. Arrange the eggplant on baking sheets, and season with sea salt and white pepper.

6 small, fresh eggplants (each about 8 ounces), rinsed and dried
Sea salt to taste
Freshly ground white pepper to taste
Several teaspoons extra-virgin olive oil
About 1 cup Tomato Sauce (page 300)
3 tablespoons freshly grated Parmigiano-Reggiano cheese

6 SERVINGS

Drizzle with oil. Spoon the Tomato Sauce over the eggplants and sprinkle with the cheese.

4. Bake until sizzling and fragrant, about 25 minutes. Serve warm or at room temperature.

I serve this with a favorite red from the Rhône, such as the spicy Domaine de l'Oratoire Saint-Martin from the charming hilltop village of Cairanne.

73

SAUTÉED ASPARAGUS WITH SPRING HERBS

Asperges Sautées à Cru
aux Herbes Printanières

I think that next to artichokes, asparagus is my favorite spring vegetable. Each year I try to add one or two new recipes to my repertoire. This one was inspired by a visit to the Richard-Lenoir market one April weekend. Serve it as a first course or as a vegetable accompaniment to a simple roast chicken.

1. In a skillet large enough to hold the asparagus in a single layer, heat the oil over moderate heat until hot but not smoking. Add the asparagus and carefully roll them to coat evenly with the oil. Add the chicken stock. Reduce the heat to low, cover, and cook until the asparagus are tender but still firm when pierced with the tip of a knife, about 5 minutes. Drizzle with a few drops of lemon juice.

2. Meanwhile, in a small saucepan, combine the butter, minced shallot, and a pinch of sea salt. Sweat (cook gently until soft but not browned) over moderate heat for about 2 minutes. Taste for seasoning. Cover and set aside.

3. Divide the asparagus among four warmed plates, sprinkle with the shallots and herbs, season to taste, and serve immediately.

3 tablespoons extra-virgin olive oil

12 spears fresh green asparagus, trimmed and peeled

6 tablespoons Homemade Chicken Stock (page 297)

Several drops freshly squeezed lemon juice

2 tablespoons unsalted butter

1 small shallot, peeled and very finely minced

Fine sea salt to taste

Freshly ground white pepper to taste

Minced fresh chives, chervil, and parsley leaves, mixed, for garnish

4 SERVINGS

Try this with a Muscat *sec* from Alsace, a much-underrated wine that is a great palate opener.

Marché Richard-Lenoir

BOULEVARD RICHARD-LENOIR,
BEGINNING AT RUE AMELOT
PARIS 11
9 A.M. TO NOON, THURSDAY
AND SUNDAY
MÉTRO: BASTILLE OR RICHARD
LENOIR

ASPARAGUS, MORELS, AND ASPARAGUS CREAM

Etuvées de Morilles, Crème aux Points d'Asperges

Guy Savoy, one of Paris's most creative and talented chefs, serves these delicate spears of green asparagus with a colorful and creamy purée of asparagus and wild morel mushrooms steeped in cream, a classic French combination that never fails to elicit raves.

1. Trim the asparagus, discarding the tips of the woody ends. Trim the tender tops to about 4 inches. Reserve the remaining ends.

2. Prepare a large bowl of ice water.

3. Fill a 4-quart pot, fitted with a colander, with 3 quarts water and bring to a boil over high heat. Add the 3 tablespoons coarse sea salt and the asparagus tops. Boil, uncovered, until the tops are crisp-tender, about 3 minutes. (The cooking time will vary according to the size of the asparagus.) Immediately remove the colander from the water, drain the asparagus, reserving the cooking water, and plunge the colander into the ice water so the asparagus will cool down as quickly as possible and retain its crispness and bright green color. As soon as the asparagus is cool (no longer than 1 to 2 minutes, or the spears will soften and begin to lose crispness and flavor), drain them and wrap in a thick towel to dry. (The asparagus can be

1 pound thin green asparagus

3 tablespoons coarse sea salt

Fine sea salt to taste

Freshly ground white pepper to taste

2 tablespoons unsalted butter

2 cups Morels in Cream (see Variation, page 85), warmed

EQUIPMENT:
A 4-quart pasta pot fitted with a colander; a food mill; a food processor

8 SERVINGS

cooked up to 2 hours in advance. Keep them wrapped in the towel and hold at room temperature.)

4. Bring the water back to a boil, add the asparagus ends, and boil, uncovered, until very tender, about 8 minutes. Drain the asparagus ends and transfer to the bowl of a food processor. Process to a smooth purée. Pass the purée through the finest grid of a food mill to remove any tough fibers. Taste for seasoning. (The purée can also be prepared up to 2 hours in advance. Transfer to a container, cover, and hold at room temperature.)

5. At serving time, melt the butter in a large skillet and gently reheat the asparagus. Arrange the morels in a mound on warmed salad plates. Spoon the asparagus purée around the morels. Arrange the asparagus spears teepee-fashion over the morels, and serve immediately.

Guy Savoy

18, RUE TROYON
PARIS 17
TELEPHONE: 01 43 80 40 61
FAX: 01 46 22 43 09
MÉTRO: CHARLES DE
GAULLE–ETOILE

RICH AND POOR: ASPARAGUS AND BABY LEEKS

Le Duo d'Asperges et Jeunes Poireaux

Come early March, the markets of Paris explode with a flourish of green. Pencil-thin spring leeks arrive, looking like lithe young ladies, while Provence steps in to provide the slimmest of green asparagus. The match is one made in heaven, for the common leek is often called "the asparagus of the poor." In this recipe, inspired by a version offered by Alain Ducasse's deputy chef Frank Cerutti, the two are anointed with a touch of butter and then a few drops of balsamic vinegar to "wake them up." (If slim leeks are not available, prepare this with all green asparagus.)

1. Trim the leeks at the root end. Rinse well under cold running water. Transfer them to a bowl of cold water and soak for 5 minutes to rid of any remaining dirt. When all the grit has settled to the bottom of the bowl, remove the leeks and dry thoroughly.

2. Place the leeks in a saucepan that will hold them in a single layer. Cover with the chicken stock, cover the pan, and simmer until tender, about 8 minutes. Drain. Set aside and keep warm.

3. Trim the asparagus, discarding the tips of the woody ends. Trim the tender tops to about 7 inches. (Reserve the less tender ends for an asparagus purée or a velouté.)

8 baby leeks, white portion only, trimmed to about 7 inches

About 2 cups Homemade Chicken Stock (page 297)

8 asparagus spears (about 8 ounces trimmed weight)

3 tablespoons coarse sea salt

2 tablespoons unsalted butter

3 tablespoons freshly grated Parmigiano-Reggiano cheese

About 1/2 teaspoon balsamic vinegar

Fleur de sel (see page 102) or fine sea salt

Minced fresh chives, for garnish

EQUIPMENT:
A 6-quart pasta pot fitted with a colander.

4 SERVINGS

4. Prepare a large bowl of ice water.

5. Fill the pasta pot, fitted with a colander, with 5 quarts water and bring to a boil over high heat. Add the 3 tablespoons salt and the asparagus, and boil, uncovered, until the spears are crisp-tender, 3 to 4 minutes. (The cooking time will vary according to the size of the asparagus.) Immediately remove the colander from the water, drain the asparagus, and plunge the colander into the ice water so the asparagus will cool down as quickly as possible and retain its crispness and bright green color. As soon as the asparagus is cool (no longer than 1 to 2 minutes, or the spears will soften and begin to lose crispness and flavor), drain them and wrap in a thick towel to dry.

6. In a skillet large enough to hold both the leeks and the asparagus in a single layer, warm the butter over moderate heat just until it begins to foam. Add the two vegetables, alternating them side by side. Sprinkle all over with the cheese, being careful to keep the vegetables in place. As the cheese melts into the vegetables and butter, it should form a thick emulsion. Cook gently just until warmed through, being careful not to burn the butter, 2 to 3 minutes. Drizzle with the balsamic vinegar. Immediately transfer the vegetables to salad plates, season with fine *fleur de sel*, garnish with minced chives, and serve.

While the slight bitterness of asparagus can make wine a difficult choice, there are solutions. I enjoy this with a young Chardonnay, any Sauvignon Blanc, an Alsatian Pinot Gris, or a Jurançon *sec*.

Restaurant Alain Ducasse au Plaza Athénée

25, AVENUE MONTAIGNE
PARIS 8
TELEPHONE: 01 53 67 65 00
FAX: 01 53 67 65 00
MÉTRO: FRANKLIN D. ROOSEVELT

GÉRARD MULOT'S GREEN BEANS WITH SNOW PEAS AND CHIVES

Les Haricots Verts, Pois Gourmands, et Ciboulette de Gérard Mulot

Paris's *boulangeries* have become great spots for picking up a carry-out lunch of sandwiches and salads. This spring-fresh salad from the excellent bakery–pastry shop run by Gérard Mulot is a favorite of mine. In it, crisp green beans are combined with equally crunchy snow peas and tossed with a touch of vinaigrette. The chives here are a welcome addition, adding a gentle hint of fresh onion. The combination of flavors is at once grassy, fresh, and springlike. The minced shallots add an almost sweet counterpoint. You can also add some sliced tomatoes for flavor and color contrast. Serve the salad as a main course with toasted country bread or as a side dish to accompany a simple fish, meat, or poultry preparation.

1. Prepare a large bowl of ice water.

2. Fill a large pasta pot, fitted with a colander, with 3 quarts water and bring to a boil over high heat. Add the 4 tablespoons sea salt and the beans, and cook until crisp-tender, about 5 minutes. (The cooking time will vary according to the size and tenderness of the beans.) Immediately remove the colander from the water, let it drain over the pot, and then plunge the colander into the ice water so the beans cool down as quickly as possible. As

4 tablespoons sea salt
8 ounces green beans, rinsed and trimmed
8 ounces snow peas, rinsed and trimmed
2 tablespoons fresh minced chives
2 shallots, peeled and finely minced
Several tablespoons Classic Vinaigrette (page 278)
Fine sea salt to taste
Freshly ground white pepper to taste

EQUIPMENT:
A large pasta pot fitted with a colander.

4 SERVINGS

soon as the beans are cool (no longer than 1 to 2 minutes, or they will become soggy and begin to lose flavor), drain them and wrap them in a thick towel to dry. (The beans can be cooked up to 4 hours in advance. Keep them wrapped in the towel, and refrigerate if desired.)

3. Repeat for the snow peas: Bring the water in the pot back to a boil over high heat. Add the snow peas and cook until they are crisp-tender, 2 to 3 minutes. (The cooking time will vary according to the size and tenderness of the peas.) Immediately remove the colander, drain, and plunge the colander into the ice water so the peas cool down as quickly as possible. As soon as the peas are cool (no more than 1 to 2 minutes, or they will become soggy and begin to lose flavor), drain them and wrap them in a thick towel to dry. (The snow peas can be cooked up to 4 hours in advance. Keep them wrapped in the towel, and refrigerate if desired.)

4. Combine the beans, snow peas, chives, and shallots in a large salad bowl. Toss gently. Add the vinaigrette and toss to coat evenly. Taste for seasoning, and serve immediately.

Boulangerie-
Pâtisserie Gérard
Mulot

76, RUE DE SEINE
PARIS 6
TELEPHONE: 01 43 26 85 11
MÉTRO: MABILLON

GALLOPIN'S GREEN BEAN, MUSHROOM, AND HAZELNUT SALAD

Le Salade de Haricots Verts, Champignons, et Noisettes de Gallopin

I last sampled this classic bistro salad at the colorful Gallopin, just across the street from the Paris *bourse*, or stock market. This is the sort of dish that depends upon freshness and care all around. It's hearty enough to serve as an entire luncheon meal, or as a first course as part of a major bistro feast.

1. Prepare a large bowl of ice water.

2. Fill a large pasta pot, fitted with a colander, with 3 quarts water and bring to a boil over high heat. Add the 4 tablespoons salt and the beans, and cook until crisp-tender, about 5 minutes. (The cooking time will vary according to the size and tenderness of the beans.) Immediately remove the colander from the water, allow the water to drain from the beans, and plunge the colander into the ice water so the beans cool down as quickly as possible. As soon as the beans are cool (no more than 1 to 2 minutes, or they will become soggy and begin to lose flavor), drain them and wrap them in a thick towel to dry. (The beans can be cooked up to 4 hours in advance. Keep them wrapped in the towel, refrigerated if desired.)

4 tablespoons fine sea salt

8 ounces green beans, rinsed and trimmed at both ends

8 ounces fresh mushrooms, wiped clean, stems removed, thinly sliced

1 small shallot, peeled and finely minced

About 3 tablespoons minced fresh chives

3 tablespoons freshly toasted hazelnuts, coarsely chopped (see Note)

HAZELNUT VINAIGRETTE

1 tablespoon best-quality sherry wine vinegar (or best-quality red wine vinegar)

Fine sea salt to taste

3. In a large bowl, combine the green beans, mushrooms, shallot, chives, and toasted hazelnuts. Set aside.

4. Prepare the vinaigrette: In a small bowl, combine the vinegar and sea salt. Whisk to blend. Add the oil, whisking to blend. Taste for seasoning.

5. At serving time, pour the vinaigrette over the salad. Toss gently to blend, and serve.

NOTE: Toasting nuts imparts a deep, rich flavor: Preheat the oven to 350 degrees F. Spread the nuts on a baking sheet, and toast in the oven until fragrant and evenly browned, about 10 minutes.

3 to 4 tablespoons best-quality hazelnut oil (or extra-virgin olive oil)

EQUIPMENT:
A large pasta pot fitted with a colander.

2 SERVINGS AS A MAIN COURSE; 4 SERVINGS AS A FIRST COURSE

Gallopin

40, RUE NOTRE-DAMES-DES-VICTOIRES
PARIS 2
TELEPHONE: 01 42 36 45 38
MÉTRO: BOURSE

WILD MOREL MUSHROOMS IN CREAM AND BOUILLON

Morilles Sauvages à la Crème et au Bouillon

Rare fresh morels arrive in the Paris markets in early March, just as the last crop of the equally rare black truffle says its farewell for the season. But I depend upon dried morel mushrooms year-round, always keeping a supply on hand for making this rich and elegant vegetable sauce, great for tossing with pasta or rice. I also serve it with Benoît's Fricassée of Chicken with Morels (page 192).

2 cups (2 ounces) dried
   morel mushrooms
3 tablespoons unsalted
   butter, softened
Fine sea salt to taste
2 shallots, peeled and
   finely minced
2 cups heavy cream
2 teaspoons freshly
   squeezed lemon juice,
   or to taste
Freshly ground white
   pepper to taste

6 TO 8 SERVINGS

1. If any of the morels are extremely large, halve them lengthwise. Place the morels in a colander and rinse well under cold running water to rid them of any grit. Transfer them to a heatproof measuring cup. Pour boiling water over the mushrooms to cover. Set aside for 20 minutes to plump them up. With a slotted spoon, carefully remove the mushrooms from the liquid, leaving behind any grit that may have fallen to the bottom.

2. Place a piece of dampened cheesecloth in a colander set over a large bowl. Carefully spoon the mushroom soaking liquid into the colander, leaving behind any grit at the bottom of the measuring cup. You should have 1½ cups of mushroom bouillon. Set it aside.

3. In a medium-size skillet, combine the butter, a pinch of sea salt, and the shallots. Sweat, covered, over moderate heat without letting the shallots color, 2 to 3 minutes. Add the drained morels and about ½ cup of the mushroom bouillon. Cook, uncovered, over moderate heat until the liquid is reduced to 2 to 3 tablespoons, about 5 minutes. Add the cream and remaining 1 cup mushroom bouillon.

4. Simmer, uncovered, over low heat until the morels have lost most of their firmness, 8 to 10 minutes. Add the lemon juice and season generously with white pepper. Taste for seasoning, and serve.

VARIATION: MORELS IN CREAM. For a richer dish, to use in the recipe for Asparagus, Morels, and Asparagus Cream (page 76), or to serve as a side vegetable dish with roast poultry, add only the ½ cup of the mushroom bouillon at Step 3. The remaining 1 cup bouillon can be frozen to enhance a mushroom soup.

IF MUSHROOMS ARE GRITTY, blanch them in salted water for 3 minutes, then rinse under cold running water and drain. This suggestion comes from the late Parisian chef Jean-Claude Ferrero, a passionate mushroom expert.

FRÉDÉRIC ANTON'S TWICE-COOKED MUSHROOMS

Les Champignons en Deux Cuissons de Frédéric Anton

I have worked with chef Frédéric Anton since the early 1980s, when he was an assistant to chef Joël Robuchon. As a Robuchon acolyte, Anton was responsible for ordering—then accepting or rejecting—every leaf of lettuce, every grain of caviar, every squiggling langoustine that entered the kitchen. A perfect dish, as any cook knows, begins with absolutely fresh, flawless ingredients. In the kitchens of the Pré Catelan, where Anton now reigns, he clearly illustrates all he learned in the school of the master, then adds his own uncanny ability to nudge ingredients, create combinations that sing on the palate, and most of all, satisfy. I love spending time with him, and I always learn a trick or two to take home to my own kitchen.

2 tablespoons extra-virgin olive oil
1 pound large fresh cèpe or porcini mushrooms (or substitute chanterelles or girolles, cremini, portobello, or cultivated mushrooms), cleaned, trimmed, and sliced
Sea salt to taste
2 tablespoon unsalted butter
Finely ground white pepper to taste
2 tablespoons minced fresh chervil leaves (or substitute minced fresh tarragon or parsley leaves)
Coarsely ground white pepper, for garnish

4 TO 6 SERVINGS

1. Heat the oil in a large nonstick skillet over moderate heat until hot but not smoking. Add the mushrooms, season lightly with sea salt, and sauté just until they begin to give up their juices, 1 to 2 minutes. Using a slotted spoon, transfer the mushrooms to a platter to drain.

2. Wipe out the skillet with paper towels. Melt the butter over moderate heat and return the mushrooms to the skillet. Season lightly with sea salt and fine white pepper. Cook for 2 minutes more. Remove the pan from the heat, sprinkle the chervil over the mushrooms, and toss to coat them with the herb. Season with coarsely ground white pepper, and serve.

FRÉDÉRICK ANTON SAYS:

"Always cook mushrooms twice:
Once to release their liquid, then again to
intensify their flavor."

Le Pré Catelan

ROUTE DE SURESNES
BOIS DE BOULOGNE
PARIS 16
TELEPHONE: 01 44 14 41 14
FAX: 01 45 24 43 25
MÉTRO: PORTE DAUPHINE

PIERRE GAGNAIRE'S JERUSALEM ARTICHOKE PURÉE

La Purée de Topinambours de Pierre Gagnaire

I have had the good fortune to know and work with chef Pierre Gagnaire since his early restaurant days in the mid 1980s. Now his restaurant is just around the corner from our apartment, and when I need some spectacular culinary inspiration, I spend a morning watching the activity in his kitchens on rue Balzac. Gagnaire is known for offering some of the zaniest, tastiest, and most astonishing combinations of ingredients. Yet the kitchen itself is one of the most classic operations, and oh so calm, quite a contrast to Gagnaire's seemingly theatrical ways. This sublime purée of nutty Jerusalem artichokes, brilliantly seasoned with a touch of vanilla, was served as part of a complex truffle dish one winter several years ago, and I have made it one of my favorite cold-weather vegetables. Serve it as a side dish with roast poultry.

3 cups whole milk

2 pounds Jerusalem artichokes

1 fresh vanilla bean, split in half lengthwise, seeds carefully scraped out and reserved

Sea salt to taste

EQUIPMENT:
A food processor, an immersion mixer.

6 SERVINGS

1. Pour the milk into a large saucepan. Peel the Jerusalem artichokes, chop coarsely, and drop instantly into the milk. (This will stop the vegetable from turning brown as it is exposed to the air.) When all the Jerusalem artichokes are prepared, place the pan over moderate heat and cook gently until soft, about 25 minutes. Watch carefully so the milk does not boil over.

2. Transfer the mixture in small batches to the bowl of a food processor. Purée. (Do not place the plunger in the

feed tube of the processor or the heat will create a vacuum and the liquid will splatter.) Purée until the mixture is perfectly smooth and silky. Professional chefs will purée for as long as 20 minutes!

3. Return the purée to the saucepan and reheat gently. At serving time, stir in the vanilla seeds. Taste for seasoning. Using an immersion mixer (a wand blender), froth the purée. Transfer to a large bowl and serve.

> WHAT I LEARNED: There are purées and there are purées. If you want a perfectly silky purée, allow your mixture to purée in the food processor for 10, 15, even 20 minutes until it is perfectly smooth.

Pierre Gagnaire

Pierre Gagnaire

HÔTEL BALZAC
6, RUE BALZAC
PARIS 8
TELEPHONE: 01 44 35 18 25
FAX: 01 44 35 18 37
MÉTRO: GEORGE V OR CHARLES
DE GAULLE–ETOILE

BENOÎT'S CARROTS WITH CUMIN AND ORANGE

Carottes à l'Orange et au Cumin de Benoît

This beautifully seasoned carrot dish was on the menu when Benoît Guichard took over Jamin in the fall of 1996. The chef's secret weapons are orange juice (which adds a point of fruity acidity to the carrots as they cook) and cumin seed, one of the vegetable's traditional accompaniments.

1. Toast the cumin seeds: Heat a small nonstick skillet over medium heat for 2 minutes. Add the cumin and toast, stirring and shaking the pan constantly to prevent burning. Watch carefully, for the seeds will brown quickly. (Lower the heat if the cumin appears to be browning too quickly.) Toast just until the cumin fills the kitchen with its fragrance and turns dark brown, about 4 minutes total. Immediately transfer the cumin seeds to a plate to cool.

2. In a large skillet, heat the oil over moderately high heat until hot but not smoking. Add the carrots, garlic, sugar, and toasted cumin seeds. Add enough water to cover the carrots by half. Add the bouquet garni and salt to taste.

3. Butter a piece of wax paper, poke several holes in the paper, and place it, butter side down, on top of the carrots. Bring to a boil over high heat. Reduce to a simmer and cook for 25 minutes. Remove and discard the wax paper and the bouquet garni. Add the orange juice and cook over low heat, uncovered, stirring from time to time, until almost all the liquid has evaporated, about 10 minutes. At serving time, stir in the butter. Taste for seasoning and serve.

2 tablespoons cumin seeds

3 tablespoons extra-virgin olive oil

1½ pounds carrots, peeled and thinly sliced

1 plump, fresh clove garlic

1 teaspoon sugar

1 bouquet garni: 2 bay leaves and a bunch of fresh thyme, tied together with household string

Sea salt to taste

½ cup freshly squeezed orange juice (juice of 3 oranges)

1 tablespoon unsalted butter

8 TO 10 SERVINGS

Jamin

32, RUE DE LONGCHAMP
PARIS 16
TELEPHONE: 01 45 53 00 07
FAX: 01 45 53 00 15
MÉTRO: TROCADÉRO

ALAIN PASSARD'S TURNIP GRATIN

Gratin de Navets Alain Passard

Each Saturday morning in *Le Figaro*, chef Alain Passard offers an incredible assortment of recipe ideas revolving around a particular ingredient. One day in February the subject was Cantal, the rich golden cheese of the Auvergne mountains. He suggested this preparation, which I promptly followed. This vegetable gratin is delicious on its own with a tossed green salad, or as a vegetable accompaniment to a roast chicken, roast pork, or veal.

1. Preheat the oven to 400 degrees F.

2. Butter a 2-quart gratin dish, and in it layer half the turnips. Season well with sea salt and black pepper, and then layer half the cheese. Season that layer. Repeat with the remaining turnips and the remaining cheese, seasoning well after each layer. Add milk just to cover. Sprinkle with the thyme and more sea salt and pepper. Place the dish in the center of the oven and bake until the turnips are soft and have absorbed most of the milk, 1 to 1¼ hours. Serve immediately.

1½ pounds round spring turnips, peeled and cut into thin rounds

Sea salt

Freshly ground black pepper

4 ounces cow's-milk cheese, such as Cantal or Cheddar, coarsely grated

1½ cups whole milk

½ teaspoon fresh thyme leaves

EQUIPMENT:
A 2-quart gratin dish.

4 TO 6 SERVINGS

Arpège

84, RUE DE VARENNE
PARIS 7
TELEPHONE: 01 45 51 47 33
FAX: 01 44 18 98 39
MÉTRO: VARENNE

SAUTÉED POTATOES LA FONTAINE DE MARS

DAVID VAN LAER'S POTATOES ANNA

CHEZ HENRI'S SAUTÉED POTATOES

POTATOES
Les Pommes de Terre

NOIRMOUTIER POTATOES WITH FLEUR DE SEL

THE ASTOR'S WARM POTATO, TRUFFLE, AND PARMESAN SALAD

Joël Robuchon

SAUTÉED POTATOES LA FONTAINE DE MARS

Pommes de Terre Sautées à Cru La Fontaine de Mars

While potatoes are sometimes precooked before they are sautéed in fat, in other preparations they are cooked raw, or *à cru,* as these are. The recipe for these golden cubes comes from one of my old-time favorite bistros, La Fontaine de Mars on the Left Bank, which is run by the outgoing Christiane Boudon and her husband, Jacques. If you go on a sunny day, try to secure a table on the terrace. If you look up in the right direction, you will see the very tip of the Eiffel Tower. These rich potatoes often accompany their *confit de canard,* duck that has been cooked and preserved in its own fat. I actually love these all on their own, with a nice simple green salad alongside. I cook them in a cast-iron Dutch oven to avoid spattering fat.

2 pounds russet potatoes
1 cup melted goose or
  duck fat
3 tablespoons unsalted
  butter
Fleur de sel (see page 102)
  or fine sea salt to taste
Freshly ground black
  pepper to taste

EQUIPMENT:
A 6-quart Dutch oven; a
  wire mesh skimmer.

4 SERVINGS

1. Peel the potatoes, rinse them well, and cut them into ½-inch cubes. Place them in a bowl of cold water.

2. Line a baking sheet with paper towels. Set it aside.

3. Place the fat in a 6-quart Dutch oven and heat over high heat until very hot. While the fat is heating, drain the potatoes and pat them dry with a clean towel. Add the potatoes to the Dutch oven, stir to prevent them from sticking together, and sauté uncovered over high heat, stirring regularly, until they are a deep golden brown, 3 to 4 minutes.

4. Using a wire skimmer, carefully transfer the potatoes to a platter. Carefully transfer the hot fat to a large dry container, such as an empty metal can. (Be careful—the fat will be very hot.) Return the potatoes to the Dutch oven, add the butter, and continue cooking over moderate heat, taking care not to burn the butter, just until the potatoes are evenly dark brown, 2 minutes. Transfer to paper towels to drain. Season with *fleur de sel* and black pepper, and serve immediately.

VARIATION: Christiane Boudon suggests that you may want to make these potatoes *bonne femme*, a term used to denote any dish prepared in a simple, family, or rustic manner. These dishes are often served in the container in which they are cooked, such as a casserole dish, plate, or pan. To make these potatoes *bonne femme*, sprinkle them with a mixture of 2 tablespoons minced parsley and 1 tablespoon minced garlic just before sautéing them in butter. Then season with *fleur de sel* and pepper, and serve them directly from the Dutch oven.

Restaurant La
Fontaine de Mars

129, RUE SAINT-DOMINIQUE
PARIS 7
TELEPHONE: 01 47 05 46 44
FAX: 01 47 05 11 13
MÉTRO: ECOLE MILITAIRE

POTATOES

DAVID VAN LAER'S POTATOES ANNA

Pommes Anna David Van Laer

This crusty, crunchy, golden potato cake comes from David Van Laer, and I first sampled it during the early years of his first Left Bank restaurant, Le Bamboche. He has since moved to a new address with a new restaurant name, Maxence, and the rich cake figures on the menu there during the winter months.

1. Preheat the oven to 425 degrees F.

2. Peel and thinly slice the potatoes, dropping them in a bowl of cold water as they are sliced. Rinse the potatoes, drain, and pat dry with a clean towel.

3. Brush the bottom and sides of a 10-inch nonstick cake pan with some of the clarified butter. Starting at the center of the pan, arrange potato slices, overlapping, in a single layer. Brush with butter. Season lightly with sea salt and white pepper. Continue layering in this manner until all the potatoes and butter have been used, occasionally pressing the layers down with the back of a spatula to form a compact cake. Cut out a piece of aluminum foil to fit exactly on top of the potatoes. Place the foil over the potatoes.

4. Place the cake pan in the center of the oven and bake for 30 minutes. Remove the foil and continue baking until the potatoes are golden brown, 25 to 30 minutes more.

2 pounds Yukon Gold or
   russet potatoes
14 tablespoons unsalted
   butter, clarified
Sea salt to taste
Freshly ground white
   pepper to taste

EQUIPMENT:
A 10-inch round nonstick
   cake pan.

8 SERVINGS

Le Maxence

9 BIS, BOULEVARD
MONTPARNASSE
PARIS 6
TELEPHONE: 01 45 67 24 88
FAX: 01 45 67 10 22
MÉTRO: Falguière

Run a small sharp knife around the edge of the pan to loosen the potatoes. Invert the cake pan over a large round serving platter with a lip (to catch any excess butter). Serve immediately, cutting the potato cake into wedges.

ON CLARIFIED BUTTER

CLARIFIED BUTTER HAS A GENTLY NUTTY AROMA and a fine, grainy texture, and can heighten the flavors of many foods. In its natural state, butter has a high water content (about 16 percent) and a small amount of nonfatty substances (about 2 percent). It is the water in butter that causes it to spoil, and the combination of water and the nonfatty substances that cause it to blacken when very hot. Clarified butter is, in essence, purified butter, because the clarification process removes the water and the nonfatty substances, leaving 100 percent pure butter, which can be stored much longer. The greatest advantage of clarified butter is that it can be heated to high temperatures without burning, and it is particularly welcome when you can achieve clean-looking, perfectly browned fruits, vegetables, or meats. Clarified butter can be used whenever butter is called for in cooking, but with care. It is the water in unclarified butter that causes it to sputter and foam when heated, a warning signal to turn down the heat. When overheated, clarified butter reacts just like overheated oil: It will only smoke.

CHEZ HENRI'S SAUTÉED POTATOES

Pommes Sautées Chez Henri

When I spent an afternoon chatting with Josette and Gérard Gélaude at their 1940s bistro, Chez Henri, Monsieur Gélaude at first flinched at the thought of sharing this recipe. He would, in fact, not tell me everything. And since he swears that part of the charm of his *pommes sautées* is that they are cooked on his 50-year-old coal-fired stove, by a chef who has cooked them for 14 years, there is no way we can duplicate them exactly. But I think I have made a pretty good stab at a home version of his potatoes—which in fact are not sautéed at all, but deep-fried. The difference here is that he fries them with the pan covered, which makes for potatoes that have a beautifully crunchy exterior and a potato-rich, moist interior, since the humidity stays inside the potato as it cooks. Chef Gélaude uses the traditional French potato, *bintje*, similar to a long, waxy-fleshed baking potato such as a russet. I also like to use a variety that combines waxy and starchy characteristics, such as Yukon Gold. Because the potatoes are cut into tiny cubes, you get more crunchy surface than in a regular French fry, and they cook through in just 3 to 4 minutes.

2 pounds russet or Yukon Gold potatoes

1 quart peanut or safflower oil

Fine sea salt

EQUIPMENT:

A 6-quart heavy-duty pot with lid or a deep-fryer; a deep-frying thermometer; a wire skimmer.

4 SERVINGS

1. Peel the potatoes, rinse them well, and cut them into ½-inch cubes. Place them in a bowl of cold water.

2. Line a baking sheet with paper towels. Set it aside.

3. Pour the oil into a 6-quart saucepan or a deep-fryer. The oil should be at least 1 inch deep. Place a deep-frying thermometer in the oil and heat the oil to 375 degrees F. While the oil is heating, drain the potatoes and pat them dry with a clean towel. Add the potatoes to the saucepan, stir to prevent them from sticking together, cover the pan, and cook until the potatoes are a deep golden brown, 3 to 4 minutes. (You may need to do this in batches. If so, keep the cooked potatoes warm in a low oven.) Remove with a wire skimmer and transfer to paper towels to drain. Season with fine sea salt, and serve immediately.

Au Moulin à Vent (Chez Henri)

20, RUE DES FOSSÉS SAINT-BERNARD
PARIS 5
TELEPHONE: 01 43 54 99 37
FAX: 01 40 46 92 23
MÉTRO: JUSSIEU OR CARDINAL LEMOINE

NOIRMOUTIER POTATOES WITH FLEUR DE SEL

Pommes de Terre de Noirmoutier à la Fleur de Sel

One spring Thursday at the avenue de Saxe market, the first-of-the-season baby potatoes (smaller than a golf ball) appeared at one stall. Each sack of precious potatoes came with a tiny bag of the equally noble *fleur de sel*, the fine crystals of sea salt that are hand-harvested on the island of Noirmoutier, not far from Nantes on the Atlantic coast. Noirmoutier potatoes are famed for their organic, earthy flavor, with a faint hint of the ocean and the salty soil in which they are grown. The merchant offered this recipe—nothing more than potatoes cooked slowly in butter and coarse salt, then seasoned with the *fleur de sel*. A few weeks later, another merchant offered the exact same recipe, warning, *"Avec les pommes de terre de Noirmoutier, surtout pas d'huile d'olive."* ("With Noirmoutier potatoes, definitely no olive oil.") I confess to loving the potatoes cooked in butter when I am in Paris, and in olive oil when in Provence. Garlic is allowed—just a few cloves in their skins to perfume the potatoes.

2 pounds baby potatoes (fingerlings or small Yukon Gold), rinsed

3 tablespoons unsalted butter (or substitute extra-virgin olive oil)

4 plump, fresh cloves garlic, unpeeled (optional)

Coarse sea salt to taste

Fleur de sel (see page 102)

4 SERVINGS

Place the potatoes in a large pot. Add the butter, garlic if using, and coarse sea salt. Cover and cook over the lowest possible heat, turning from time to time, until the potatoes are tender when pierced with a fork and are browned in patches, about 20 minutes. (The cooking time will vary according to the size of the potatoes.) Using a slotted spoon, transfer the potatoes to a serving bowl. Serve, passing a small dish of *fleur de sel* at the table.

Marché de Breteuil

AVENUE DE SAXE, FROM AVENUE
DE SÉGUR TO PLACE DE
BRETEUIL
PARIS 7
9 A.M. TO NOON, THURSDAY
AND SUNDAY
MÉTRO: SÉGUR

FLEUR DE SEL, CAVIAR OF THE OCEAN

It is an essential ingredient as old as the Romans, so how is it that elementary sea salt—really nothing more than sea-water evaporated by the sun and the wind—has become one of the modern world's gastronomic treasures?

The story of *fleur de sel* actually begins on the windswept Guérande peninsula in the Brittany region of France. Since the Middle Ages it is here, on this jagged body of marshy land jutting out into the Atlantic Ocean, that man has captured the saline water in an intricate series of winding canals and tiny ponds until it is decanted and evaporated into one of the world's most precious commodities, *sel marin,* or sea salt.

Although France's salt trade has been important for centuries, the practice in Brittany had all but died out in recent times. With increasing from large commercial salt operations in the Mediter-ranean, and the ports and salt marshes in poor repair, Brittany's production had almost closed down a few decades ago. In hopes of rescuing their dying craft, a small number of salt-marsh workers—called *paludiers* and *paludières*—banded together in the late 1970s. Today there are about 220 artisans harvesting a total of 10,000 tons of sea salt each year in Brittany.

The rugged men and women who harvest the salt daily from mid-June to mid-September are also known as "gardeners of the Atlantic." Trapping the ocean water at high tide, the salt-marsh workers store the seawater in giant reservoirs for up to one month. Then, pushed by an iodine-rich wind, the increasingly saline water is directed into a labyrinth of smaller and smaller pools or basins, square reservoirs known as *oeillets.* The salt that crystallizes on the surface of the water is carefully raked off and piled into giant alabaster mounds of what we know as *sel gris,* or coarse gray sea salt, also called *sel de mer.* On a good day, a *paludier* working with as many as 60 to 80 *oeillets* can gather up to 100 pounds of salt. This natural product—a source of sodium, potassium, calcium, magne-sium, copper, and zinc—is totally unrefined and unwashed.

At certain times of the year, when the temperature is just right, a dry wind blows in from the east and a very, very fine film of crystals settles at the very edge of those small pools. This, the caviar of the ocean, *fleur de sel*, is traditionally harvested by women, wives of the salt-marsh workers, whose delicate job it is to rake off only the *fleur de sel*, taking none of the larger crystals of *gros sel* with it. The practice is not only a delicate one, but one that is dependent on the vagaries of nature, for the entire day's harvest can be destroyed by a sudden change in the weather. With a faint aroma of iodine—some even say violets—this precious commodity accounts for only 5 percent of the total Breton sea salt production, which is why it is prized and in France costs four times as much as coarse salt. The French like to call it *la fille du vent et du soleil*, "daughter of the wind and the sun," for the moist, delicate, shiny crystals are set in wicker baskets to dry naturally in the sun.

Fleur de sel is the darling of chefs and bakers as well as home cooks. The famed chef Joël Robuchon likes to use both *gros sel* and *fleur de sel* to season his homemade French fried potatoes, since each salt imparts its own flavor and texture on the palate. However one utilizes this gift from the sea, there is one solid rule: *Fleur de sel* is never actually cooked. It is only added as a last-minute seasoning, for everything from a green salad to a resting roasted leg of lamb.

While the *fleur de sel* from Brittany's Guérande peninsula is the most famous in France, there are other excellent small-production salts that come from both the Ile de Noirmoutier and the Ile de Ré on the Atlantic coast, and from the Camargue region along the Mediterranean. Today creative packaging (some are even dated and signed by the salt rakers) has rocketed sea salt into the realm of rare French gastronomic treasures.

Both coarse and fine sea salt are essential to any cook's larder. To my palate, sea salt makes food taste seasoned, while regular table salt (refined and plumped up with additives to prevent clumping) makes food just taste salty.

THE ASTOR'S WARM POTATO, TRUFFLE, AND PARMESAN SALAD

Salade de Pommes de Terre aux Truffes et au Parmesan l'Astor

Joël Robuchon first offered a version of this dish during the last days of his restaurant on avenue Raymond Poincaré in 1996. It has become a family favorite, with or without truffles. When preparing it with the truffles, omit the herb garnish. Without truffles, the garnish serves to provide a fresh herbal note.

1. Scrub the potatoes but do not peel them.

2. Bring 1 quart of water to a simmer in the bottom of a vegetable steamer. Place the potatoes on the steaming rack, place the rack over the simmering water, cover, and steam until a knife inserted in a potato comes away easily, 20 to 30 minutes. Drain the potatoes. As soon as they are cool enough to handle, peel them. Slice the potatoes thin and transfer them to four small individual serving bowls that are safe for a microwave oven. Drizzle the potatoes with olive oil and toss gently to coat lightly with the oil. Season lightly with sea salt and white pepper.

3. With a vegetable peeler, a sharp knife, or a mandoline, very thinly slice the truffles. Transfer the slices to a large plate. Cover the slices with a damp cloth or with plastic wrap to prevent them from drying out. Set aside.

1 pound tiny yellow-flesh potatoes, such as Yukon Gold

About 1 tablespoon extra-virgin olive oil

Sea salt to taste

Freshly ground white pepper to taste

2 fresh black truffles (about 1½ ounces total), cleaned (optional)

12 Oven-Roasted Tomatoes (page 298)

A 2-ounce chunk of Parmigiano-Reggiano cheese

Coarse sea salt

A mix of minced fresh herbs, such as tarragon, dill, and chives, for garnish (optional)

EQUIPMENT:

A microwave oven; a vegetable steamer.

4 SERVINGS

4. Place 3 oven-roasted tomatoes on top of each serving of potatoes. Using a vegetable peeler, shave the Parmesan cheese into long thin strips. Arrange half of the Parmesan shavings on top of the tomatoes. Arrange the truffle slices on top of the cheese. Arrange the rest of the cheese on top of the truffles. Drizzle with oil just to moisten. Cover loosely with plastic wrap.

5. Place the bowls in a microwave oven and microwave at high until just warmed through but not cooked, about 30 seconds.

6. Remove from the oven. Remove the plastic wrap. Drizzle with a few drops of oil. Sprinkle with coarse sea salt and white pepper. Garnish with the herbs, if using. Serve immediately.

I enjoy a sturdy white with this—why not a Châteauneuf-du-Pape Beaucastel Cru du Coudelet Côtes-du-Rhône? This powerful, rich, dry white is a complex and successful blend of Viognier, Marsanne, Bourboulenc, and Clairette grapes.

L'AMBROISIE'S WHITE BEANS WITH MUSTARD AND SAGE

WILLIAM'S SALAD OF FRESH WHITE BEANS, MUSHROOMS,

MIMOLETTE, ARUGULA, AND PISTACHIO OIL

GUY SAVOY'S LENTIL RAGOUT WITH BLACK TRUFFLES

AMBASSADE D'AUVERGNE'S LENTIL SALAD WITH WALNUT OIL

BENOÎT GUICHARD'S MACARONI GRATIN

PASTA, RICE, BEANS, AND GRAINS
Les Pâtes, Riz, Légumes Sec, et Céréales

JOËL ROBUCHON'S MACARONI WITH FRESH TRUFFLES

PENNE WITH MUSTARD AND CHIVES

FLORA'S POLENTA FRIES

HÉLÈNE'S "POLENTA" WITH SHEEP'S-MILK CHEESE

MONSIEUR LAPIN'S POLENTA SAVOYARDE

SPELT "RISOTTO"

FRÉDÉRIC ANTON'S RISOTTO WITH WILD MUSHROOMS

L'AMBROISIE'S WHITE BEANS WITH MUSTARD AND SAGE

Cocos Blancs à la Moutarde et à la Sauge L'Ambroisie

One November evening at a celebratory birthday dinner at L'Ambroisie—Paris's most romantic dining room—we feasted on roasted lamb and these wholesome white beans, touched with a hit of sharp mustard and a hint of fresh sage. The dish is typical of chef Bernard Pacaud's light and subtle touch: That trace of mustard transforms what could be a ho-hum dish into one that elevates the lowly bean to an ingredient of elegance and sophistication. If you can find fresh white beans in the market, by all means use them—they will reward you with a creaminess and nutty flavor that dried beans cannot match.

1. In a large, heavy-bottomed saucepan, combine the olive oil and garlic and stir to coat the garlic with the oil. Place over moderate heat and cook, stirring from time to time, until the garlic is fragrant, about 2 minutes. Do not let the garlic brown. Add the fresh or soaked dried beans, stir to coat with the oil, and cook for 1 minute. Add just enough stock to cover the beans. Add the bay leaves, sage, and fine sea salt. Cover and bring to a simmer over moderate heat. Simmer gently until the beans are tender, about 30 minutes for fresh beans, about 1 hour for soaked dried beans. (The cooking time will vary according to the freshness of the beans.) Stir from time to time to make

3 tablespoons extra-virgin olive oil

20 plump, fresh cloves garlic, peeled and halved lengthwise

2 pounds fresh small white beans in the pod, shelled; or 1 pound dried white *cocos blancs*, flageolets, cannellini, navy, or Great Northern beans, soaked (see Note)

1 quart Homemade Chicken Stock (page 297)

2 fresh or dried bay leaves

Large bunch of fresh sage

Fine sea salt

About 3 tablespoons coarse-grain French Dijon mustard

Extra-virgin olive oil for seasoning at the table

8 SERVINGS

sure the beans do not stick to the bottom of the pan. The beans should be just covered with liquid. Add additional stock or water if necessary as they cook.

2. Remove and discard the bay leaves and sage. Add the mustard to taste, stirring to distribute it evenly throughout the beans. Taste again for seasoning. Serve piping hot. Pass a cruet of extra-virgin olive oil to drizzle over the beans.

NOTE: To prepare dried beans, rinse them, picking them over to remove any pebbles. Place the beans in a large saucepan. Cover with boiling water by 2 inches. Cover and let stand until the beans swell to at least twice their size and have absorbed most of the liquid, about 1 hour. Drain the beans in a colander, discarding the soaking liquid. Proceed with the recipe.

L'Ambroisie

9, PLACE DES VOSGES
PARIS 4
TELEPHONE: 01 42 78 51 45
MÉTRO: SAINT-PAUL

MEMORY LANE

BERNARD AND DANIELLE PACAUD opened their first incarnation of L'Ambroisie along the Left Bank Quai de la Tournelle in the early 1980s, just after my arrival in Paris. Those were heady days of culinary minimalism and *nouvelle cuisine*, when diners flocked to L'Ambroisie for Pacaud's ethereal red pepper mousse, skate with cabbage, and feather-light *mille-feuilles*, or puff pastry. I remember one evening in this contemporary nine-table restaurant when my friend Susy Davidson and I swooned over a particular white Burgundy served that night and Susy remarked, "I wish I could bathe in Meursault."

Later on, it became a custom to stop by L'Ambroisie at the end of the evening, for a nightcap and a chat about the Parisian food world. I remember that once we stopped in with Chicago food writer Bill Rice, after dining at the renowned Tour d'Argent down the street. Now that the Pacauds have moved to the grand Place des Vosges, my husband, Walter, and I continue the tradition, stopping in for a sip of champagne and a chat after a late-night stroll around the Marais.

PASTA, RICE, BEANS, AND GRAINS

WILLIAM'S SALAD OF FRESH WHITE BEANS, MUSHROOMS, MIMOLETTE, ARUGULA, AND PISTACHIO OIL

La Salade de Cocos de Paimpol, Champignons, Huile de Pistache, et Mimolette de William

I have known chef William Ledeuil since the late 1980s, when he was chef at Guy Savoy's first bistro, Le Bistro de l'Etoile, across from Savoy's elegant restaurant near the Arc de Triomphe. I would follow him anywhere, and have, and am a regular customer now at Les Bookinistes, where he cooks some of the most inventive and modern bistro fare in the world. This dish—complex in its evolution but not in execution—is typical of his full-flavored, imaginative fare.

For years Mimolette, the sweet and almost caramel-like cheese from the north of France, was known only to aficionados and wrongly neglected by everyone else. Today chefs are finding that its richness, color, and sweet edge make it a brilliant cheese to be used in place of the more common Italian Parmigiano-Reggiano.

If you can secure fresh shell beans (fresh cranberry or borlotti beans, fresh white cannellini or white kidney beans), by all means buy them. They can be shelled and frozen, then cooked like fresh beans. Their smooth, rich nuttiness and firm sweet flavor will make you a convert forever. Note here that chef Ledeuil, like many French chefs, loves to use Italian balsamic vinegar as a last-minute seasoning.

THE BEANS

1 tablespoon extra-virgin olive oil

3 plump, fresh cloves garlic, peeled and halved lengthwise

Several bay leaves, preferably fresh

Sea salt to taste

1 pound fresh small white (navy) beans or red (cranberry) beans in the pod, shelled; or 8 ounces dried small white beans (such as cannellini, Great Northern, or marrow beans), soaked (see Note)

2 cups Homemade Chicken Stock (page 297)

2 ounces smoked bacon, cut into matchsticks (about ½ cup)

1. In a large saucepan, combine the oil, garlic, bay leaves, and sea salt. Stir to coat with the oil. Sweat—cook, covered, over low heat—until the garlic is fragrant and soft, about 2 minutes. Add the fresh or soaked dried beans and stir to coat with the oil. Add the chicken stock and bacon. Simmer gently, uncovered, until the beans are tender, about 35 minutes. (The cooking time will vary according to the freshness of the beans.) Add additional stock or water if necessary. Let the beans cool in the cooking liquid.

2. Cut each mushroom lengthwise into ⅛-inch-thick slices. Brush both sides of each mushroom slice with olive oil. Season with sea salt, white pepper, and thyme.

3. Preheat a gas, electric, or ridged cast-iron stovetop grill. Or, prepare a wood or charcoal fire. The fire is ready when the coals glow red and are covered with ash.

4. Place the mushroom slices on the grill at a 45-degree angle to the ridges. Grill for 1 minute, pressing down firmly on the mushrooms with a baking sheet to accentuate the impression of the grill marks. Turn the mushrooms to the opposite 45-degree angle and grill for 1 minute more, pressing them firmly with the baking sheet (this will form an even and attractive crosshatch grill mark on the mushrooms). Then turn the mushrooms over and grill in the same way on the other side, pressing down firmly on the mushrooms with the baking sheet, for 2 minutes. Season lightly with sea salt and white pepper. Set aside.

5. Using a vegetable peeler, shave the cheese into long thin strips. (If the chunk of cheese becomes too small to

THE MUSHROOMS

1 pound meaty fresh
  mushrooms, rinsed and
  trimmed, such as
  portobello, sliced
2 tablespoons extra-
  virgin olive oil
Sea salt to taste
Freshly ground white
  pepper to taste
½ teaspoon fresh thyme
  leaves

A 3-ounce chunk of
  French Mimolette or
  Parmigiano-Reggiano
  cheese
1½ ounces arugula leaves,
  stemmed, washed, and
  dried (about 3 cups)
Balsamic vinegar to taste
Sea salt to taste
Several drops of
  pistachio, walnut, or
  olive oil
1 shallot, peeled and
  finely minced
About 1 tablespoon finely
  minced fresh chives
Celery salt

4 SERVINGS

shave, grate the remainder and place it in a bowl.) You should have about 1 cup of shaved cheese. Set aside.

6. Place the arugula leaves in a small bowl. Season to taste with balsamic vinegar, sea salt, and pistachio oil. Toss to evenly coat the greens. Set aside.

7. Using a slotted spoon, transfer the beans to the center of four warmed, shallow soup bowls. Drizzle with balsamic vinegar, pistachio oil, the shallots, and the chives. Spoon several teaspoons of the bean cooking liquid around the edge of the beans. Top the beans with the mushrooms. Arrange several shavings of cheese and any grated cheese on top of the mushrooms. Arrange several dressed arugula leaves around the edge of each bowl, sprinkle with celery salt, and serve.

NOTE: To prepare dried beans, rinse them, picking them over to remove any pebbles. Place the beans in a large saucepan. Cover with boiling water by 2 inches. Cover and let stand until the beans swell to at least twice their size and have absorbed most of the liquid, about 1 hour. Drain the beans in a colander, discarding the soaking liquid. Proceed with the recipe.

THE REGAL FRENCH BEAN

STUDENTS IN MY COOKING SCHOOL are always amazed at the quality and variety of France's fresh white beans. From May until October, one finds the creamy white *cocos blancs* encased in their pale celadon-green pods. Come September, Brittany's prized *haricots de Paimpol* appear in the market and find their way onto many of the city's menus. Whichever variety I find, I use them the day they are purchased, carefully shelling them just before cooking to preserve moisture and freshness. One November day I found them freshly shelled at a vegetable stand at the market along the avenue de Saxe. The merchant suggested that they could be frozen, for a real treat come Christmastime. A revelation, and a *truc* I followed and will never forget.

And when there are no fresh white beans at all, I can still find the incomparably creamy dried *haricots blanc Tarbais*, beans from the southwestern city of Tarbes, at La Grande Epicerie de Paris, 38, rue de Sèvres, Paris 7; telephone: 01 44 39 81 00. Be prepared to pay the price of these luxurious beans. At last purchase, they cost a good 160 francs (about $30) a kilo.

Les Bookinistes

53, QUAI GRANDS-AUGUSTINS
PARIS 6
TELEPHONE: 01 43 25 45 94
FAX: 01 43 25 23 07
MÉTRO: RER SAINT-MICHEL

William Ledeuil and Eric Bruyelle of Les Bookinistes

GUY SAVOY'S LENTIL RAGOUT WITH BLACK TRUFFLES

Petit Ragoût de Lentilles à la Truffe Noire Guy Savoy

The flinty, dusty flavor of the homey lentil creates a remarkable alliance with the elegantly earthy essence of the truffle. This unforgettable, haunting dish has long been on the menu at one of my favorite Paris restaurants, Guy Savoy. I sample this each winter during his memorable truffle feast.

1. Place the lentils in a large fine-mesh sieve and rinse under cold running water. Transfer them to a large heavy-duty saucepan, cover with cold water, and bring to a boil over high heat. When the water boils, remove the saucepan from the heat. Transfer the lentils to a fine-mesh sieve and drain over the sink. Rinse the lentils under cold running water. Return the lentils to the saucepan, add the chicken stock, and bring just to a boil over high heat. Reduce the heat to a simmer. Using a slotted spoon, skim off any impurities that rise to the surface. Once the liquid is clear of impurities, add the carrot and onion. Simmer gently, uncovered, over low heat until the lentils are cooked yet still firm in the center, about 30 minutes. (The cooking time will vary according to the freshness of the lentils: The fresher they are, the more quickly they will cook.) Remove and discard the onion and carrot.

1½ cups French lentils, preferably *lentilles du Puy*

2 cups Homemade Chicken Stock (page 297)

1 carrot, peeled

1 onion, peeled and stuck with a clove

Sea salt

Freshly ground black pepper to taste

4 tablespoons unsalted butter, chilled, cut into small cubes

2 fresh black truffles (about 1½ ounces total), cleaned: one third minced, two thirds cut into small triangles

EQUIPMENT:
A food processor.

4 SERVINGS

2. Transfer the lentils to a fine-mesh sieve set over a bowl. Drain, reserving the cooking liquid. Transfer the reserved liquid and a ladleful of lentils to the bowl of a food processor, and purée. Return the whole lentils and the purée to the saucepan. Add sea salt and black pepper to taste. Add the butter and the minced truffle, and warm over low heat just until the flavors are blended. Taste for seasoning. Transfer the mixture to small warmed plates, sprinkle with the truffle triangles, and serve immediately.

THE MYSTERIOUS BLACK TRUFFLE

Why make such a fuss over a rather gnarled and unprepossessing black tuber? Because of its rarity, its unpredictable nature, its overwhelming and unique fragrance, and its clean, crisp texture. The black truffle also plays an essential historical role in French gastronomy, finding its way into the menus of the most renowned and memorable tables. The fact that production in France has declined over the past hundred years, that man has not been able to reproduce it in laboratories, and that its sale remains a rather clandestine and secret affair adds an air of mystery and excitement.

Guy Savoy

18, RUE TROYON
PARIS 17
TELEPHONE: 01 43 80 40 61
FAX: 01 46 22 43 09
MÉTRO: CHARLES DE
GAULLE–ETOILE

PASTA, RICE, BEANS, AND GRAINS

115

AMBASSADE D'AUVERGNE'S LENTIL SALAD WITH WALNUT OIL

Salade de Lentilles à l'Huile de Noix Ambassade d'Auvergne

When I moved to Paris in 1980, L'Ambassade d'Auvergne was one of my favorite early haunts, serving as a spot for gastronomic discovery. Then so many dishes—such as giant platters of sausages and warming plates of flinty green lentils from the heart of France—were a revelation to me. I can't make lentils without thinking of this lively family restaurant, where regional favorites remain a cornerstone. I like to serve this as a main-course salad accompanied by a tossed green salad.

1. In a large, heavy saucepan, melt the goose fat over medium-high heat. Add the onion and ham and sweat—cook, covered, over low heat—without coloring until soft and translucent, about 5 minutes. Transfer the mixture to a small bowl. Set it aside.

2. Place the lentils in a large fine-mesh sieve and rinse under cold running water. Transfer them to the same heavy saucepan. Cover with cold water, and bring to a boil over high heat. When the water boils, remove the saucepan from the heat. Transfer the lentils to a fine-mesh sieve and drain over the sink. Rinse the lentils under cold running water. Return the lentils to the saucepan, add the chicken stock, and bring just to a boil over high heat. Reduce the heat to a simmer. With a slotted spoon, skim off any impurities that rise to the surface.

THE LENTILS

2 tablespoons goose fat or extra-virgin olive oil

1 onion, peeled and minced

2 ounces smoked ham, cut into tiny dice (½ cup)

3 cups (1 pound) French lentils, preferably *lentilles du Puy*

1 quart Homemade Chicken Stock (page 297)

THE VINAIGRETTE

1 tablespoon French Dijon mustard

2 tablespoons best-quality red wine vinegar or sherry vinegar

⅔ cup best-quality walnut oil or extra-virgin olive oil

1 shallot, peeled and finely minced

Sea salt to taste

Freshly ground black pepper to taste

Once the liquid is clear of impurities, simmer gently, uncovered, over low heat until the lentils are cooked yet still firm in the center, about 30 minutes. (The cooking time will vary according to the freshness of the lentils: The fresher they are, the more quickly they will cook.)

3. Meanwhile, prepare the vinaigrette: In a large salad bowl, combine the mustard and vinegar and whisk to blend. Add the walnut oil and shallots, and whisk again. Season with sea salt and black pepper to taste. Set aside.

4. Place the bacon in a large nonstick skillet and fry over moderate heat until golden brown, 5 to 6 minutes. Using a slotted spoon, transfer the bacon cubes to a plate covered with a double thickness of paper towels.

5. Pour the lentils into a fine-mesh sieve, draining and discarding any remaining liquid. Transfer them to the salad bowl and toss with the vinaigrette until evenly and thoroughly coated. Let the lentils sit until they have absorbed the vinaigrette, about 10 minutes. Sprinkle with the cubed bacon and chives. Taste for seasoning, and serve warm.

Ambassade d'Auvergne

22, RUE DU GRENIER SAINT-
LAZARE
PARIS 3
TELEPHONE: 01 42 72 31 22
FAX: 01 42 78 85 47
MÉTRO: RAMBUTEAU

4 ounces lean slab bacon, rind removed, cubed (1 cup)
3 tablespoons minced fresh chives
Sea salt
Freshly ground black pepper

8 SERVINGS

 A chilled young Beaujolais

THE FAMED *LENTILLES DU PUY*

The best lentils in the world are a deep green, almost black, and have a mysteriously flinty, sometimes peppery flavor. And when they are cooking on top of the stove, they fill the house with an almost pungent earthiness. These qualities are no surprise, for the lentils are grown on the volcanic soil of the rocky Auvergne region in the center of France, a soil that transmits all of its qualities to the well-known *lentilles vertes du Puy*. It's a lentil with an Appellation d'Origine Contrôlée, a quality standard recognized by the French government and given only to products grown according to certain standards and traditions and on certain soils.

WHAT I LEARNED: When was the last time you bought a costly bottle of walnut or hazelnut oil and when you opened it found that the oil was rancid? It happens all the time—and it should not. Nut oils such as walnut and hazelnut are far more perishable than cold-pressed olive oils. And there is a reason: No heat is necessary when pressing an olive to obtain its oil. Nuts, on the other hand, need to be gently nudged to give up their precious oils, so heat is applied when they are pressed. Unfortunately heat also destroys a natural preservative in the oil, which is why nut oils go rancid more quickly than olive oil. There are also other reasons that oils go rancid: The fruit or nut was spoiled from the beginning; the materials used to press it were not totally sanitary; or the container in which the oil was put was not totally sanitary. When you bring a bottle of nut oil home, keep it stored in the refrigerator and use it up within a year.

BENOÎT SAYS:

*"A white sauce is not made in two minutes!
It must be cooked until no flavor of raw flour
remains."*

BENOÎT GUICHARD'S MACARONI GRATIN

Le Gratin de Macaroni
Benoît Guichard

This rich macaroni gratin—a far cry from the macaroni and cheese of my youth—is deliciously moist. Benoît Guichard, Joël Robuchon protégé and chef at the famed Jamin restaurant, cooks the pasta, to plump it, in milk, then cools the cooking liquid down with ice cubes, which prevents the macaroni from drying out. Like so many French dishes, this one is embellished—here by the enrichment of a golden cheese crust and the added sharpness of fresh chives and coarsely ground black pepper. This can be served as a main pasta course accompanied by a salad, or as an accompaniment to grilled or roasted meats or poultry.

1. Prepare the white sauce, or *béchamel*: In a large saucepan scald the milk over high heat, bringing it just to the boiling point. Remove the pan from the heat, add the bay leaves, cover, and set aside to infuse for 10 minutes. Then strain the milk through a fine-mesh sieve into a measuring cup with a pouring spout, and discard the bay leaves.

2. In a large saucepan, melt the butter over moderate heat. Whisk in the flour and cook, stirring constantly, for 1 minute. Do not let the flour brown. Remove the saucepan from the heat and whisk in the hot strained milk, a few tablespoons at a time, stirring constantly until all the milk has been incorporated into the flour mixture.

THE WHITE SAUCE

1 cup whole milk

2 fresh or dried bay leaves

1 tablespoon unsalted butter

1 tablespoon all-purpose flour

Fine sea salt to taste

Freshly grated nutmeg to taste

¾ cup heavy cream

Freshly ground white pepper

THE PASTA

3 quarts whole milk

4 plump, fresh cloves garlic, peeled

4 tablespoons sea salt

12 ounces imported Italian penne pasta

1 cup freshly grated Swiss Gruyère cheese

Coarsely ground white pepper, for garnish

4 tablespoons minced fresh chives, for garnish

3. Return the saucepan to the heat. Add sea salt and a generous grating of nutmeg. Cook over low heat, whisking constantly, until the sauce thickens, 1 to 2 minutes. Continue to cook over the lowest possible heat, whisking constantly, until the sauce is thick and any taste of raw flour is eliminated, another 3 to 4 minutes. Set aside. Once the sauce has cooled, stir in the heavy cream. Season with freshly ground white pepper. Set aside.

4. Preheat the broiler. Place an oven rack about 3 inches from the heat.

5. Prepare the pasta: In a 6-quart pasta pot fitted with a colander, combine the milk and garlic. Scald the milk over high heat, bringing it just to the bubbling point. Remove from the heat, cover, and set aside to infuse for 10 minutes. Remove and discard the garlic. Bring the milk back to a simmer, add the pasta, and cook at a gentle simmer until still firm but *al dente* (you should just be able to cut the pasta with a knife), about 8 minutes. Remove the pot from the heat and add about 12 ice cubes to stop the cooking. Once it has cooled, use a slotted spoon to transfer the pasta to a large bowl. Discard the milk. Toss the drained pasta with the white sauce, and transfer the mixture to a 1½-quart gratin dish. Sprinkle with the cheese.

6. Place the gratin dish on the oven rack, and broil until the cheese is melted and golden, 2 to 3 minutes. Remove the dish from the oven and season generously with coarsely ground white pepper. Garnish with minced chives, and serve immediately.

EQUIPMENT:
A 6-quart pasta pot fitted with a colander; a 1½-quart gratin dish.

8 SERVINGS

This gratin is delicious on its own, or it could be served with a simple roast lamb or veal. In that case, Benoît Guichard suggests a Sociando-Mallet Bordeaux with a few years of age, or a similar *grand cru bourgeois* from the Haut Médoc.

Jamin

32, RUE DE LONGCHAMP
PARIS 16
TELEPHONE: 01 45 53 00 07
FAX: 01 45 53 00 15
MÉTRO: TROCADÉRO

JOËL ROBUCHON'S MACARONI WITH FRESH TRUFFLES

Macaroni aux Truffes Joël Robuchon

Revered chef Joël Robuchon may have closed his restaurant in Paris, but his presence is evident in many of the city's kitchens. Two lieutenants—Benoît Guichard at Jamin and Frédéric Anton at Le Pré Catelan—are following admirably in his footsteps. This elegant macaroni dish was on the menu at Robuchon's final restaurant on the avenue Raymond-Poincaré, served with a simple but sublime roast chicken.

1. Prepare reduced chicken stock: In a 6-quart saucepan, bring the chicken stock to a boil over high heat. (Make sure you use a large saucepan, to prevent the stock from boiling over.) Boil until the mixture is thick and syrupy, reduced to about ½ cup, 10 to 12 minutes. Transfer the liquid to the top of a double boiler, set it over simmering water, cover, and keep warm.

2. In a 6-quart pasta pot fitted with a colander, bring 3 quarts water and the milk, sea salt, and oil to a gentle simmer over moderate heat. (Do not allow the liquid to boil, or it will boil over.) Add the macaroni and cook just until tender, 8 to 10 minutes. Lift the colander from the pot and shake gently to drain well, eliminating as much water as possible. Reserve the cooking water. Set the pasta aside.

2 cups Homemade Chicken Stock (page 297)

1¼ cups whole milk

3 tablespoons sea salt

3 tablespoons extra-virgin olive oil

16 large macaroni, such as zitoni (about 5 ounces total)

3 tablespoons Truffle Butter (page 286)

¾ cup freshly grated Swiss Gruyère cheese

Freshly ground white pepper

4 fresh black truffles (about 3 ounces total), cleaned and sliced into thick rounds

Minced fresh chives, for garnish

EQUIPMENT:

A 6-quart saucepan; a 6-quart pasta pot fitted with a colander; a double boiler.

4 SERVINGS

3. In a large nonstick skillet, melt the truffle butter over moderate heat. Add the macaroni, taking care not to break the pasta. Add a few ladlefuls of the pasta cooking liquid to create a sauce. Sprinkle the cheese evenly over the macaroni and cook, without turning, for 2 minutes.

4. Transfer the macaroni pieces to warmed individual dinner plates. Season with white pepper. Arrange the truffles between the macaroni, and spoon the sauce over the pasta. Spoon the reserved chicken stock around the edge of the dish. Sprinkle with chives, and serve immediately.

I enjoy this dish with a lovely Burgundy, such as a Savigny-lès-Beaune.

TRUC: Having spent a good deal of time in Paris kitchens, I have picked up a number of tips a home cook can copy. One of these is reduced chicken stock, which has become my secret weapon in the kitchen. Often there is a need for a glossy, rich, yet light sauce to accompany a roast, a pasta, a risotto. A swirl of beautiful reduced chicken stock is the answer. My freezer is always well supplied with chicken stock, which I thaw and reduce as needed.

Variations on this dish can often be found at:

Jamin

32, RUE DE LONGCHAMP
PARIS 16
TELEPHONE: 01 45 53 00 07
FAX: 01 45 53 00 15
MÉTRO: TROCADÉRO

Le Pré Catelan

ROUTE DE SURESNES
BOIS DE BOULOGNE
PARIS 16
TELEPHONE: 01 44 14 41 14
FAX: 01 45 24 43 25
MÉTRO: PORTE DAUPHINE

Joël Robuchon

PENNE WITH MUSTARD AND CHIVES

Penne à la Moutarde et à la Ciboulette

Years ago I clipped a version of this recipe from a French magazine article on the history of mustard. It seemed implausible, but since I love pasta and mustard, I gave it a try. I love it! This is definitely a French touch with pasta; you might also be tempted to toss in bits of cubed smoked bacon, ham, or mushrooms. This is a rich dish, so don't plan on it as a main course, but rather a side dish that goes well with roast chicken or lamb. You might even be tempted to play around with different mustards to go with different dishes, shopping at what I call Mustard Heaven, the charming Maille mustard boutique on the place de la Madeleine. Think of an herb mustard for roast chicken, a spicy mustard to pair with grilled pork sausages, a smooth and golden version for rabbit with mustard sauce. I think you can put mustard on anything and everything. Sometimes while I am waiting for my food in a café or bistro, I slather the bread with mustard to assuage my hunger.

3 tablespoons coarse sea salt

8 ounces penne pasta

1 cup heavy cream

1 large egg yolk, lightly beaten

2 tablespoons French Dijon mustard

Sea salt to taste

Freshly ground white pepper to taste

3 tablespoons finely minced fresh chives, for garnish

Freshly grated Parmigiano-Reggiano cheese, for garnish

EQUIPMENT:

A 6-quart pasta pot fitted with a colander.

6 TO 8 SERVINGS

1. In a 6-quart pasta pot fitted with a colander, bring 5 quarts of water to a rolling boil over high heat. Add the 3 tablespoons sea salt and the pasta, stirring to prevent the pasta from sticking. Cook until tender but firm to the bite, about 11 minutes.

2. Meanwhile, in a saucepan that is large enough to hold the pasta, combine the cream, egg yolk, and mustard. Whisk to blend. Season to taste with sea salt and white pepper. Bring to a simmer over low heat. Remove from the heat, cover, and keep warm.

3. Remove the colander and drain the pasta, shaking to remove excess water. Immediately transfer the drained pasta to the sauce in the saucepan. Toss to evenly coat the pasta. Cover, and let rest for 1 to 2 minutes to allow the pasta to thoroughly absorb the sauce. Taste for seasoning. Transfer to warmed salad plates, individual gratin dishes, or a large bowl. Garnish with minced chives and freshly grated cheese, and serve immediately.

This simple pasta dish calls out for a cru Beaujolais—a Brouilly, Morgon, or Fleurie.

Boutique Maille

6, PLACE DE LA MADELEINE
PARIS 8
TELEPHONE: 01 40 15 06 00
MÉTRO: MADELEINE

FLORA'S POLENTA FRIES

Les Frites de Polenta de Flora

Flora Mikula, chef-owner of Les Olivades, is one of my favorite Paris chefs, and one of the few authentically Provençal cooks in the capital. She is a native of Nîmes, a city that straddles the regions of Provence and the Languedoc. Flora trained in Provence, studied in London and New York, was sous-chef to Alain Passard at Arpège, and finally flew off on her own. Her international approach to food is reflected in her menus. Flora served us these amazing, not very French, "fries" one spring afternoon, teamed up with her Spicy Spareribs (page 210). The flavors are explosive: a perfect marriage of the rich corn essence of polenta and the creamy, lactic pungency of Parmigiano-Reggiano cheese. The fries offer three qualities we tend to crave in our foods: crusty, crunchy, salty. These are such a hit, I often serve them as an appetizer at room temperature, stacked up like Lincoln Logs on a serving tray.

1. Lightly oil the jelly-roll pan. Set it aside.

2. In a large, heavy saucepan, bring the milk, rosemary, and sea salt to a boil over high heat. (Watch it carefully, because milk will boil over quickly.) Add the polenta in a steady stream; stirring constantly with a wooden spoon, cook until it is thickened and leaves the side of the pan as it is stirred, about 20 minutes.

1 quart whole milk, plus more if needed

1 tablespoon finely chopped fresh rosemary leaves

1½ teaspoons fine sea salt

1½ cups coarse-grain yellow cornmeal (polenta)

⅓ cup extra-virgin olive oil

1¼ cups freshly grated Parmigiano-Reggiano cheese

3 quarts grapeseed or canola oil, for deep-frying

Fleur de sel or fine sea salt, for garnish

EQUIPMENT:
An electric deep-fat fryer (optional); a jelly-roll pan.

8 SERVINGS

3. Remove from the heat. Add the olive oil and the cheese, stirring to blend thoroughly. If the mixture seems too thick, thin it out with a little additional milk. Pour the polenta onto the oiled jelly-roll pan, and even it out with a spatula. The mixture should be about ½ inch thick. Refrigerate until firm, about 1 hour.

TRUC: While I am a firm believer in chopping as many ingredients as I can by hand (for better control and authenticity of flavor as well as texture), there are some items that do better chopped or minced by mechanical means. Rosemary is one of those. I love the flavor the pungent, aromatic herb emits when it is chopped very very fine. I strip all the leaves off of a branch of fresh rosemary and chop them in my spice grinder; ending up with a fine green powder with a crisp, woodsy perfume.

4. Remove the polenta from the refrigerator and cut it into rectangles measuring about 3½ inches by 1 inch.

5. Pour the grapeseed oil into an electric deep-fat fryer or a heavy 5-quart saucepan. The oil should be at least 2 inches deep. Place a deep-frying thermometer and a wire skimmer in the oil and heat the oil to 375 degrees F. Fry the polenta in batches, about four at a time, until crisp and a deep golden brown, about 2 minutes. (Be careful as you drop the polenta in, and always allow several seconds before adding another, to prevent the fries from sticking together.) Remove and transfer to paper towels to drain. Sprinkle with *fleur de sel*. Serve warm or at room temperature.

Les Olivades

41, AVENUE DE SÉGUR
PARIS 7
TELEPHONE: 01 47 83 70 09
FAX: 01 42 73 04 75
MÉTRO: SÉGUR

HÉLÈNE'S "POLENTA" WITH SHEEP'S-MILK CHEESE

L'Escaoutoun d'Hélène

We are so accustomed to polenta from Italy, we tend to forget that two important regions of France—the Savoy and the Landes in the southwest—are great producers and consumers of corn and corn products. This recipe comes from young Parisian chef Hélène Darroze, a native of the Landes. It is a luscious corn flour preparation lavishly laced with Basque sheep's-milk cheese and Italian mascarpone. The dish is about as dreamy as food like this can get. The first time I sampled this, I dreamed that I had just a few bites of it for dinner every night. While Hélène prepares this with her local corn flour, not cornmeal, I have found the dish works beautifully with imported Italian cornmeal, or polenta. The resulting mixture is much thinner, and richer, than a classic Italian polenta and does not require the traditional lengthy cooking time.

3²⁄₃ cups Homemade Chicken Stock (page 297), or more as needed

¾ cup corn flour or fine-grain yellow cornmeal (polenta)

7 ounces French Basque sheep's-milk cheese, freshly grated (2½ cups)

8 ounces mascarpone cheese

EQUIPMENT:
A 6-quart saucepan; a double boiler.

4 SERVINGS

1. Reduce the chicken stock: In a 6-quart saucepan, bring 2 cups of the stock to a boil over high heat. (Make sure you use a large saucepan, to prevent the stock from boiling over.) Boil until the mixture is thick and syrupy, reduced to about ½ cup, 10 to 12 minutes. Transfer the liquid to the top of a double boiler, set it over simmering water, cover, and keep warm.

2. In a large, heavy saucepan, combine the cornmeal and the remaining 1⅔ cups chicken stock. Stir with a wooden spoon to blend. Cook the mixture over high heat, stirring, until it is thickened and leaves the side of the pan as it is stirred, about 2 minutes. Reduce the heat to low, add both cheeses, and stir to blend. Cook, stirring to melt the cheeses and thoroughly combine the mixture, about 2 minutes more. The mixture should be soft and pourable. (If it is not, thin it out with additional chicken stock.)

3. Pour the mixture into warmed shallow soup bowls. Drizzle with the reduced chicken stock, and serve.

This is delicious paired with Alain Brumont's fruity and elegant red Madiran Domaine de Bouscassé.

Restaurant Hélène Darroze

4, RUE D'ASSAS
PARIS 6
TELEPHONE: 01 42 22 00 11
FAX: 01 42 22 25 40
MÉTRO: SÈVRES-BABYLONE

The Cousin brothers at Au Petit Marguery

MONSIEUR LAPIN'S POLENTA SAVOYARDE

La Polenta Savoyarde de Monsieur Lapin

Monsieur Lapin is the name of a sweet Montparnasse restaurant run by the professional and outgoing Yves Plantard and his partner, chef Francois Ract. Their specialties, of course, include *lapin*, or rabbit, but also rotisserie-grilled rack of lamb with preserved lemons, and a rich bitter-chocolate cake. Also available are several dishes from Chef Ract's childhood village in the mountainous Savoy region of France, known for its yellow-cornmeal dishes, or polenta, the food that feeds the skiers and mountain climbers of the area. In this dish, Chef Ract uses instant polenta, which, he insists, is as good as the one his mother used to make, standing at the stove for hours on end. I enjoy serving this as a main luncheon dish, accompanied by homemade Tomato Sauce (page 300) and a tossed green salad.

3 cups whole milk

1 teaspoon fine sea salt

Freshly grated nutmeg to taste

1 cup instant polenta

1/2 cup heavy cream

1 cup freshly grated Swiss Gruyère cheese

About 2 cups Tomato Sauce (page 300), warmed

EQUIPMENT:
A 1-quart gratin dish.

4 TO 6 SERVINGS

1. Preheat the broiler. Set the oven rack about 3 inches from the heat.

2. In a large, heavy saucepan, bring the milk, sea salt, and nutmeg to a boil over high heat. (Watch it carefully, because milk will boil over quickly.) Add the polenta in a steady stream; stirring constantly with a wooden spoon, cook until it is thickened and leaves the side of the pan as it is stirred, about 2 minutes.

Monsieur Lapin

11, RUE RAYMOND LOSSERAND
PARIS 14
TELEPHONE: 01 43 20 21 39
FAX: 01 43 21 84 86
MÉTRO: GAÎTÉ

3. Remove the pan from the heat. Stir in the cream and half of the cheese, stirring to blend thoroughly. Pour into a 1-quart gratin dish, evening out the top with a spatula. Sprinkle with the remaining cheese.

A light, soft white from the shores of Lake Geneva, such as a Crépy from the Savoy.

4. Place the gratin dish on the oven rack and broil until the cheese is golden and bubbling, 1 to 2 minutes. Serve, with warm tomato sauce alongside.

ON POLENTA

Polenta—Italian cornmeal—can be found in many textures (from coarse to medium to fine ground) as well as natural and instant versions. I use both in my kitchen. When I am making a pure polenta that will stand on its own and be seasoned only with a touch of butter or oil, I take the time to use the natural variety that will take a minimum of 20 minutes to cook. When I am in a hurry and am using it as it is used here, in essentially a casserole that will be baked and then served with a tomato sauce, I opt for the instant version.

SPELT "RISOTTO"

Risotto d'Épeautre

During the 1990s, when Mediterranean cuisine became the rage all over France, Parisian chefs took a fancy to *épeautre*, the Provençal grain that resembles spelt. *Épeautre* is always referred to as "the poor man's wheat," for it will grow in the poor, rocky soil of the south. Parisian chefs cook *épeautre* much like risotto, resulting in a dish that is at once chewy, wholesome, and creamy. This recipe was given to me by Emmanuel Leblay, a talented chef who has worked in the best restaurants in Paris, London, and Provence. I love his idea of adding whipped cream, which has a soufflé-like effect in aerating this elegant dish of simple, peasant origin. Serve it as an accompaniment to roast chicken, lamb, or squab.

1. Place the *épeautre* in a large fine-mesh sieve and rinse it thoroughly under cold running water. Transfer it to a large bowl, cover with cold water, and soak for 2 hours. Rinse again, drain, and set aside.

2. In a large, deep skillet, combine the oil, butter, onions, shallots, and a pinch of sea salt. Sweat—cook, covered, over low heat without coloring—until soft and translucent, about 5 minutes. Add the *épeautre*, chicken stock, bay leaves, and 1 teaspoon sea salt. Bring to a boil over high heat; then reduce the heat to a simmer. Cook, uncovered, until tender, about 30 minutes, stirring from time to time to keep the grain from sticking to the pan.

3 cups (1 pound) *épeautre* or spelt

3 tablespoons extra-virgin olive oil

2 tablespoons unsalted butter

2 onions, peeled and minced

1 shallot, peeled and minced

Fine sea salt

1½ quarts Homemade Chicken Stock (page 297)

2 fresh or dried bay leaves

1 cup heavy cream

EQUIPMENT:

A large deep skillet with lid; a heavy-duty mixer.

6 TO 8 SERVINGS

3. While the *épeautre* is cooking, whip the cream: In the bowl of a heavy-duty mixer fitted with the whisk (or with a handheld mixer), whip the cream at moderate speed until soft peaks form. Gradually increase the speed to high, whisking until stiff peaks form. Scrape down the sides of the bowl. Set aside.

4. When the *épeautre* is cooked, place a large sieve over a large bowl and drain the *épeautre* in the sieve, discarding the cooking liquid.

5. At serving time, return the cooked *épeautre* to the skillet and sauté over moderate heat to toast it lightly, 2 to 3 minutes. Add sea salt to taste. Stir in the whipped cream, and serve.

Épeautre can be found in most fine supermarkets

Oliviers & Co.

28, RUE DE BUCI
PARIS 6
TELEPHONE: 01 44 07 15 43
MÉTRO: SAINT-GERMAIN DES
PRÉS OR ODÉON

FRÉDÉRIC ANTON'S RISOTTO WITH WILD MUSHROOMS

Le Risotto Crémeux aux Champignons Sauvages de Frédéric Anton

Rarely does a French chef get the point of risotto, but Joël Robuchon protégé Frédéric Anton understands it in the way only a pro can: One bite of his smooth, alabaster, creamy risotto layered with parchment-thin slices of pancetta, a good dose of Parmesan, and powerfully intense tiny fresh girolle mushrooms and you almost want to stop right there. For a second bite means you'll be on your way to finishing this ingenious, ephemeral dish, a meal all on its own. The texture, flavor, aroma, and essence of each ingredient shine through, yet each plays an essential note in a minor culinary symphony. The first time I sampled this dish—during Anton's first months at Le Pré Catelan in 1997—I was in ecstasy. The risotto has all the Robuchon trademarks of full flavors and complexity, yet remains faithful to its Italian heritage. Textures here are paramount: the salty crunch of the pancetta serves as a palate-pleasing counterpoint to the tooth-tenderness of the mushrooms, while the risotto serves as a midpoint between the two. The reduced chicken stock adds that extra attentive touch that is now one of chef Anton's signatures.

THE PANCETTA

8 paper-thin slices pancetta or bacon, each measuring about 1 by 5 inches

THE MUSHROOMS

1 tablespoon extra-virgin olive oil

4 large fresh cèpe (porcini) or girolle (chanterelle) mushrooms (or substitute cremini, portobello, or standard cultivated mushrooms), cleaned, trimmed, and sliced

Sea salt

1 tablespoon unsalted butter

Finely ground white pepper

Minced fresh chervil leaves (or substitute minced fresh tarragon or parsley leaves)

2 cups Homemade Chicken Stock (page 297)

1. Preheat the broiler. Set an oven rack 3 inches from the heat.

2. Arrange the slices of pancetta side by side on a baking sheet, and place the baking sheet on the oven rack. Broil until the pancetta is golden and sizzling, 1 to 2 minutes. Transfer to a double thickness of paper towels to drain. Turn off the oven. Return the pancetta to the oven to keep warm.

3. Cook the mushrooms: Heat the oil in a large nonstick skillet over moderate heat until hot but not smoking. Add the mushrooms, season lightly with sea salt, and sauté just until they begin to give up their juices, 1 to 2 minutes. Transfer the mushrooms to a fine-mesh sieve to drain. Wipe out the skillet with paper towels. Melt the butter in the skillet over moderate heat and return the mushrooms to the skillet. Season lightly with sea salt and white pepper. Cook for 2 minutes more. Remove the skillet from the heat, sprinkle the mushrooms with chervil, and toss to coat with the herb. Transfer the mushrooms to the turned-off oven to keep warm.

4. Reduce the chicken stock: In a 6-quart saucepan, bring the stock to a boil over high heat. (Make sure you use a large saucepan, to prevent the stock from boiling over.) Boil until the mixture is thick and syrupy, reduced to about ½ cup, 10 to 12 minutes. Transfer the liquid to the top of a double boiler, set it over simmering water, cover, and keep warm.

5. Next, prepare the rice: In a large saucepan, heat the 5 cups stock. Keep it barely simmering while you prepare the risotto.

THE RICE

About 5 cups Homemade Chicken Stock (page 297)
1 tablespoon goose fat or unsalted butter
1 plump, fresh clove garlic, peeled, halved lengthwise, green germ removed
1 shallot, peeled and minced
Sea salt
1½ cups Italian Arborio rice
½ cup freshly grated Parmigiano-Reggiano cheese
1 tablespoon extra-virgin olive oil
2 tablespoons heavy cream
Freshly ground white pepper

A chunk of Parmigiano-Reggiano cheese, for shaving as garnish
Coarsely ground white pepper, for garnish

EQUIPMENT:
A 6-quart saucepan; a double boiler.

4 TO 6 SERVINGS

6. In a large nonstick skillet, melt the goose fat over low heat. Add the garlic to perfume the fat. Add the shallots and sea salt to taste, and sweat—cook, covered, over low heat without coloring—until soft and translucent, 3 to 4 minutes. Remove and discard the garlic.

THE GLORIES OF GOOSE FAT

NOTHING REPLACES GOOSE FAT for a luxurious feel on the tongue, a richness that neither oil nor butter can supply. Goose fat (which can be refrigerated for a year in a well-sealed container) can be used in place of just about any fat, although it is most often used with starchy dishes such as potatoes or rice. Since fat actually "fixes" the flavor of foods—makes them come alive in a way they can't on their own—using more than one kind of fat in a dish, as Frédéric Anton does here, only intensifies the flavors.

Add the rice, and stir until it is well coated with the fat, glistening, and semitranslucent, 1 to 2 minutes. (This step is important for good risotto: The heat and fat will help separate the grains of rice, ensuring a creamy consistency in the end.)

7. When the rice is glistening and semitranslucent, add a ladleful of the hot stock. Cook, stirring constantly, until the rice has absorbed most of the stock, 1 to 2 minutes. Add another ladleful of the stock, and stir regularly until all the stock is absorbed. Adjust the heat as necessary to maintain a gentle simmer. The rice should cook slowly and should always be covered with a veil of stock. Continue adding ladlefuls of stock, stirring frequently and tasting regularly, until the rice is almost tender but firm to the bite, about 17 minutes total. The risotto should have a creamy, porridgelike consistency.

The wild mushrooms in this dish suggest a good red, such as an Italian Barolo or Chianti, or a fine Bordeaux, such as a Saint-Estèphe or a Pauillac.

8. Remove the saucepan from the heat and stir in the cheese, olive oil, and cream. Taste, and season with sea salt and white pepper to taste. Transfer the risotto to warmed shallow soup bowls. Garnish with the mushrooms, shavings of fresh Parmesan, and the pancetta. Carefully spoon the reduced chicken stock around the edge of the risotto. Season with coarsely ground white pepper, and serve immediately.

TRUC: When boiling any liquid over high heat to reduce it, always use an extra-large saucepan to prevent it from boiling over.

Le Pré Catelan

ROUTE DE SURESNES
BOIS DE BOULOGNE
PARIS 16
TELEPHONE: 01 44 14 41 14
FAX: 01 45 24 43 25
MÉTRO: PORTE-DAUPHINE

The Market Gardener's Zucchini and Curry Soup

Boulevard Raspail Cream of Mushroom Soup

Taillevent's Cream of Watercress Soup with Caviar

Gazpacho: Arpège and Port Alma

Tante Louise's Caramelized Cauliflower Soup with Foie Gras

Olivier & Co.'s Provençal Three-Grain Soup

Les Bookinistes's Cream of Corn Soup

SOUPS
Les Soupes et les Potages

Joël Robuchon's Creamy White Bean Soup

Brasserie Balzar's Midnight Onion Soup

Potato, Leek, and Oyster Soup Le Maxence

Pumpkin Soup for Halloween

Spicy Langoustine Broth

Fresh Crab Soup

Rue Bayen Fish Soup

THE MARKET GARDENER'S ZUCCHINI AND CURRY SOUP

Potage de Courgettes au Curry Les Maraîchers

Fragrant with a gentle touch of curry, verdant as a vegetable garden in August, and smooth as silk, this versatile zucchini soup can be served piping hot or refreshingly cold. The curry helps accentuate the sweet and almost grassy flavor of the zucchini, and adds an elegantly piquant touch. Firm, unblemished, top-quality zucchini is plentiful in the Paris markets from June to September, when I make this soup regularly, freezing any extra for a quick meal when I'm pressed for time. My husband, Walter, prefers a mild curry flavor (about 2 teaspoons), while I crave a greater hit of spice (1 tablespoon). Season your soup to meet your taste.

1. In a stockpot, combine the onions, oil, curry powder, and a pinch of sea salt. Stir to coat the onions. Cook, covered, over low heat, stirring, until the onions are soft, 3 to 4 minutes.

2. Add the stock and zucchini and stir to blend. Bring to a simmer over moderate heat, cover, and simmer gently for 20 minutes.

3. Process the liquid in a blender, food processor, or with a handheld immersion blender until emulsified into a smooth-textured mixture. (The soup may be prepared ahead of time up to this point. Cool and refrigerate.)

4. At serving time, reheat the soup, and serve it in warm shallow soup bowls.

1 large onion, peeled, halved lengthwise, and cut into thin half-moons

2 tablespoons extra-virgin olive oil

2 teaspoons curry powder, or to taste

Fine sea salt to taste

1 quart Homemade Chicken Stock (page 297)

4 small zucchini (about 12 ounces total), rinsed and cut into thin rounds

EQUIPMENT:
A stockpot.

6 TO 8 SERVINGS

PARIS MARKETS

PARIS ESSENTIALLY HAS three kinds of markets: a handful of covered markets, a dozen or so market streets, and the roving markets that set up shop on schedule two or three days a week around town. The roving markets offer some of the best variety and greatest freshness, since many of the merchants are *maraîchers,* or market gardeners, with small plots of land just outside of town.

For fresh produce, try

Marché Carmes

PLACE MAUBERT
PARIS 5
7 A.M. TO 1:30 P.M. TUESDAY,
THURSDAY, AND SATURDAY
MÉTRO: MAUBERT-MUTUALTIÉ

BOULEVARD RASPAIL CREAM OF MUSHROOM SOUP

Crème de Champignons Boulevard Raspail

At once elegant and classic, this is a favorite come autumn, when every gastronome in France begins to think of mushrooms. The famed Paris mushroom—*champignon de Paris*—was originally cultivated in caves located beneath the subways and sewers of the city, caves that were excavated for the stone with which many of Paris's buildings are constructed. Today the mushrooms are more likely to be grown by farmers outside of Paris. I often find superbly fresh mushrooms at the organic produce market held each Sunday morning along the boulevard Raspail. While the French revere the variety of wild mushrooms found all over the nation's woods and forests, one should not underestimate the flavor and value of the common cultivated mushroom, used here for a simple but exquisite mushroom soup.

1. In a 6-quart stockpot, combine the leeks, butter, and a pinch of salt. Sweat—cook, covered, over low heat—until soft but not brown, about 3 minutes.

2. Add the mushrooms and cook, stirring often, for another 5 minutes. Add the chicken stock. Cover and simmer gently for about 35 minutes. Taste for seasoning.

2 leeks, white and tender green portions, rinsed and coarsely chopped

3 tablespoons unsalted butter

Sea salt

1½ pounds mushrooms, trimmed, washed, and thinly sliced

1½ quarts Homemade Chicken Stock (page 297)

3 cups heavy cream, or a mix of half cream and half whole milk

Freshly ground white pepper

EQUIPMENT:

A 6-quart stockpot; a blender, food processor, or immersion blender.

6 SERVINGS

3. Process the soup in a blender, food processor, or with a handheld immersion blender until emulsified into a smooth-textured mixture. (The soup may be prepared ahead of time up to this point. Reheat at serving time.)

4. At serving time, add the cream and simmer gently, uncovered, over low heat until thickened, about 5 minutes. To serve, ladle the soup into warmed soup bowls.

Marché Biologique Boulevard Raspail

BOULEVARD RASPAIL, BETWEEN
RUE DU CHERCHE-MIDI AND
RUE DE RENNES
PARIS 6
9 A.M. TO 1 P.M. SUNDAY
MÉTRO: RENNES OR SÈVRES-
BABYLONE

TAILLEVENT'S CREAM OF WATERCRESS SOUP WITH CAVIAR

La Crème de Cresson au Caviar de Taillevent

For more than twenty years, Taillevent has been one of our favorite restaurants, a place that my husband, Walter, and I reserve for special occasions. Owner Jean-Claude Vrinat is one of the city's finest hosts, a model restaurateur if there ever was one. He kindly shared the recipe for this festive soup, one that seems the perfect choice for a celebratory New Year's Eve dinner. Like so much of the fare at this august restaurant, this soup shines with simple elegance.

1. In a 6-quart stockpot, combine the butter, leeks, onions, and a pinch of sea salt. Sweat—cook, covered, over low heat—until soft but not browned, about 3 minutes. Add the chicken stock and cream. Simmer gently, uncovered, for 30 minutes.

2. Process the soup in a blender, food processor, or with a handheld immersion blender until emulsified into a smooth-textured mixture.

3. Return the mixture to the saucepan, increase the heat to high, and bring to a gentle boil. Using a slotted spoon, skim off any impurities that may rise to the surface. Set this base aside. (This mixture can be prepared up to 1 day in advance. To store, cover and refrigerate.)

4. Prepare a large bowl full of ice water.

THE LEEK AND STOCK BASE

3 tablespoons unsalted butter

1 pound leeks, white and tender green portions, rinsed, halved, and thinly sliced

1 onion, peeled and finely chopped

Fine sea salt

1 quart Homemade Chicken Stock (page 297)

2 cups heavy cream (or substitute whole milk)

THE WATERCRESS

3 tablespoons coarse sea salt

4 bunches watercress, stems removed, leaves rinsed

5. In a 6-quart pasta pot fitted with a colander, bring 4 quarts water to a boil over high heat. Add the coarse sea salt and the watercress leaves. Blanch, uncovered, until soft and wilted, 2 to 3 minutes. Immediately remove the colander from the water, drain the watercress, and plunge the colander into the ice water to stop the cooking. Drain again, and purée the watercress in a food processor. Place the purée in a fine-mesh sieve, and carefully press out any remaining liquid. Set it aside.

6. In the bowl of a heavy-duty mixer fitted with a whisk (or with a handheld mixer), whip the cream at high speed until stiff. Add the lemon juice, and season to taste with sea salt and white pepper. Set aside.

7. At serving time, reheat the creamy soup base. Remove it from the heat and add the watercress purée, stirring until thoroughly blended. Serve the soup in warm, shallow soup bowls, placing a scoop of the whipped cream in the center of each bowl. Top with a small spoonful of caviar, and serve.

THE CREAM
1 cup heavy cream
Juice of 1 lemon
Sea salt
Freshly ground white
 pepper

2 tablespoons caviar,
 preferably Osetra

EQUIPMENT:
A 6-quart stockpot; a 6-
 quart pasta pot fitted
 with a colander; a food
 processor.

6 SERVINGS

Taillevent owner Jean-Claude Vrinat (left) and Chef Michel Delburgo

Taillevent

15, RUE LAMENNAIS
PARIS 8
TELEPHONE: 01 44 95 15 01
FAX: 01 42 25 95 18
MÉTRO: CHARLES DE
 GAULLE–ETOILE OR GEORGE V

GAZPACHO: ARPÈGE AND PORT ALMA

Les Gaspachos d'Arpège et de Port Alma

Even though it is Spanish in origin, French chefs adore gazpacho, and this brilliant red summer soup can be found at many of the city's best tables in the warm months. At home, I like to make it with the giant Russian heirloom tomatoes that one finds at farmers' markets in late summer. Russian heirlooms are huge, weighing up to 2 pounds each, and are a brilliant, deep red, making for a truly colorful soup. For even more color and panache, serve the gazpacho with a dollop of Mustard Ice Cream. Or try Port Alma chef Paul Canal's delicious version with fresh crabmeat.

Place the tomatoes in the bowl of a food processor, and purée them. Then add the remaining ingredients, except the ice cream, and purée. Taste for seasoning. Pass the mixture through a fine-mesh sieve, discarding the solids that remain in the sieve. Transfer the soup to a bowl, cover, and refrigerate for at least 3 hours and up to 24 hours. Serve it in chilled bowls, with a spoonful of Mustard Ice Cream if desired.

VARIATION: Paul Canal's Gazpacho with Crabmeat: Add several spoonfuls of fresh lump crabmeat—drained, picked over, and flaked into generous bite-size pieces.

3 pounds ripe tomatoes, cored and quartered

1 red bell pepper, trimmed and quartered

1 green bell pepper, trimmed and quartered

1 medium cucumber, peeled, seeded, and coarsely chopped

2 plump, fresh cloves garlic, peeled, quartered, green germ removed

¼ cup best-quality sherry vinegar

3 tablespoons extra-virgin olive oil

Sea salt to taste

Mustard Ice Cream (optional; recipe follows)

8 SERVINGS

Port Alma

10, AVENUE DE NEW YORK
PARIS 16
TELEPHONE: 01 47 23 75 11
MÉTRO: ALMA-MARCEAU

MUSTARD ICE CREAM

Crème Glacée à la Moutarde

It was a steamy day in July when my good friend Susan Loomis and I lunched at Arpège, home of Alain Passard, one of France's most creative chefs. When the waiter set before us a tiny bowl of gazpacho laced with this golden mustard ice cream, we were first taken by shock, then joy, as we devoured this original, creative combination. Wacky, you say? Try it—you will be an instant convert! The rich creaminess of the ice cream, with the tang of mustard, melting into the cool and smooth gazpacho is a marriage you will never forget. Top it all off with a chiffonade of fresh basil.

6 large egg yolks
2 cups whole milk
1 cup heavy cream
1½ tablespoons French Dijon mustard

EQUIPMENT:
An ice cream maker.

8 SERVINGS

1. Place the egg yolks in a medium-size bowl and whisk to blend.

2. In a heavy saucepan, cook the milk over medium heat until bubbles form around the edges. Slowly whisk the hot milk into the egg yolks. Return this mixture to the saucepan.

3. Rinse out and dry the mixing bowl; then set a fine-mesh sieve on top. Set it aside.

4. Place the saucepan over low heat. Using a wooden spoon, stir the sauce gently but constantly, sweeping the entire pan bottom and reaching into the corners. As soon as the sauce is slightly thickened, remove the pan from the heat and stir gently for 2 minutes to complete the

cooking. The sauce should be the consistency of heavy cream and register around 170 degrees F on an instant-read thermometer.

5. Immediately stir in the cream to stop the cooking. Stir in the mustard. Pass through the fine-mesh sieve. Cool completely.

6. When the mixture is thoroughly cooled, transfer it to an ice cream maker and freeze according to the manufacturer's instructions.

TANTE LOUISE'S CARAMELIZED CAULIFLOWER SOUP WITH FOIE GRAS

La Crème de Chou-fleur Caramélisé au Foie Gras Chez Tante Louise

Several years ago chef Bernard Loiseau, who comes from Burgundy, expanded his holdings by adding Tante Louise—a cozy, old-fashioned bistro near the Madeleine—to his empire. There, chef Arnaud Magnier has a fine hand, producing classic bistro fare as well as elegant modern dishes like this soup. Come the cold gray days of November in Paris, this hearty soup is there to cheer me up. The nutlike flavor of cauliflower, enhanced by the nutlike flavor of brown butter, pairs perfectly with the richness of the foie gras. You can, of course, prepare it without the foie gras garnish, but why deprive yourself?

1. Prepare the cauliflower: Cut the head in quarters, removing the core from each piece. Cut or break the florets into small pieces.

2. In a pasta pot fitted with a colander, bring 4 quarts water to a boil over high heat. Add 2 tablespoons sea salt and the lemon juice. Add the cauliflower florets and cook, uncovered, for 15 minutes. Drain. Transfer to a blender or food processor and purée until smooth.

3. Melt the butter in a 6-quart soup pot over moderately high heat. Watch it carefully: The butter will go through

1 large head cauliflower
   (about 2½ pounds)
Sea salt
Juice of 1 lemon
4 tablespoons unsalted
   butter
1 quart Homemade
   Chicken Stock (page
   297)
Freshly ground white
   pepper
4 ounces fresh duck liver
   (foie gras), cut into tiny
   cubes

EQUIPMENT:

A 6-quart pasta pot
   fitted with a colander;
   a 6-quart soup pot;
   a blender, food
   processor, or
   immersion blender.

6 SERVINGS

several stages, from a foamy white liquid to one that is al-most clear and golden, with big airy bubbles. When the butter begins to brown and gives off a nutty aroma (about 2 minutes), add the cauliflower purée (do not delay or the butter could burn) and stir to blend. Add the chicken stock and stir to blend. Simmer, covered, for 5 minutes.

4. Process the soup in a blender, food processor, or with a handheld immersion blender until emulsified into a smooth-textured mixture. Add sea salt and white pepper to taste. (The soup may be prepared ahead of time up to this point. Reheat at serving time.)

5. At serving time, ladle the soup into warmed shallow soup bowls. Sprinkle with the cubed foie gras, and serve immediately.

Tante Louise

41, RUE BOISSY-D'ANGLAS
PARIS 8
TELEPHONE: 01 42 65 06 85
FAX: 01 42 65 28 19
MÉTRO: MADELEINE

SOUPS

OLIVIERS & CO.'S PROVENÇAL THREE-GRAIN SOUP

La Soupe Provençale aux Trois Céréales Oliviers & Co.

This cold-weather soup sings of the wholesomeness of Provence, perfect for days when a wintry Mistral wind blows down the Rhône Valley. It is inspired by the beautiful products found at Oliviers & Co., a Left Bank shop that offers an extraordinary array of olive oils from all over the Mediterranean, as well as a fine line of organic grains. Here a trio of grains—pearl barley, lentils, and the Provençal *épeautre,* or spelt—team up with tomatoes and leeks, carrots and garlic, for what the French call *"la bonne cuisine des familles."*

1. Place the spelt, barley, and lentils in a fine-mesh sieve and rinse under cold running water. Drain and set aside.

2. In a soup pot, combine the oil, bay leaves, thyme, leeks, carrots, and 1 teaspoon fine sea salt. Sweat—cook, covered, over low heat without coloring—until soft, about 5 minutes. Add the canned tomatoes (do not drain them) and 5 cups cold water. Bring to a boil over moderate heat. Add the grains, and garlic, stir, and simmer, covered, until they are tender, about 45 minutes. (The cooking time will depend upon the freshness of the grains—older grains take longer to cook.) Remove and discard the bay leaves.

$\frac{1}{3}$ cup *épeautre* or spelt

$\frac{1}{3}$ cup pearl barley

$\frac{1}{3}$ cup dark green imported lentils, preferably *lentilles de Puy*

1 tablespoon extra-virgin olive oil

2 fresh or dried bay leaves

$\frac{1}{2}$ teaspoon fresh or dried thyme leaves

3 leeks, white portion only, rinsed and minced

2 carrots, peeled and cubed

Fine sea salt

One 28-ounce can peeled Italian plum tomatoes in their juice

1 head garlic, cloves peeled, halved, and green germ removed

A cruet of olive oil for the table

EQUIPMENT:

A soup pot.

8 SERVINGS

Taste for seasoning. (This soup is even more delicious the second day, after the flavors have had time to ripen.)

3. Serve piping hot, drizzled with extra-virgin olive oil.

Oliviers & Co.

28, RUE DE BUCI
PARIS 6
TELEPHONE: 01 44 07 15 43
MÉTRO: SAINT-GERMAIN DES
PRÉS OR ODÉON

Jacques Cousin of Au Petit Marguery

LES BOOKINISTES'S CREAM OF CORN SOUP

Crème de Maïs aux Champignons d'Automne Les Bookinistes

The first time chef William Ledeuil proposed this creamy, fragrant, endearing soup, I wanted to say, "You've got to be kidding." Cream of corn soup seemed so American—I couldn't imagine it on a French bistro table. But leave it to the talented William to come up with a sophisticated, elegant soup, embellished with a trio of wild mushrooms and the unforgettable grilled peanut oil from the house of Leblanc in southern France. Note that for this recipe you need both the corn kernels and the cobs, which give a great depth of flavor to the soup.

1. Using a sharp knife, scrape the kernels from the corn cobs. Place the corn and the scraped cobs in a shallow pot that is large enough to hold the corn in two layers. Cover with the milk. Cover, bring to a simmer over moderate heat, and simmer for 1½ hours.

2. Remove the corn from the pot. Discard the cobs. Reserve the kernels and the milk.

3. In batches, transfer the corn kernels and cooking liquid to a food processor and purée. Place a food mill fitted with the finest disc over a large saucepan. Pass the purée through the food mill into the saucepan. Stir in 8 tablespoons of the butter and all of the cream. Add sea salt and white pepper to taste. Keep warm over the lowest possible heat.

6 ears fresh corn (about 4 pounds total)

2 quarts whole milk

9 tablespoons unsalted butter

⅓ cup heavy cream

Sea salt

Freshly ground white pepper

3 ounces fresh shiitake mushrooms, cleaned and dried

1 tablespoon extra-virgin olive oil

3 ounces fresh chanterelle mushrooms, cleaned and dried

2 shallots, peeled and finely minced

1 tablespoon finely minced fresh chives

About 2 teaspoons grilled peanut oil (see Note; or substitute hazelnut or walnut oil)

Celery salt

4. Heat the oil in a large nonstick skillet over moderate heat until hot but not smoking. Add the shiitake mushrooms, season lightly with salt, and sauté just until they begin to give up their juices, 1 to 2 minutes. Using a slotted spoon, transfer the mushrooms to a platter to drain.

5. With paper towels, wipe out the skillet. Melt the remaining 1 tablespoon of butter over moderate heat. Add the chanterelle mushrooms and the shallots, season lightly with salt, and sauté just until the mushrooms begin to give up their juices, 1 to 2 minutes. Using a slotted spoon, transfer the mushrooms and shallots to a platter to drain.

6. At serving time, return both the shiitake and chantarelle mushroom mixtures to the pan to rewarm lightly. Off the heat, sprinkle the mushrooms with chives, and toss to coat with the herb. Season with freshly ground white pepper.

Chef Ledeuil suggests a Domaine de la Passière Blanc Corbières.

7. Process the corn soup with a handheld immersion blender until emulsified into a smooth-textured mixture.

8. Arrange the mushrooms in the bottom of warmed shallow soup bowls. Pour the soup over the mushrooms. Drizzle with the grilled peanut oil, season with celery salt, and serve.

NOTE: Grilled peanut oil can be found at Huilerie Leblanc, 6, rue Jacob, Paris 6. Telephone: 01 46 34 61 55. Métro: Saint-Germain des Prés.

EQUIPMENT:
A food processor; a food mill; a handheld immersion blender.

8 SERVINGS

Les Bookinistes

53, QUAI DES GRANDS-AUGUSTINS
PARIS 6
TELEPHONE: 01 43 25 45 94
FAX: 01 43 25 23 07
MÉTRO: RER SAINT-MICHEL

SOUPS

155

JOËL ROBUCHON'S CREAMY WHITE BEAN SOUP

Crème de Cocos Blancs Joël Robuchon

During the last years of his chiefdom on the rue de Longchamp, Joël Robuchon served this rich, soul-warming white bean cream as part of his all-truffle menu. With a faintly smoky flavor and that creamy richness of good white beans, this should be served in small portions. I like to serve it as a small first course, which can be drunk from a simple white demitasse cup. The soup can be anointed with finely minced truffles or with a drizzling of hazelnut oil. I only recently learned that fresh white beans, such as the French *cocos blancs*, which can be found from May to September, can easily be frozen. So when you find the beans in your farmers' market, freeze them for one of those cool winter days when bean soup is all that will do!

1. In a 6-quart stockpot, combine the fresh or soaked dried beans with the carrots, onion, garlic cloves, bouquet garni, bacon, and 1 teaspoon sea salt. Cover with cold water, bring to a boil, and cover the pot. Simmer gently over low heat until the beans are very tender, about 30 minutes for fresh beans, 1 to 1½ hours for dried beans. (The cooking time will vary according to the freshness of the beans.) Add additional stock or water if necessary.

2. Drain the beans. Remove and discard the carrot, onion, garlic, bouquet garni, and bacon. Transfer the beans to a

2 pounds fresh small white (navy) beans or red (cranberry) beans in the pod, shelled; or 1 pound dried small white beans (such as cannellini, Great Northern, or marrow beans), soaked (see Note)

2 carrots, peeled and halved

1 onion, peeled and stuck with a clove

4 cloves garlic: 3 peeled, 1 very finely minced

1 bouquet garni: several sprigs of parsley and thyme, and several bay leaves, tied together with cotton string

3 ounces smoked bacon, in one piece

Sea salt

2 cups Homemade

food processor and purée. Pass the purée through the finest grid of a food mill. (The soup can be prepared ahead of time up to this point. Cool and refrigerate.)

3. At serving time, reheat the purée. Add the chicken stock and cream, stir to blend, and bring just to a simmer. Stir in the butter and the minced garlic. Add sea salt and white pepper to taste. Serve piping hot, in very small warmed soup bowls or in demitasse cups. Sprinkle with minced truffles or drizzle with hazelnut oil, if desired.

NOTE: To prepare dried beans, rinse them, picking them over to remove any pebbles. Place the beans in a large saucepan. Cover with boiling water by 2 inches. Cover and let stand until the beans swell to at least twice their size and have absorbed most of the liquid, about 1 hour. Drain the beans in a colander, discarding the soaking liquid. Proceed with the recipe.

This is delicious with a floral white, such as a Condrieu or a Viognier from Domaine les Gouberts.

Chicken Stock (page 297)

1 cup heavy cream

6 tablespoons unsalted butter, softened

Freshly ground white pepper

1 small fresh black truffle (about 1 ounce), cleaned and minced (optional); or several teaspoons best-quality hazelnut or pistachio oil (optional)

EQUIPMENT:

A 6-quart stockpot; a food processor; a food mill; 12 demitasse cups or other very small bowls.

12 DEMITASSE SERVINGS

BRASSERIE BALZAR'S MIDNIGHT ONION SOUP

La Gratinée de Minuit
Brasserie Balzar

There are few Parisian traditions as solid as the late-night onion soup feast at the Brasserie Balzar on the Left Bank. Unlike many heartier versions that call for deep, dark, caramelized onions and rich beef stock, this is prepared with chicken stock, making for a very delicate, highly digestible soup. The onions are cooked to a pale golden color and are enriched with a mixture of chicken stock, white wine, and water. Be sure to use the best-quality imported Swiss Gruyère you can find. You won't regret it.

1. Peel the onions and halve them vertically. Cut the halves lengthwise into thin slices.

2. In a 10-quart stockpot, melt the butter over low heat. Add the oil, onions, and salt, and stir to coat the onions. Cook, covered, over low heat—stirring occasionally so the onions do not scorch—just until the onions are soft but still pale, about 15 minutes.

3. Sprinkle the flour over the onions and stir to coat the onions. Immediately add the stock, wine, 4 quarts water, the white pepper, thyme sprigs, and bay leaves. Bring just to a boil. Immediately reduce the heat to low. Simmer, partially covered, for 30 minutes. Taste for seasoning.

3 pounds onions

6 tablespoons unsalted butter

6 tablespoons peanut oil

1 tablespoon fine sea salt

4 tablespoons all-purpose flour

2 cups Homemade Chicken Stock (page 297)

⅔ cup dry white wine, such as Sancerre

1½ teaspoons freshly ground white pepper

Several sprigs fresh thyme, wrapped in cheesecloth

Several fresh or dried bay leaves

8 thin slices baguette, toasted

1 pound Swiss Gruyère cheese, freshly grated

EQUIPMENT:

A 10-quart stockpot; ovenproof soup bowls.

8 TO 10 SERVINGS

(The soup can be prepared up to this point 1 day in advance. Refrigerate in a covered container. Reheat gently at serving time.)

4. Preheat the broiler.

5. Ladle the soup into individual ovenproof soup bowls. Top each serving with a slice of toasted baguette. Cover the bread with a thick coating of grated Gruyère. Place under the broiler. As soon as the cheese begins to bubble, serve the soup.

While most soups don't call out for wine, I do like a sip of the same young Sancerre (from the house of Sautereau) I use to make this soup. It comes from my favorite Paris wine merchant, Juan Sanchez, at La Dernière Goutte, on the Left Bank: 6, rue Bourbon-le-Château, Paris 6; telephone: 01 43 29 11 62. Métro: Saint-Germain des Prés or Odéon.

Brasserie Balzar

49, RUE DES ECOLES
PARIS 5
TELEPHONE: 01 43 54 13 67
FAX: 01 44 07 14 91
MÉTRO: ODÉON OR CLUNY–
LA-SORBONNE

POTATO, LEEK, AND OYSTER SOUP LE MAXENCE

Potage Parmentier aux Huîtres
Le Maxence

Potato soups have long been a French favorite, and the classic combination of leeks and potatoes—named after eighteenth-century agronomist Antoine-Auguste Parmentier—is one of the most obvious winter warm-ups. I sampled this restorative soup one October evening at the diminutive Bamboche, then the newly created restaurant of chef David Van Laer. That evening we ordered a brisk white Burgundian Marsannay wine: The circle of flavors was complete, with the briny oysters, the creamy warm soup, and the chilled white wine. Chef Van Laer has since moved, but you can still find this soup on the menu at his new restaurant, Le Maxence.

1. In a 6-quart stockpot, combine the butter, leeks, and 1 teaspoon fine sea salt. Sweat—cook, covered, over low heat—until the leeks are soft but not browned, about 3 minutes. Add the potatoes, milk, cream, and several gratings of nutmeg. Simmer, covered, stirring often to prevent the starchy soup from sticking to the bottom of the pot, for about 20 minutes. Taste for seasoning.

2. Process the soup in a food processor or with a handheld immersion blender until emulsified into a smooth-textured mixture. (The soup may be prepared ahead of time up to this point. Cool and refrigerate.)

3. Reheat the soup to serve. Pour it into warmed shallow soup bowls, and float 2 fresh oysters in each bowl. The oysters will cook slightly in the heat of the soup as it is served.

2 tablespoons unsalted butter

2 leeks, white and tender green portions, rinsed, halved lengthwise, and thinly sliced

Fine sea salt to taste

8 ounces baking potatoes, such as russets, peeled and thinly sliced

1 quart whole milk

1/3 cup heavy cream

Freshly grated nutmeg

8 large fresh oysters, freshly shucked and removed from their shells

EQUIPMENT:
A 6-quart stockpot.

4 SERVINGS

Le Maxence

9 BIS, BOULEVARD
MONTPARNASSE
PARIS 6
TELEPHONE: 01 45 67 24 88
FAX: 01 45 67 10 22
MÉTRO: FALGUIÈRE

PUMPKIN SOUP FOR HALLOWEEN

Velouté de Potiron "Halloween"

In recent years, the French have gone crazy over Halloween. Now pumpkins carved with wonderfully expressive faces can be found piled high at my market on rue Poncelet. A vegetable merchant suggested this simple soup to celebrate what has become an international holiday. This combination of a few ingredients looks and tastes as though you have been working for days on the ultimate pumpkin soup.

1. In a 6-quart stockpot, combine the pumpkin, chicken stock, and sugar. Bring to a boil over high heat, cover, and boil for 18 minutes. (The pumpkin should cook quickly to avoid any bitterness.)

2. Process the soup in a food processor or with a handheld immersion blender until emulsified into a smooth-textured mixture. (The soup may be prepared ahead of time up to this point. Cool and refrigerate.)

3. At serving time, return the soup to the stockpot and bring to a boil again. With a flat sieve, skim off any scum that rises to the top. Add the *crème fraîche* and bring back to a boil. Add sea salt and white pepper to taste. Serve immediately in warmed shallow soup bowls.

VARIATION: At Guy Savoy's bistros, they often serve pumpkin soup with very thin slices of Fourme d'Ambert—the blue cow's-milk cheese from the Auvergne—floating on top.

2 pounds fresh pumpkin, cubed

1 quart Homemade Chicken Stock (page 297)

1 tablespoon sugar

3 tablespoons *crème fraîche* or heavy cream

Sea salt

Freshly ground white pepper

EQUIPMENT:

A 6-quart stockpot.

4 SERVINGS

SPICY LANGOUSTINE BROTH

Bouillon de Langoustines Epicé

When I made this for my cooking class in Paris, the students declared it a Hummer, meaning it's the kind of restorative broth that makes you hum with satisfaction. I serve this whenever I make any dish with langoustines, since I hate the thought of tossing out the shells that give up such a rich, elusive flavor. Like so many of what I call my "little soups," I serve this in demitasse cups as people come in the door, or as we gather around the kitchen island before sitting down to dinner.

1. In a heavy-duty roasting pan or in a large, deep skillet, heat the oil over moderate heat until hot but not smoking. Add the shells and sear until they turn bright pink, 2 to 3 minutes. Add the orange quarters, fennel seeds, star anise, 4 quarts cold water, the tomatoes, bay leaves, garlic, chile peppers, sea salt, and tomato paste. Bring to a boil, uncovered, and boil vigorously for 30 minutes. To extract the maximum flavor from the shells, use a wooden mallet to crush and break them up while the soup is cooking.

2. Line a large colander with a double layer of dampened cheesecloth, and place the colander over a large bowl. Ladle the broth into the colander, discarding the solids.

3. Taste for seasoning. Serve warm in small cups as an appetizer, or in warmed shallow soup bowls as a first course.

2 tablespoons extra-virgin olive oil

2 pounds langoustine shells, rinsed but left whole (or substitute shrimp or lobster shells)

2 oranges, preferably organic, rinsed and quartered

1 tablespoon fennel seeds

2 whole pieces star anise

One 28-ounce can peeled Italian plum tomatoes in their juice (do not drain)

Several fresh or dried bay leaves

1 plump, moist head garlic, halved crosswise but not peeled

1/4 teaspoon ground chile pepper, or *piment d'Espelette*

1 teaspoon fine sea salt

1 tablespoon tomato paste

WE SAY "Too many cooks spoil the broth," and the French say *"On n'arrive à rien quand tout le monde s'en mêle,"* meaning "Nothing happens when everyone gets involved."

EQUIPMENT:

A large heavy-duty roasting pan or large deep skillet; cheesecloth.

8 SERVINGS

A chilled fruity Chenin Blanc, such as a Cappellet Chenin Blanc with the flavors of melon and citrus.

For the best langoustines in Paris, go to

Poissonnerie
Daguerre Marée

4, RUE BAYEN
PARIS 17
TELEPHONE: 01 43 80 16 29
FAX: 01 43 80 76 97
MÉTRO: TERNES

FRESH CRAB SOUP

Soupe de Favouilles

In France the tiniest of hard-shell crabs—with a greenish back and measuring no more than 3 inches in length—are prized for crab soup. Known in Italy as *granchio comune,* and in Spain as *cangrejo de mar,* these crabs can be found in Paris markets in spring and autumn, sold live as *favouilles.* In this recipe, the tiny crabs (too small to eat on their own) are used to flavor the soup, then are discarded after cooking. This soup is brilliant with simplicity, and wonderful with toast prepared from homemade Parmesan Bread (page 56).

1. In a 6-quart Dutch oven, combine the oil, leeks, fennel, celery, and a pinch of sea salt. Sweat—cook, covered, over low heat—until soft, stirring from time to time, about 5 minutes. Increase the heat to high, add the crabs, and cover. Cook until colored, about 2 minutes. Then add the tomatoes, wine, 2 quarts hot water, and the bouquet garni. Season to taste with sea salt and cayenne. Bring to a rapid boil and boil, covered, for 20 minutes. To extract the maximum flavor from the shells, use a wooden mallet to crush and break them up while the crabs are cooking.

2. Remove the pan from the heat and strain the mixture through a fine-mesh sieve or a food mill, pressing down on the crabs to extract as much liquid as possible. Return

3 tablespoons extra-virgin olive oil

2 leeks, tender white portion only, rinsed, halved lengthwise, and thinly sliced

1 bulb fennel, finely chopped

1 rib celery, finely chopped

Sea salt

2 pounds live baby crabs (rock crab or blue crab), rinsed but left whole

3 fresh tomatoes, cored and chopped

½ cup white wine

1 bouquet garni: several sprigs of parsley, fennel leaves, bay leaves, and thyme, wrapped in the green part of the leek and secured with cotton string

⅛ teaspoon cayenne pepper, or to taste

the liquid to the pan, and place over high heat. Taste for seasoning, and add the saffron and the pasta. Simmer until the pasta is cooked through, about 5 minutes. Taste again for seasoning. Serve hot.

1/8 teaspoon saffron
   threads
1/4 cup small pasta, such
   as rosmarino or orzo

EQUIPMENT:
A 6-quart Dutch oven.

6 SERVINGS

RUE BAYEN FISH SOUP

Soupe de Poissons de Roche Rue Bayen

There are as many versions of fish soup as there are cooks. At my fish market on the rue Bayen, the fishmonger occasionally sells a varied selection of tiny, freshly caught Mediterranean rockfish, called *poissons de roche*. When I see fresh, glistening, oftentimes squiggling varieties of these fish and shellfish, I grab a batch and rush them home for a quick luncheon soup. The tiny fish should be neither washed nor gutted. The same soup can be prepared with larger fish (one might include whiting, red mullet, small monkfish, baby crabs, and conger eel), which would need to be scaled, gutted, and washed. This soup does not need *rouille* or *aïoli* or cheese—just a few thin slices of sourdough bread, toasted and rubbed with garlic.

1. In a 6-quart stockpot, combine the oil, garlic, bouquet garni, and sea salt. Soften the garlic over moderate heat for 3 to 4 minutes. Add the fish, increase the heat to high, and let the ingredients sweat for 5 minutes. Add the fresh and canned tomatoes. If using, add the cayenne pepper, fennel branches, and orange zest. Add 6 cups water. Bring to a vigorous boil and cook, uncovered, at a galloping boil for 25 minutes. Carefully skim off any impurities to avoid any bitterness.

3 tablespoons extra-virgin olive oil

1 plump, fresh head garlic, halved horizontally but not peeled

1 bouquet garni: a generous bunch of flat-leaf parsley, celery leaves, fresh or dried bay leaves, and sprigs of thyme tied in a bundle with cotton string

2 teaspoons sea salt, or to taste

2 pounds very fresh rockfish, including small *rascasse* (scorpion fish), *galinettes* (tub gurnard), rock or blue crabs, small crustaceans, conger eel

5 large ripe tomatoes, rinsed and quartered (do not peel)

2. Remove and discard the bouquet garni and fennel branches. Place a food mill fitted with the coarse blade over another saucepan, and pass the contents through the food mill. Discard the solids. Add the saffron to the strained soup, and bring it just to a boil. Serve in warmed shallow soup bowls.

Any flowery, herbal Provençal white wine, such as Cassis, Côtes-de-Provence, Côtes-du-Rhône, or Costières de Nîmes.

One 14-ounce can peeled
    tomatoes in their juice
    (do not drain)
⅛ teaspoon cayenne
    pepper, or to taste
    (optional)
4 dried fennel branches
    (optional) or 1 teaspoon
    fennel seeds
Fresh or dried zest of 1
    orange (optional)

EQUIPMENT:
A 6-quart stockpot; a food
    mill.

6 SERVINGS

Poissonnerie
Daguerre Marée

4, RUE BAYEN
PARIS 17
TELEPHONE: 01 43 80 16 29
FAX: 01 43 80 76 97
MÉTRO: TERNES

Le Dôme's Sole Meunière

The Bistrot du Dôme's Clams with Fresh Thyme

Les Bookinistes's Fresh Cod Brandade

Memories of Brittany Lobster with Cream

The Taxi Driver's Wife's Secret Mussels

FISH AND SHELLFISH
Les Poissons, Coquillages, et Fruits de Mer

La Cagouille's Sea Scallops with Warm Vinaigrette

Slow-Roasted Salmon

Le Duc's Hot Curried Oysters

Clams in Vinaigrette

Ledoyen's Langoustines

LE DÔME'S SOLE MEUNIÈRE

Sole Meunière Le Dôme

For years I traveled from Paris restaurant to Paris restaurant in search of the best *sole à la meunière*—a simple and sublime panfried fish embellished with nothing more than its buttery cooking juices, a sprinkling of parsley, and a shower of lemon juice. As I sampled the sweet fish here and there, I studied the moistness and size at one restaurant, the color and fragrance of the brown butter at another, the dexterity of the server in filleting the fish at yet another. Finally I determined that the famous Montparnasse Art Deco brasserie Le Dôme—whose prized fish comes from the Ile d'Yeu on the Brittany coast—had the best of all, so I set aside a morning to spend in the kitchen with the Dôme's chef, Frank Graux. I expected to pick up a few tips, but I hardly expected him to take all the classic ideas about cooking this delicate fish and throw them out the window! See the box on page 172 for his secrets.

1. Season the fish with sea salt. Heat a dry nonstick pan over high heat until it is smoking. Add the butter and let it begin to melt for about 10 seconds. Then add the fish (if it is sole, place it light-skinned-side down). Reduce the heat to low. Cook, undisturbed, until the skin near the tail portion begins to pull away from the flesh, about 4 minutes. During this time, the butter will turn brown and emit an aroma of grilled hazelnuts. (If it looks as though

2 sole (or substitute any firm white-fleshed fish, such as flounder, trout, or perch), each about 12 ounces, trimmed, gutted, and scaled

Sea salt to taste

8 tablespoons lightly salted butter

Finely minced fresh curly parsley, for garnish

Freshly squeezed lemon juice, for garnish

EQUIPMENT:
An oval, heavy nonstick skillet large enough to hold the fish.

SERVES 2 AS A MAIN COURSE

the butter is getting too brown, instantly add more butter to cool it down and stop it from burning. Should the butter burn, discard it and begin again with fresh butter.)

2. Using a flexible spatula, turn the fish over, and cook for 4 minutes more.

3. Remove the pan from the heat. Transfer the fish to a serving platter, and fillet it. Transfer the fillets to warm dinner plates. Pour the brown butter from the skillet all over the fish. (For *sole sèche*, or dry sole without the butter sauce, delete this step, discarding the brown butter.) Season with parsley and lemon juice, and serve.

The elegance of the fish, the sweetness of the flesh, and the nuttiness of the butter make me want a rich wine, such as a white Burgundy or a golden Meursault, whose own nuttiness echoes the best elements of this classic dish.

WHAT IS A MEUNIÈRE:

THE TERM *MEUNIÈRE* translates literally as "in the style of the miller's wife." This refers, of course, to the flour miller, and anything called *meunière* means that the dish, usually fish, is first dusted with flour and then cooked in butter. Anything cooked *meunière* is also generally sprinkled with lemon juice and chopped parsley.

WHAT I LEARNED: I think the most astonishing thing I learned from this recipe is that butter can cook for a long time, up to 10 minutes, without burning, as long as you carefully regulate the heat.

Le Dôme

108, BOULEVARD MONTPARNASSE
PARIS 14
TELEPHONE: 01 43 35 25 81
FAX: 01 42 79 01 19
MÉTRO: VAVIN

CHEF FRANK GRAUX'S TIPS FOR PERFECT PANFRIED FLATFISH

JUST WHEN YOU THINK you know everything about a dish, you realize you know nothing. While traditional recipes for sole suggest that you skin the fish, dust it with flour, and cook it in clarified butter, Graux does none of the above. In fact, the idea for leaving the skin intact came from his children. One day he served them turbot with the skin, and one of the children cleaned his plate and asked if there was some more skin left over! Here, then, are some of the lessons I learned at Le Dôme, lessons that can apply to the panfrying of any flatfish. This is a simple preparation, but one that requires a bit of practice. The practice is worth it, and the rewards incredible.

· Use the best-quality lightly salted butter you can find. While many cooks recommend using clarified butter (clarifying removes the water and solids that burn and discolor when the butter is heated to a high temperature), Graux feels that clarifying denatures the flavor of the butter, and the butter flavor is important to this dish. He prefers to use lightly salted butter, which burns less quickly than unsalted butter.

· Do not skin the fish—just scale, gut, and trim it. The skin acts as a natural protective barrier. By leaving the skin on, you do not need the "artificial" barrier of the commonly used coating of flour.

· Use the right pan: He uses a heavy-duty aluminum nonstick oval pan that leaves generous room for the fish. You need to seal the fish first to prevent the butter from saturating the inside. If the pan is too small or the heat too low, the fish will be soggy with fat, rather than crisp on the outside and juicy on the inside.

· Begin at a high heat and then reduce the heat to low. Once the fish is "sealed" over high heat, reduce the heat to low to finish cooking and to prevent the outside from burning.

THE BISTROT DU DÔME'S CLAMS WITH FRESH THYME

Palourdes au Thym Bistrot du Dôme

The first time I visited the bustling all-fish Bistrot du Dôme in 1989, I fell in love with this dish. It is one of those simple four-ingredient preparations that emerges with a multitude of flavors and aromas. The iodine-rich juices of the clams merge with the sweet tang of the cream, all punctuated with the herbal zest of fresh thyme. A hit of black pepper serves to wake up and round out the flavors. Serve this with plenty of toasted country bread to absorb the sauce.

2 pounds small fresh little-
    neck or Manila clams,
    purged (see Note)
1 teaspoon fresh thyme leaves
3/4 cup heavy cream
Freshly ground black pepper
    to taste

4 SERVINGS AS A FIRST
COURSE, 2 SERVINGS AS
A MAIN COURSE

In a large, shallow skillet, combine the purged clams, thyme, and cream. Stir to coat the clam shells with the cream. Cover. Cook over high heat, shaking the skillet occasionally, until all the clams are open, 2 to 3 minutes. Transfer the clams in their shells, with the sauce, to warmed shallow soup bowls. (Discard any clams that do not open.) Season with black pepper and serve.

WHAT I LEARNED: Do not try to make this dish with low-fat cream. It doesn't contain enough fat to bind the cream to the clam liquor, and the sauce will separate and curdle when heated.

One of my favorite wines at Le Bistrot du Dôme is their lovely dry Vouvray from the house of Huet.

NOTE: To purge clams, scrub the shells under cold running water. Discard any broken shells or shells that do not close when tapped. In a large bowl, combine 1½ quarts cold water and 3 tablespoons fine sea salt. Stir to dissolve the salt. Add the rinsed clams and purge them in the saltwater in the refrigerator for at least 3 hours. Once they are purged, remove the clams with your fingers, leaving behind the sand and grit.

Le Bistrot du Dôme

1, RUE DELAMBRE
PARIS 14
TELEPHONE: 01 43 35 32 00
MÉTRO: VAVIN

LES BOOKINISTES'S FRESH COD BRANDADE

Brandade du Morue Fraîche Les Bookinistes

William Ledeuil is a truly talented chef in the employ of the gifted Guy Savoy. Ledeuil has been at the helm at Les Bookinistes—with its colorful modern decor mimicking old-time bistros—since it first opened in 1994. On one of my earliest visits, he offered us this delicious and simple first course of fresh cod and potatoes. I make it often, embellishing it with chives for a touch of green and the gentle bite of that versatile herb.

1. In a large saucepan, combine the cream, milk, and the cod.

2. Wrap the garlic, bay leaf, thyme sprigs, and white peppercorns in a small piece of cheesecloth and tie in a bundle. Add the herb bundle to the saucepan. Add the coarse sea salt. Bring the liquid just to a boil over medium heat. Then lower the heat and simmer until the fish flakes easily with a fork, 3 to 4 minutes. Drain the fish, reserving the cooking liquid. Transfer the fish to a large bowl and set aside. Discard the herb bundle. Return the cooking liquid to the large saucepan.

3. Prepare the potatoes: Place the potatoes in the reserved cooking liquid and place over moderate heat. Simmer, uncovered, stirring regularly, until a knife inserted into a potato comes away easily, 15 to 20 minutes. Watch

2 cups heavy cream

2 cups whole milk

1 pound skinned fresh cod, cut into 2-inch cubes

5 cloves garlic, peeled, halved, green germ removed

1 bay leaf

2 sprigs fresh thyme

1 teaspoon white peppercorns

2 tablespoons coarse sea salt

1 pound waxy yellow-fleshed potatoes, peeled and cut into 1-inch cubes

Sea salt

Freshly ground white pepper to taste

½ cup minced fresh parsley leaves

½ cup minced fresh chives

carefully, for the liquid can easily boil over. As soon as they are cooked, drain the potatoes, reserving the cooking liquid. Pass the potatoes through the coarse grid of a food mill into a large bowl. Reserve. Pass the cooking liquid through a fine-mesh sieve into a container with a pouring spout. Reserve.

4. Add the potatoes to the cod, and stirring regularly, gradually add enough of the cooking liquid to make a soft, moist mixture. The cod and potatoes will quickly absorb the liquid. The *brandade* should have the consistency of loose mashed potatoes. Add sea salt and white pepper to taste. Stir in the parsley and chives.

5. Preheat the broiler.

6. Divide the *brandade* among six individual gratin dishes or place it in a single large gratin dish. Sprinkle lightly with the breadcrumbs. Place under the broiler until lightly browned. Season with additional minced chives and fine sea salt, and serve.

3 tablespoons fresh
   breadcrumbs
Minced chives, for
   garnish
Fine sea salt, for garnish

EQUIPMENT:
A food mill.

6 SERVINGS

A Condrieu from Georges Vernay.

Les Bookinistes

53, QUAI GRANDS-AUGUSTINS
PARIS 6
TELEPHONE: 01 43 25 45 94
FAX: 01 43 25 23 07
MÉTRO: RER SAINT-MICHEL

MEMORIES OF BRITTANY LOBSTER WITH CREAM

Homard à la Crème Retour de Bretagne

Often the memory of a dish plays as much of a role in enjoyment as the dish itself. One of my fondest food memories is the lobster I ate at l'Etrave, a casual fish restaurant in Brittany in the town of Cléden Cap Sizun, where the lobster was halved and doused with cream and grilled under a fierce fire until golden and bubbly. In Paris, this is the only way I prepare lobster—often in the winter, when we feast on the dish in front of a roaring fire with a glass of chilled bubbling champagne.

1 lobster, about 2 pounds
3 tablespoons coarse sea salt
1 cup heavy cream

EQUIPMENT:
A 6-quart pasta pot fitted with a colander.

2 SERVINGS

1. Preheat the broiler. Place an oven rack about 3 inches from the heat.

2. Parboil the lobster: Fill a 6-quart pasta pot, fitted with a colander, with water and bring to a boil over high heat. Add the coarse sea salt, and plunge the lobster head first into the pot. Cover, and cook for 5 minutes for the first pound, plus 3 minutes for each additional pound.

3. Remove the colander from the water, drain, and let the lobster cool for a few minutes. Then transfer the lobster to a cutting board, laying it on its back. Split the lobster in half: Plunge a sturdy chef's knife through the back of the head. Cut forward through the head and back through the

body and tail. Remove the head sac and intestines. Crack the claws and legs slightly with the back of the knife. Place the halves, cut side up, side by side on a baking sheet. Pour the cream into the claws and the tail.

4. Place the baking sheet on the oven rack and broil until the lobster flesh is firm and the cream is brown and bubbling, 6 to 10 minutes. Transfer each lobster half to a warmed dinner plate, and serve.

The rich combination of lobster and cream cries out for a rich and elegant wine. Why not a creamy vintage champagne? Other suggestions include a top California Chardonnay or a fine white Burgundy.

WHAT I LEARNED: This dish taught me not to be afraid of cooking lobster. It is a dish that is simple and clear—and in fact the only lobster recipe I find I need in my repertoire.

THE TAXI DRIVER'S WIFE'S SECRET MUSSELS

Les Moules Secrètes de la Femme du Chauffeur de Taxi

I feel as though I am a magnet for guarded culinary secrets: Wherever I am in Paris, it seems, people want me to know about their special recipes. One day while a taxi driver was taking me from restaurant to market to specialty shop, he confided that his wife made the best mussels in the world. So delicious that everyone, he said, raved about them and his wife never, ever, revealed her secret. I did not even have to pop the question, and pretty soon he had shared his spouse's most guarded recipe: The key is Gewürztraminer, the aromatic wine from France's Alsace region. At first I was a bit doubtful, for acidic white wines, such as those from the Loire, are most commonly used with mussels. Well, now I am a convert. The faint sweetness of Gewürztraminer mirrors the sweetness of the finest mussels.

I always look for the tiniest mussels in the market, for I find them to be the most flavorful. Some of the best in Paris are the *moules de bouchot* from Le Baie du Mont-St. Michel. Don't forget the crusty baguette to soak up the memorable sauce.

1. Thoroughly scrub the mussels, and rinse with several changes of water. If an open mussel closes when you press on it, it is good; if it stays open, the mussel should be discarded. Beard the mussels. (Do not beard the mussels more

2 pounds fresh mussels

2 shallots, peeled and finely minced

3 tablespoons unsalted butter

¼ teaspoon fine sea salt

2 cups Alsatian Gewürztraminer wine

Freshly ground black pepper

2 teaspoons fresh or dried thyme leaves

A handful of fresh flat-leaf parsley leaves, minced

EQUIPMENT:
A large deep skillet with a lid.

4 SERVINGS AS A FIRST COURSE, 2 SERVINGS AS A MAIN COURSE

than a few minutes in advance or they will die and spoil. Note that in some markets mussels are preprepared, in that the small black beard that hangs from the mussel has been clipped off but not entirely removed. These mussels do not need further attention.) Set them aside.

2. In a large, deep skillet, combine the shallots, butter, and sea salt. Sweat—cook, covered, over low heat—until softened, about 3 minutes. Add the wine, bring to a boil over high heat, and boil, uncovered, until reduced by half, about 5 minutes.

3. Add the mussels, sprinkle generously with black pepper, and stir. Cover, and cook just until the mussels open, about 3 minutes. Remove the mussels as they open. Do not overcook. Discard any mussels that do not open.

4. Transfer the mussels and liquid to four warmed shallow soup bowls. Sprinkle each with thyme, parsley, and black pepper. Serve immediately, with finger bowls.

I use an inexpensive Gewürztraminer when preparing this dish, and I serve the same wine with the mussels.

WHAT I LEARNED: Years ago, a fishmonger warned me against taking mussels home in a plastic bag and storing them in the refrigerator. Mussels stored in a sealed bag will suffocate and die. Rather, when you get home from the market, either place the mussels on a shelf in the refrigerator with the bag opened or, better yet, transfer them to a large bowl and cover the bowl with a damp cloth.

One of the best places to buy fish and shellfish on the Left Bank is

Poissonnerie du Bac

69, RUE DU BAC
PARIS 7
TELEPHONE: 01 45 48 06 64
MÉTRO: RUE DU BAC

LA CAGOUILLE'S SEA SCALLOPS WITH WARM VINAIGRETTE

Coquilles Saint-Jacques Vinaigrette Tiède La Cagouille

To my mind, this is one of the finest ways to cook scallops: Simply seared in a hot pan, the rich, golden, nutty, almost caramelized sweet aroma and flavor of these rich muscles from the sea are allowed to shine, unadorned and unsmothered. The vinaigrette—here prepared with about half the amount of acid used in a classic vinaigrette—is there just to gently coat the scallops and add the slightest touch of acid to balance the richness of the scallops' meat. In dictating this recipe, La Cagouille owner Gérard Allemandou noted: "Delicate, subtle, with a meat that is dense and velvety, the scallop allows unlimited preparations, but the cook must always look to respect the delicacy of its smooth, soft, sweet flavor."

Noirmoutier Potatoes with Fleur de Sel (page 100) are the perfect accompaniment.

1. Rinse the scallops and pat them dry. Remove the little muscle on the side of the scallop, and discard. Cut each scallop in half horizontally, and set aside.

2. Prepare the vinaigrette: In a small jar, combine the vinegar and sea salt to taste. Cover and shake to dissolve the salt. Add the grapeseed oil, cover, and shake to form an emulsion. Taste for seasoning. Set aside.

8 large sea scallops (about 8 ounces total)
Sea salt
Freshly ground white pepper

THE VINAIGRETTE

1 tablespoon best-quality sherry vinegar
Fine sea salt
8 to 10 tablespoons grapeseed or mild extra-virgin olive oil

About 2 tablespoons finely minced fresh chives
About 2 tablespoons finely minced fresh flat-leaf parsley leaves
About 2 tablespoons finely minced fresh chervil or tarragon leaves
Fleur de sel (see page 102) or fine sea salt
Freshly ground white pepper

4 SERVINGS AS A FIRST COURSE

3. Heat a large nonstick skillet over high heat. When it is hot, add the scallops and sear just until they brown around the edges, 30 seconds to 1 minute on each side. Season each side with sea salt and white pepper after it has cooked. (The cooking time will vary according to the size of the scallops. For scallops that are cooked all the way through, sear for 1 minute or more on each side.)

4. Spoon 2 tablespoons of the vinaigrette and ½ teaspoon of each of the herbs on each warmed dinner plate. Carefully transfer four scallop halves to each of the prepared plates. Sprinkle the scallops with the remaining herbs. Season with *fleur de sel* and white pepper, and serve.

As chef Allemandou suggests: "A great white wine will help this dish reach its apotheosis—a Condrieu from Georges Vernay, for example."

WHAT I LEARNED: This is one of those simplest of dishes that must be followed to the letter. Be sure that your herbs are minced as fine as possible, so that they do not overwhelm the delicate scallops. Take your time in preparing the herbs and you will be justly rewarded.

La Cagouille

10–12, PLACE BRANCUSI
(ACROSS FROM 23, RUE DE
L'OUEST)
PARIS 14
TELEPHONE: 01 43 22 09 01
FAX: 01 45 38 57 29
MÉTRO: GAÎTÉ

SLOW-ROASTED SALMON

Saumon Confit

I first tasted a version of this dish while sampling the sublime, simple, straightforward cuisine of Dominique Bouchet, who now mans the stoves at the Hôtel Crillon and one of the city's most romantic dining rooms, Les Ambassadeurs. In this recipe, the salmon is cooked in a low oven for 17 minutes, making for an extremely moist fish, one that tastes neither raw nor cooked, but rather a perfect stage in between. I like to serve it as a first course, with a chiffonnade of sorrel and a sorrel sauce.

1. Preheat the oven to 275 degrees F.

2. Run your fingers over the top of the salmon fillet to detect any tiny bones that remain. Use tweezers to remove them. Cut the salmon into four equal pieces.

3. Place the salmon in an ovenproof dish that will hold the fish snugly. Using a pastry brush, brush the salmon on all sides with the oil. Place the baking dish in the center of the oven and roast until the fish is a bright pinkish orange and flakes easily, 17 minutes. Remove the dish from the oven, and trim off and discard any white milky portions or darkened edges around the fish. Using a wide spatula, transfer the fish to a small rack set on top of a plate, and allow it to drain.

4. Serve at room temperature (never hot or cold or it will lose its essence), with Sorrel Sauce.

1 pound fresh salmon
    fillet, skinned
Several teaspoons extra-
    virgin olive oil
Fine sea salt
Freshly ground white
    pepper to taste
Sorrel Sauce (page 296)

4 SERVINGS AS A MAIN
COURSE

I enjoy this with a fresh and fragrant Viognier, such as one made by one of my favorite winemakers, Jean-Pierre Cartier in Gigondas.

Les Ambassadeurs

HÔTEL CRILLON
10, PLACE DE LA CONCORDE
PARIS 8
TELEPHONE: 01 44 71 16 16
FAX: 01 44 71 15 02
MÉTRO: CONCORDE

LE DUC'S HOT CURRIED OYSTERS

Huîtres Chaudes au Curry Le Duc

Le Duc is one of Paris's finest fish restaurants, and this is one of its classic dishes. These hot oysters are great to pass as an appetizer or to serve as a first-course palate opener. The salt and the curry stimulate the appetite and get you ready for more!

1. Preheat the broiler.

2. Sprinkle an ovenproof gratin dish with coarse salt to cover the bottom and form a cushion for the oysters. Arrange the oysters, on their shells, on the bed of salt. Set aside.

3. In a small saucepan, combine the shallots, garlic, and butter. Sweat—cook, covered, over low heat without coloring—until soft and translucent, 1 to 2 minutes. Stir in the cream and spices and cook until thick and creamy, 1 to 2 minutes. Stir in the lemon juice and reserved oyster liquor. Add white pepper to taste.

4. Spoon the sauce over the oysters. Place the gratin dish under the broiler and cook just until the sauce melts and begins to sizzle, about 45 seconds. Serve immediately.

Serve with champagne or a young, crisp, dry, almost sparkling (the French call it *perlant*) Muscadet de Sèvre-et-Maine, an underrated Atlantic coast wine made near the town of Nantes.

About 1 cup coarse sea salt
8 ultra-fresh oysters, scrubbed, shucked, the liquor strained and reserved
2 shallots, peeled and minced
1 plump, fresh clove garlic, peeled and minced
1 tablespoon unsalted butter
1/4 cup heavy cream
1/2 teaspoon cayenne pepper
1/2 teaspoon powdered saffron
3/4 teaspoon Homemade Curry Powder (page 289)
1 tablespoon freshly squeezed lemon juice
Freshly ground white pepper

4 APPETIZER SERVINGS

Le Duc

243, BOULEVARD RASPAIL
PARIS 14
TELEPHONE: 01 43 20 96 30
FAX: 01 43 20 46 73
MÉTRO: RASPAIL

CLAMS IN VINAIGRETTE

Palourdes à la Vinaigrette

Paris probably offers the best and freshest shellfish in France. Thanks to modern transportation and popular enthusiasm for the abundance of food from the nation's waters, the capital offers an embarrassment of riches. Much of the year one can find tiny *coques*—miniature clams that are sweet, almondy, and satisfying—and when I want to prepare a quick meal, I put *coques* on the menu. Although this dish is made in just 3 or 4 minutes, you do have to think ahead: Clams tend to be sandy, and must always be purged in a cold saltwater bath. Serve these with plenty of toasted country bread to absorb the sauce.

1. Prepare the vinaigrette: In a small bowl, combine the vinegars and sea salt, and stir to dissolve the salt. Add the oil, whisking to blend. Add the chives, shallots, and black pepper. Set aside.

2. Place the purged clams in a large, shallow skillet. Cover and cook over high high, shaking occasionally, until all the clams are open, 2 to 3 minutes. With a large slotted spoon, transfer the clams, in their shells, to warmed shallow soup bowls. Discard any clams that do not open. Whisk the vinaigrette one more time, and pour it over the clams. Toss well to coat the clams with the dressing. Serve immediately.

THE VINAIGRETTE

2 tablespoons balsamic vinegar

2 tablespoons best-quality sherry vinegar

Sea salt to taste

4 tablespoons extra-virgin olive oil

3 tablespoons minced fresh chives

1 shallot, peeled and finely minced

Freshly ground black pepper to taste

2 pounds small fresh littleneck or Manila clams, purged (see Note)

2 SERVINGS AS A MAIN COURSE; 4 SERVINGS AS A FIRST COURSE

NOTE: To purge clams, scrub the shells under cold running water. Discard any broken shells or shells that do not close when tapped. In a large bowl, combine 1½ quarts cold water and 3 tablespoons fine sea salt. Stir to dissolve the salt. Add the rinsed clams and purge them in the saltwater in the refrigerator for at least 3 hours. Once they are purged, remove the clams with your fingers, leaving behind the sand and grit.

Any good, acidic white wine goes well here. Mardon's Quincy, with its pure, distinctive grassiness, is one of my favorites.

Oysterman at Prunier

An excellent source for fresh clams is

Poissonnerie Bruno Gauvain

16, RUE DUPIN
PARIS 6
TEL: 01 42 22 46 65
MÉTRO: SÈVRES-BABYLONE

LEDOYEN'S LANGOUSTINES

Langoustines Ledoyen

Chef Christian Le Squer, of the restaurant Ledoyen, considers langoustines "refined lobsters." I agree with him, for they are one of my top ten favorite foods, up there with oysters, artichokes, asparagus, and squab. Langoustines have a more delicate flavor than lobster, they satisfy instantly in the way only pure protein can, and when properly cooked, they have a delicate texture that reminds me of plump down pillows. This is one recipe that allows you to enjoy to the fullest the pure, unadulterated flavor and texture of the langoustines. Where langoustines are not available, the dish is just as delicious prepared with the freshest of giant shrimp.

1. Prepare the three-spice blend: Combine the coriander seeds, star anise, and fennel seeds in a spice mill and grind until fine. Transfer to a spice jar and seal.

2. Prepare the citrus emulsion: Combine the lemon juice and sea salt in a small bowl. Stir to dissolve the salt. Whisk in the oil. Taste for seasoning, and set aside.

3. Prepare three plates: one with 2 tablespoons of the olive oil, one with the minced basil, and one with the *kadaif*. Sprinkle the three-spice blend over the langoustines. Roll the seasoned langoustines in the oil to coat evenly. Roll them in the basil, then in the *kadaif*.

THE THREE-SPICE BLEND

1 tablespoon coriander seeds

3 whole star anise

1 tablespoon fennel seeds

THE CITRUS EMULSION

2 tablespoons freshly squeezed lemon juice

Fine sea salt to taste

1/2 cup hazelnut or extra-virgin olive oil

THE LANGOUSTINES

5 tablespoons extra-virgin olive oil

4 tablespoons very finely minced fresh basil leaves

3 ounces *kadaif* (shredded Greek pastry, found in specialty stores)

24 raw langoustines (or substitute extra-large shrimp, shelled and deveined)

4. Heat the remaining 3 tablespoons olive oil in a large nonstick skillet. Add the langoustines, and brown them evenly on all sides, about 1 minute per side.

5. Transfer four langoustines to the center of each warm dinner plate. Drizzle the citrus emulsion over the langoustines. Garnish with the basil chiffonnade, and serve immediately.

Several tablespoons very finely shredded fresh basil (chiffonnade) for garnish

6 SERVINGS AS A MAIN COURSE

My choice is a Viognier, such as the regal white from the *caves* of Jean-Pierre Cartier, Domaine les Gouberts, in Gigondas.

Ledoyen

CARRÉ CHAMPS-ELYSÉES
PARIS 8
TELEPHONE: 01 53 05 10 01
FAX: 01 47 42 55 01
MÉTRO: CHAMPS ELYSÉES–
CLÉMENCEAU

Lemon Chicken

Benoît's Fricassee of Chicken with Morels

Chicken Fricassee with Two Vinegars

Chicken Fricassee with Morels and Vin Jaune

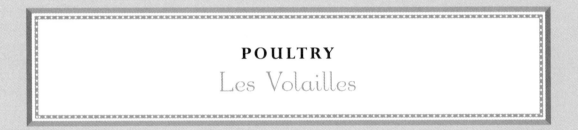

POULTRY
Les Volailles

Grilled Chicken with Mustard and Red Pepper

Place Monge Market Guinea Hen with Sauerkraut and Sausages

Manu's Grilled and Roasted Squab

Parisian Roasted Turkey

Alain Dutourier of Carré des Feuilants

LEMON CHICKEN

Poulet au Citron

When I can't think of what to cook, I cook chicken. When there is chicken on a restaurant menu, I order it. I think that I could eat moist, healthy, chewy roast farm chicken almost every day. There is something so simple and sublime about well-bred, free-range poultry. This is the simplest of recipes, and one I credit to my husband, Walter. Actually, I cooked the chicken; he discovered the *truc*. He walked in from work one evening as I was taking a roast chicken from the oven. The chicken was particularly small, and so rather than putting a whole lemon in the cavity as is my custom, I had quartered the citrus lengthwise. As Walter carved the chicken, he squeezed the juices from the lemons over the meat. The juice itself had become a rich, complex *confit*—thick, dense, and fragrant. We swooned over that little touch of genius. Ever since, this has been one of our weeknight treats, which we usually team up with a simple green salad, two or three cheeses, some Poilâne bread, and of course a glass or two of good French wine.

1 best-quality farm chicken (about 5 pounds)

Sea salt to taste

Freshly ground black pepper to taste

2 lemons, preferably organic, scrubbed, dried, and quartered lengthwise

Several sprigs fresh thyme

5 tablespoons unsalted butter, softened

EQUIPMENT:

An oval roasting pan, just slightly larger than the chicken, fitted with a roasting rack.

4 TO 6 SERVINGS

1. Preheat the oven to 425 degrees F.

2. Generously season the cavity of the chicken with sea salt and black pepper. Place the giblets, the lemon quarters, and the thyme inside. Truss. Rub the skin with the butter. Season all over with sea salt and black pepper.

3. Place the chicken on its side on a rack in a roasting pan. Place in the center of the oven and roast, uncovered, for 20 minutes. Turn the chicken to the other side, and

roast for 20 minutes more. Turn the chicken breast side up, and roast for 20 minutes more, for a total of 1 hour's roasting time. By this time the skin should be a deep golden color. Reduce the heat to 375 degrees F. Turn the chicken breast side down, at an angle if at all possible, so its head end is down and its tail end is in the air. (This heightens the flavor by allowing the juices to flow down through the breast meat.) Roast until the juices run clear when you pierce a thigh with a skewer, about 15 minutes.

The lemony tang of this chicken suggests a simple white, such as an Alsatian Riesling.

4. Remove the pan from the oven and season the chicken generously with sea salt and black pepper. Transfer the chicken to a platter, and place it on an angle against the edge of an overturned plate, with its head down and tail in the air. Cover loosely with foil. Turn off the oven and place the platter in the oven, with the door open. Let the chicken rest for a minimum of 10 minutes and up to 30 minutes. It will continue to cook during this resting time.

5. Meanwhile, prepare the sauce: Place the roasting pan over moderate heat and cook, scraping up any bits that cling to the bottom and stirring until the liquid is almost caramelized, 2 to 3 minutes. Do not let it burn. Spoon off and discard any excess fat. Add several tablespoons cold water to deglaze the pan (hot water will cloud the sauce). Bring to a boil. Reduce the heat to low and simmer until thickened, about 5 minutes.

6. While the sauce is cooking, remove the lemons from the cavity of the chicken. Carve the chicken into serving pieces and transfer them to a warmed platter. Squeeze the lemons all over the chicken pieces, extracting as much juice as possible. Strain the sauce through a fine-mesh sieve and pour it into a sauceboat. Serve immediately.

BENOÎT'S FRICASSEE OF CHICKEN WITH MORELS

Fricassée de Poulet aux Morilles Benoît

This recipe was dictated to me one morning as I worked behind the stove with Benoît Guichard at his Michelin two-star restaurant, Jamin. Despite the luxurious surroundings, Jamin has at its soul a very solid "home" style of French cooking. I love this dish—the mahogany tones of the morel sauce permeate the chicken as it cooks, resulting in a penetrating, welcoming color. The recipe allows for plenty of sauce, so the dish is ideal for pairing with strands of fresh pasta or fluffy white rice.

1. Slice the onions in half lengthwise. Place each half, cut side down, on a cutting board and cut crosswise into very thin slices.

2. In a large skillet, combine 2 tablespoons of the oil, 1 tablespoon of the butter, and a pinch of sea salt. Add the onions and sweat—cook, covered, over low heat without coloring—for about 5 minutes. With a slotted spoon, transfer the onions to a clean plate. Set them aside.

3. Liberally season the chicken on all sides with sea salt and white pepper. Add the remaining 2 tablespoons oil and 1 tablespoon butter to the skillet, and place over moderate heat. When the fats are hot, add the chicken, skin side down, and brown until it turns an even golden color,

2 medium onions, peeled
4 tablespoons extra-virgin olive oil
2 tablespoons unsalted butter
Sea salt to taste
4 chicken legs, thighs attached (about 3 pounds total), at room temperature
Freshly ground white pepper to taste
1 recipe Wild Morel Mushrooms in Cream and Bouillon, prepared through Step 3 (page 84)

4 SERVINGS

about 5 minutes. Turn the pieces and brown them on the other side, 5 minutes more. Carefully regulate the heat to avoid scorching the skin. When all the pieces are browned, use tongs (to avoid piercing the meat) to transfer them to a platter.

4. Pour off and discard the fat in the skillet. Return the chicken to the skillet. Add the onions and the Wild Morel Mushrooms in Cream and Bouillon. Cover, and simmer over the lowest possible heat for 20 minutes. Taste for seasoning, and serve.

This classic dish deserves a classic wine. If you can find it, try an Arbois *vin jaune* Côtes du Jura, a golden wine much like a *fino* sherry. Or even better is the rare Château-Chalon, a strong and dry sherrylike wine that is bottled only after six years of aging.

Jacques Melac at his wine bar

Jamin

32, RUE DE LONGCHAMP
PARIS 16
TELEPHONE: 01 45 53 00 07
FAX: 01 45 53 00 15
MÉTRO: TROCADÉRO

POULTRY

CHICKEN FRICASSEE WITH TWO VINEGARS

Fricassée de Poulet aux Deux Vinaigres

$\mathcal{A}$ perfect farm chicken, properly cut into serving pieces and sautéed to a golden tenderness, sauced with a luscious blend of cream, tomatoes, vinegar, and stock, is a culinary triumph. This recipe, typical of the sort of traditional bistro fare that makes French food so appealing and satisfying, appeared in my shopping bag one day as part of a promotion for the delicate, creamy-fleshed *poulet de Bresse*, the king of French chicken. The first time I made this for my husband, Walter, and myself, there were a few leftovers. The next day Walter asked what I did with the chicken. When I said I had frozen it, he replied, "Oh, good. It makes me happy to know that I have it in my future." Then he added, "But I really think you need to test that again, soon." I did, and it's been a family favorite ever since. At home I serve this with steamed rice or fresh pasta.

Where Bresse poultry is not available, use a good, meaty, free-range chicken, organic if you can find it: It will be firmer, less fatty, and certainly more flavorful than the smaller, battery-raised variety.

1. Liberally season the chicken on all sides with sea salt and white pepper.

1 fresh farm chicken (3 to 4 pounds), cut into 8 serving pieces, at room temperature

Sea salt to taste

Freshly ground white pepper to taste

3 tablespoons extra-virgin olive oil

4 tablespoons unsalted butter

⅓ cup best-quality white champagne vinegar

⅓ cup best-quality red wine vinegar

⅓ cup white wine

2 shallots, peeled and finely minced

¾ cup Tomato Sauce (page 300)

1⅔ cups Homemade Chicken Stock (page 297)

1 cup heavy cream

EQUIPMENT:
A deep skillet with a lid.

4 SERVINGS

2. In a deep skillet, combine the oil and butter, and heat over moderate heat. When the fats are hot but not smoking, add the chicken, skin side down, and brown until it turns an even golden color, about 5 minutes. Turn the pieces and brown them on the other side, 5 minutes more. Carefully regulate the heat to avoid scorching the skin. (This may have to be done in batches.) When all the pieces are browned, use tongs (to avoid piercing the meat) to transfer them to a platter.

3. Pour off and discard the fat in the skillet. Off the heat, add the two vinegars and deglaze the pan. Add the wine. Add the shallots and cook, covered, over low heat until softened, 2 to 3 minutes. Return the chicken to the pan. Cover and simmer over low heat for 15 minutes. Transfer the chicken pieces to a large warmed platter and cover with aluminum foil to keep warm.

4. Add the tomato sauce and the stock to the skillet; stir to blend thoroughly. Add the cream and cook, uncovered, over medium heat for 5 minutes. Return the chicken to the skillet, cover, and cook over low heat, turning the pieces from time to time to absorb the sauce, for about 10 minutes. Taste for seasoning, and serve.

This dish from the Bresse region is tailor-made for a simple, fruity Beaujolais.

Bresse poultry can be found at any good Parisian butcher shop. I often buy mine at

La Grande Epicerie de Paris

LE BON MARCHÉ DEPARTMENT STORE
38, RUE DE SÈVRES
PARIS 7
TELEPHONE: 01 44 39 81 00
MÉTRO: SÈVRES-BABYLONE

CHICKEN FRICASSEE WITH MORELS AND VIN JAUNE

Fricassée de Poulet aux Morilles et Vin Jaune

My good friend Hervé Poron is the truffle king of Provence. Throughout the year, he also supplies me with extraordinary dried morels, which I use to prepare this luscious chicken dish. This is one of my husband's favorite Sunday suppers, perfect for sitting around a fire on a chilly Paris night. Serve it with rice or fresh pasta.

1. Prepare the morels: Place the morels in a colander and rinse well under cold running water to rid them of any grit. Transfer them to a heatproof measuring cup. Pour boiling water over the mushrooms to cover. Set aside for 20 minutes to plump them up. Then, using a slotted spoon, carefully remove the mushrooms from the liquid, leaving behind any grit that may have fallen to the bottom. If any of the morels are extremely large, halve them lengthwise.

2. Liberally season the chicken pieces on all sides with sea salt and white pepper.

3. In a deep 12-inch skillet, combine the oil and 4 tablespoons of the butter. Place over moderate heat. When the fats are hot but not smoking, add the chicken, skin side down, and brown until it turns an even golden color, about 5 minutes. Turn the pieces and brown them on the other side, 5 minutes more. Carefully regulate the heat to

2 cups (2 ounces) dried morel mushrooms

1 fresh farm chicken (3 to 4 pounds), cut into 8 serving pieces, at room temperature

Fine sea salt to taste

Freshly ground white pepper to taste

3 tablespoons extra-virgin olive oil

5 tablespoons unsalted butter

2 shallots, peeled and finely minced

2 plump, fresh cloves garlic, peeled and finely minced

2 cups *vin jaune* from the Jura, sherry, or oaky Chardonnay

1 cup heavy cream

EQUIPMENT:

A large deep skillet with a lid.

4 SERVINGS

avoid scorching the skin. (This may have to be done in batches.) When all the pieces are browned, use tongs (to avoid piercing the meat) to transfer them to a platter. Season once again with sea salt and white pepper.

4. Pour off and discard the fat in the skillet. Add the remaining 1 tablespoon butter, the shallots, and the garlic. Sweat—cook, covered, over low heat—until soft but not browned, about 3 minutes. Add the wine and boil, uncovered, over high heat for 5 minutes to burn off the alcohol, which could make the sauce bitter. Add the cream and the morels, and stir to blend. Return the chicken and any juices that have accumulated to the skillet. Cover, and cook over low heat, turning the pieces in the sauce once or twice, until the chicken is cooked through and has thoroughly absorbed the sauce, about 20 minutes. Taste for seasoning, and serve.

There is no choice here—the wine must be the golden, sherrylike *vin jaune* from the Jura, the best being from Château-Chalon.

TRUC: You can save the mushroom "bouillon." When I make this dish, I serve rice with it, and I use the bouillon in place of water. I also like to freeze the bouillon to enhance a mushroom soup. Place a piece of dampened cheesecloth in a colander set over a large bowl. Carefully spoon the mushroom liquid into the colander, leaving behind any grit at the bottom of the measuring cup.

THE PAMPERED BRESSE CHICKEN

ON ONE OF MY EARLY TRIPS to France in the 1970s, I spent a day researching the life of the pampered Bresse chicken. I didn't speak a word of French at the time, and my husband, Walter, who had studied French for years, served as my translator. It was our luck that the sweet gentleman who took us around spoke about the fastest French I had ever witnessed. He would speak for about five minutes without taking a breath. When I would ask Walter to translate, the speech would be condensed into a sentence or two! Thank goodness one can report with one's eyes as well as one's ears. What can I say about Bresse poultry: They are the *crème de la crème* of the poultry world. Their delicate, meltingly tender meat is white as alabaster. It is no surprise that Bresse poultry loves creamy sauces and delicate flavors. *Bresse* is actually the name of a breed of poultry grown in the region just south of Lyon; the birds are identified by their red, white, and blue tricolor seal and a numbered leg band. The chicken lives freely—free range, just as the name implies—for the early part of its life, then rests indoors for one week to obtain that white, white meat. But the quality of the poultry comes from what it is fed: cereal grains, corn, and dairy products, not to mention all the insects it finds on its wanderings about the yard.

GRILLED CHICKEN WITH MUSTARD AND RED PEPPER

Poulet Grillé à la Diable

In French cooking, any meat or poultry seasoned with mustard and hot pepper and then coated with bread-crumbs is called *à la diable*, since the devil, or *diable*, is associated with anything hot and fiery. Cafés and bistros all over Paris offer versions of this classic. I like to make mine with a combination of sharp Dijon and coarse-grain Dijon mustard, and with a good hit of spice, usually what the French call *piments langues d'oiseaux*, or bird's-tongue peppers. This is a great picnic dish as well, and I often make it for our lunch when we take the train to Provence. When we eat at home, I serve this chicken with steamed rice or sautéed potatoes and a green salad.

2 tablespoons French
  Dijon mustard
1 tablespoon coarse-grain
  French Dijon mustard
¼ teaspoon finely ground
  dried hot red pepper
2 eggs
6 chicken legs, thighs
  attached
½ cup fine homemade
  breadcrumbs
3 tablespoons unsalted
  butter

6 SERVINGS

1. Preheat the oven to 375 degrees F.

2. In a small bowl, combine the mustards and red pepper; stir to blend.

3. Place the eggs in a shallow platter, and whisk lightly with a fork to blend.

4. Using a pastry brush, brush the mustard mixture all over the chicken legs and thighs. Dip them in the eggs, coating evenly on all sides. Sprinkle with the bread-crumbs, coating as evenly as possible. Place the chicken pieces side by side in a roasting pan. Dot with the butter.

Place in the oven and bake for 30 to 35 minutes, basting frequently. The chicken is done when the juices run clear when pierced with a fork. Remove the chicken from the oven and transfer the pieces to a wire rack to help firm up the coating, about 5 minutes.

5. Serve hot or cold.

This simple dish suggests a simple red, either a Saumur-Champigny or a young Côtes-du-Rhône. I love Michel Richaud's rich reds from the village of Cairanne.

PLACE MONGE MARKET GUINEA HEN WITH SAUERKRAUT AND SAUSAGES

Pintade à la Choucroute et aux Saucisses Marché Place Monge

One chilly day in March at the Place Monge market in the student quarter of the 5th arrondissement, I happened to spy a variation of this warming winter dish: The poultry merchant had boned a plump farm guinea hen, stuffed it with sauerkraut and wrapped it with bacon. He advised me to brown the poultry, then braise it with beer. I knew I didn't have time to prepare his pintade that night, so a few days later created this version at home. It's now become one of our favorite winter dishes: The entire house takes on a beautifully smoky aroma from the meats, as appetites rise in wait for dinner. If you can, use fresh rather than canned sauerkraut. Fresh sauerkraut can usually be found in delicatessens or in the deli section of the supermarket.

1. Generously season the inside of the guinea hen with sea salt and black pepper. Place the giblets, 2 bay leaves, 5 juniper berries, and 1 teaspoon cumin seeds inside the guinea hen. Truss.

2. In a cast-iron casserole that is large enough to hold the guinea hen, heat the oil until hot but not smoking. Add the hen and brown evenly on all sides, about 7 minutes total. Remove the guinea hen from the casserole. Discard the fat in the pan. Generously season the hen all over with sea salt and black pepper. Return the hen, breast side up,

1 guinea hen (about 3 pounds), giblets reserved

Sea salt to taste

Freshly ground black pepper to taste

6 bay leaves

15 juniper berries

3 teaspoons cumin seeds

3 tablespoons extra-virgin olive oil

4 cups (12 ounces) fresh sauerkraut

2 cups beer

4 smoked pork sausages (each about 4 ounces), such as kielbasa

4 thick slices smoked bacon

EQUIPMENT:

A large cast-iron casserole with a lid or a Dutch oven.

4 SERVINGS

to the casserole, and spoon the sauerkraut all around it. Sprinkle with the remaining 4 bay leaves, 10 juniper berries, and 2 teaspoons cumin seeds. Pour the beer all over the hen and the sauerkraut. Cover, and braise over low heat, stirring from time to time, until the hen is cooked through, about 1 hour.

3. While the guinea hen is cooking, fill a large saucepan with water and bring just to a boil. Add the sausages. Immediately remove the pan from the heat and cover it. Let the sausages sit until firm to the touch and heated through, 10 to 15 minutes.

4. Just before the guinea hen is finished cooking, grill or broil the smoked bacon until crisp and cooked to the desired doneness. Drain on paper towels and set aside.

5. Remove and discard the bay leaves. Arrange the sauerkraut and the sausages on a large warmed platter. Carve the guinea hen and serve it with the sausages and sauerkraut. Garnish each plate with a slice of grilled bacon.

Serve with a chilled Alsatian Pinot Blanc, Pinot Gris, or Riesling, or with an icy, frothy glass of beer.

Marché
Place Monge

PLACE MONGE
PARIS 5
WEDNESDAY, FRIDAY, AND SUNDAY MORNINGS
MÉTRO: MONGE

MANU'S GRILLED AND ROASTED SQUAB

Le Pigeon Grillé et Rôti de Manu

This classic preparation was taught to me by chef Emmanuel Leblay—known as Manu—who has worked in some of Paris's best kitchens, from Guy Savoy to Arpège to Lucas Carton. He is a talented and exacting cook: Follow this simple preparation to the letter and your palate will be richly rewarded! Since a whole squab can be awkward to eat, I find it best to partially debone the bird (this can be done by your butcher). When prepared in this manner, the tender breast portion cooks quickly while the firm dark meat retains all its natural flavor and moisture by being cooked on the bone. Be sure to offer finger bowls so your guests can enjoy every morsel.

About 7 tablespoons extra-virgin olive oil

1 large onion, peeled and chopped

6 squabs (each about 1 pound), cleaned and partially deboned, livers and carcasses reserved

3 tablespoons best-quality sherry vinegar

Sea salt to taste

Freshly ground white pepper to taste

6 SERVINGS

1. Prepare the stock: In a large, deep skillet, heat 3 tablespoons of the oil until hot but not smoking. Add the onions, reduce the heat, and cook until lightly browned, about 5 minutes. Add the squab carcasses and cook until the bones are browned, about 5 minutes. Cover with water and cook over moderately high heat for about 20 minutes, skimming off any impurities that rise to the surface. Strain the stock through a fine-mesh sieve and set it aside.

2. Place the poultry livers on a large plate and using a fork, crush them to a purée. Place the purée in a bowl, and with a small whisk, whisk until smooth.

3. In a large skillet, heat 3 tablespoons of the oil until hot but not smoking. Add the puréed livers and cook, stirring regularly with a whisk, until cooked through, 3 to 4 minutes. Add the sherry vinegar and cook 3 minutes more. Add the reserved stock and cook over moderate heat until the mixture is reduced to a thick, reddish-black, syrupy sauce, about 15 minutes. Set aside and keep warm.

4. Heat a grill or broiler. Preheat the oven to 425 degrees F (optional—see Step 6).

5. Place the squabs on a baking sheet and coat them with the remaining 1 tablespoon olive oil. Season generously with sea salt and white pepper.

6. Place the squabs under the broiler, skin side toward the heat. Broil just until the meat begins to weep a bit, 3 to 4 minutes. Turn the squabs and broil until cooked through but still moist, about 5 minutes. Immediately season with sea salt and white pepper. Place the squabs in the oven, turn off the heat, and, with the door ajar, let the squabs rest for 5 minutes.

7. To serve, place a squab in the center of each plate and spoon the sauce over the crevice in the center of each bird. Serve immediately.

The richness of squab cries out for an equally rich and majestic wine, such as Gérard Chave's pure-syrah Hermitage.

PARISIAN ROASTED TURKEY

Dinde Rôtie à la Parisienne

When I first moved to Paris, turkeys were impossible to find at the end of November. Since the French do not celebrate our Thanksgiving holiday, most birds were raised to be ready for the Christmas table. Today the French have adopted our fall celebrations of Halloween and Thanksgiving, so finding a late-November turkey is less of a trauma. I love to prepare it with this delicious sausage, rosemary, and fennel stuffing, which keeps the bird beautifully moist as it roasts. By tenting the turkey with foil for the first hour of cooking, the stuffing cooks first, allowing the bird to cook evenly and slowly from the inside out. It also prevents excessive browning. Rather than traditional American gravy, I serve this with a simple sauce prepared with the roasting juices.

1. Preheat the oven to 425 degrees F.

2. In a large bowl, combine all the stuffing ingredients except the pepper. Using your hands, blend the ingredients thoroughly, breaking up any remaining large pieces of sausage meat. Season with pepper and mix to blend. Still using your hands, pack the stuffing into the cavity of the turkey. Don't be afraid to push the stuffing slightly as you go, so there are no air pockets. Truss. Rub the skin of the turkey with the butter and season generously with sea salt and white pepper.

STUFFING

The heart, liver, and gizzard of the turkey, chopped into bite-size pieces
1 pound bulk pork sausage meat
2 large eggs, lightly beaten
2 teaspoons fennel seeds
1 cup (4 ounces) very fine fresh breadcrumbs
3 tablespoons fresh rosemary leaves, minced
Freshly ground white pepper to taste

1 free-range roasting turkey (6 to 8 pounds), at room temperature, heart, liver, gizzard, and neck reserved
1½ tablespoons unsalted butter, softened
Sea salt to taste
Freshly ground white pepper to taste

8 TO 10 SERVINGS

POULTRY

205

3. Place the turkey, breast side up, on a rack in the roasting pan. Add the neck to the pan. Lightly tent the turkey with aluminum foil (to prevent the skin from browning before the turkey is fully cooked). Place the roasting pan in the center of the oven and roast for 30 minutes. Remove the pan from the oven and carefully remove the foil. Baste the turkey thoroughly, cover with the foil, and return the pan to the oven. Roast for another 30 minutes, basting from time to time. By this time, the skin should be a deep golden color. Reduce the heat to 375 degrees F and baste again. Remove the foil, and roast the turkey uncovered until the juices run clear when you pierce a thigh with a skewer, about 30 minutes more.

4. Remove the pan from the oven and immediately season the turkey generously with sea salt and white pepper. Transfer the turkey to a platter, placing it at an angle against the edge of an overturned plate, with its head down and its tail in the air. (This heightens the flavor by allowing the juices to flow down through the breast meat.) Cover the turkey loosely with foil. Return the turkey to the oven and turn off the heat. With the door ajar, let the turkey rest for at least 10 minutes or up to 30 minutes. The turkey will continue to cook as it rests.

5. Meanwhile, prepare the sauce: Discard the turkey neck. Place the roasting pan over moderate heat, scraping up any bits that cling to the bottom. Cook for 2 to 3 minutes, scraping and stirring until the liquid is almost caramelized. Do not let it burn. Spoon off and discard any excess fat. Add several tablespoons cold water to deglaze

At our last Thanksgiving celebration, we sampled a rich white Rhône, the Châteauneuf-du-Pape from Château Beaucastel. The clean, fruity, and floral flavors stand up nicely to the rich sausage stuffing.

the pan (hot water would cloud the sauce), and bring to a boil. Reduce the heat to low and simmer until thickened, about 5 minutes. Taste for seasoning.

6. While the sauce is cooking, carve the turkey and arrange it on a warmed platter. Spoon the stuffing into a warmed serving bowl.

7. Strain the sauce through a fine-mesh sieve, and pour it into a sauceboat. Serve immediately with the turkey and stuffing.

FLORA'S SPICY SPARERIBS

L'ALSACO'S SAUERKRAUT, PORK, AND SAUSAGES

FRÉDÉRIC ANTON'S FOUR-HOUR PORK ROAST

LE MAUZAC'S HANGER STEAK

MEATS
Les Viandes

LES ALLOBROGES'S BRAISED LAMB SHANKS WITH GARLIC

ERIC LECERF'S BRAISED LEG OF LAMB

JEAN-GUY'S BASQUE-SPICED LEG OF LAMB

VEAL FLANK STEAK BOUCHERIE DUCIEL

FLORA'S SPICY SPARERIBS

Travers de Cochon Fermier
au Miel et aux Epices

Frankly, the French are not very creative with spareribs. In the 20 years I have been in France, only once was I served them, and that was at Flora Mikula's charming Provençal restaurant, Les Olivades. They were unfatty ribs—meaty, chewy, and tender—and they were bathed in a glistening sauce of honey and spices that was so shiny, you wanted to don ice skates and go for a spin!

Later, I decided to research what happens to all those ribs from French pigs: Since you rarely see ribs for sale in the butcher shops, I wondered whether they stuffed them under the bed or fed them to their cats! Then one day a butcher explained that this cut is traditionally reserved for terrines and pâtés. So if you want ribs in France, you need to ask the butcher to save you some the next time he butchers a pig.

This recipe has become a favorite around our house: French ribs are moist, not too fatty (but not so lean that you think you are eating cardboard), and, oh, the sauce is a delight—just enough spice, just enough of that elegant French touch. So the French do know a few things about some of our favorite foods! I love it when American food and traditions—such as Halloween, Thanksgiving, and ribs—are embraced by the French and given a new twist and a French accent. Whenever I prepare these, which is often in the cool fall and winter months, I accompany the ribs with Flora's thoroughly irresistible Polenta Fries (page 126).

THE SAUCE

½ cup honey

4 tablespoons tomato paste

2 tablespoons Thai curry paste, homemade (page 288) or a commercial variety

3 tablespoons extra-virgin olive oil

2 racks baby back pork ribs (about 4 pounds total)

1 cup dry white wine

3 tablespoons freshly squeezed lemon juice

EQUIPMENT:

A roasting pan large enough to hold the meat in a single layer.

4 SERVINGS

1. Preheat the oven to 300 degrees F.

2. Prepare the sauce: In a small bowl, combine the honey, tomato paste, and curry paste. Mix with a fork to blend.

3. In a large roasting pan over moderate heat, heat the oil until hot but not smoking. Add the pork ribs and brown well on each side, about 2 minutes per side. With a pastry brush, brush the ribs with about half of the sauce (reserve the remaining sauce to serve at the table). Sear for 1 minute more per side. Pour the wine and lemon juice over the ribs. Cover the roasting pan tightly with aluminum foil.

4. Place the roasting pan in the center of the oven. Cook until the meat is very tender and you can wiggle the bone from the meat with little effort, about 1½ hours. Cut the ribs into serving portions and serve, passing the remaining sauce.

In honor of the chef, Flora Mikula, I would serve one of the up-and-coming wines from her home region of Nîmes, such as a Costières de Nîmes: Some good finds include wines from Château de la Tuileries, Mas des Bressades, or Domaine du Vieux Relais.

WHAT I LEARNED: While traditionally spareribs are simply roasted, Flora had the idea of searing the ribs before roasting them. It's brilliant! In typical French style, the searing adds a dimension to the meat that roasting alone cannot impart. The searing locks in a depth of flavor and a moistness that makes these ribs memorable.

Les Olivades

41, AVENUE DE SÉGUR
PARIS 7
TELEPHONE: 01 42 83 70 09
FAX: 01 42 73 04 75
MÉTRO: SÉGUR

L'ALSACO'S SAUERKRAUT, PORK, AND SAUSAGES

Choucroute L'Alsaco

I admit to a passion for both sauerkraut and sausages from an early age. As a child I could easily eat an entire can of sauerkraut at a single sitting. It was, I am sure, the combination of the saltiness and tanginess of the cured cabbage that pleased my palate. When I lived in New York City, my husband, Walter, and I even used to make homemade sauerkraut in our Central Park West apartment. As for sausages, well, I confess that during my sojourn as a vegetarian, I still craved them and occasionally broke with my diet and dug into a plateful of earthy smoked pork sausages.

This is *the* quintessential *choucroute* recipe: Use the finest sausages, pork products, and sauerkraut, and you and your guests will be in for a real treat, or as the French say, *"un vrai régal." Choucroute* is a perfect dish for entertaining—the only difficult part is shopping for the various sausages and kinds of pork. This recipe comes from L'Alsaco, one of my favorite Parisian restaurants specializing in the food of the Alsace region of France. When the outgoing owner-chef Claude Steger shared this recipe with me, he noted, "This is for ten people, with no first course, and all good eaters, or *bons mangeurs*!" Well, I have cut his recipe in half and I think that it would still feed an army.

2 tablespoons pork fat or goose fat

2 onions, peeled, halved lengthwise, and finely sliced

Fine sea salt to taste

1 pound salt pork

10 ounces smoked pork butt, bone in

3 pounds fresh sauerkraut

THE SEASONING MIX, WRAPPED SECURELY IN A CHEESECLOTH BAG

2 teaspoons coriander seeds

5 whole cloves

2 teaspoons juniper berries

1 tablespoon black peppercorns

1 tablespoon cumin seeds

½ head garlic, unpeeled, crushed

Use as many of the meats and sausages as you can find, and be sure to use all the seasonings. The result is crisp and fragrant sauerkraut that has mingled for a good hour with the essence of the delicious cured meats, creating a harmonious and surprisingly light and digestible meal. When I prepare this, I use a young (and usually less expensive) Alsatian Riesling wine in cooking and serve an older, more mature Riesling with the meal. If you can, use fresh, rather than canned, sauerkraut. Fresh sauerkraut can usually be found in delicatessens or in the deli section of the supermarket.

1. In a large heavy pot, combine the fat, onions, and a pinch of sea salt. Sweat—cook, covered, over low heat without coloring—until soft and translucent, about 5 minutes. Arrange the salt pork and smoked pork butt on top of the onions. Spoon the sauerkraut on top. Add the seasoning mix, salt, and the wine. Add just enough water to cover (about 1 quart), cover the pot, and cook at the very gentlest of a simmer for 1 hour and 20 minutes. Stir the sauerkraut from time to time to distribute the seasoning. Add the smoked pork sausages (kielbasa), cover, and simmer for 10 minutes.

2. Meanwhile, fill a large saucepan with water and bring just to a boil. Add the frankfurters. Immediately turn off the heat and cover the pan. Let the frankfurters sit until firm to the touch and heated through, 10 to 15 minutes.

3. In a large, dry nonstick skillet over medium heat, lightly panfry the grilling sausage (knockwurst) and the

1 bottle Alsatian Sylvaner or Riesling wine

6 coarse-textured smoked pork sausages, such as small kielbasa

6 fine-textured precooked sausages, such as frankfurters

6 fine-textured precooked grilling sausages, such as knockwurst

1 plump coarse-textured smoked pork sausage, such as kielbasa, cut in half lengthwise

A variety of mustards, for the table

EQUIPMENT:
A large heavy pot with a lid or a Dutch oven.

10 SERVINGS

halved pork sausage (kielbasa) until browned, shaking the pan from time to time so they cook evenly, 7 to 10 minutes total.

4. Using a large slotted spoon, transfer the sauerkraut to several large warmed serving platters. Cut the meats into serving pieces. Halve or quarter the sausages. Arrange the meats and sausages all around. Serve with a variety of mustards.

Do not *dare* drink anything other than a Grand Cru Riesling from Alsace. With a truly brilliant balance of sweet and acid, and a touch of dryness, the wine totally rounds out the complex salty, smoky, acid flavors of the sauerkraut, sausages, and meats. I especially like a Riesling from Ostertag, Vignoble d'Epfig.

CHEF STEGER SAYS:

"Sauerkraut must always remain just lightly crunchy. Too cooked, and it is indigestible."

L'Alsaco

10, RUE CONDORCET
PARIS 9
TELEPHONE: 01 45 26 44 31
FAX: 01 42 85 11 05
MÉTRO: POISSONIÈRE

FRÉDÉRIC ANTON'S FOUR-HOUR ROAST PORK

Le Rôti de Porc de Quatre Heures de Frédéric Anton

Over the past several years, braised meats have become increasingly popular among Parisian chefs: Rare lamb, rosy pork, duck with a touch of pink all have their place, but the homey, wholesome flavors of meat and poultry cooked until meltingly tender and falling off the bone are once again in vogue. Here Frédéric Anton, chef at the romantic restaurant Pré Catelan in the Bois de Boulogne, offers universally appealing roasted pork loin, flavored simply with thyme. This is delicious accompanied by sautéed mushrooms or a potato gratin.

1. Preheat the oven to 275 degrees F.

2. Season the pork all over with sea salt, white pepper, and the 2 teaspoons thyme. In a large heavy-duty casserole that will hold the pork snugly, heat the oil over moderate heat until hot but not smoking. Add the pork and sear well on all sides, about 10 minutes total. Transfer the pork to a platter and discard the fat in the casserole. Wipe the casserole clean with paper towels. Return the pork to the casserole, bone side down. Set it aside.

3. In a large, heavy skillet, combine the butter, carrots, onions, garlic, celery, and sea salt to taste. Sweat—cook, covered, over low heat without coloring—until the vegeta-

One 4-pound pork loin roast, bone in (do not trim off fat)

Sea salt to taste

Freshly ground white pepper to taste

2 teaspoons fresh or dried thyme leaves

4 tablespoons extra-virgin olive oil

3 tablespoons unsalted butter

2 carrots, peeled and finely chopped

2 onions, peeled and finely chopped

6 plump, fresh cloves garlic, peeled and minced

2 ribs celery, finely chopped

2 cups Homemade Chicken Stock (page 297)

bles are soft and cooked through, about 10 minutes. Spoon the vegetables around and on top of the pork. Add the chicken stock to the casserole. Add the bunches of thyme, and cover.

4. Place the casserole in the center of the oven and braise, basting every 30 minutes, for about 4 hours, or until the pork is just about falling off the bone. Remove the casserole from the oven. Carefully transfer the meat to a carving board and season it generously with sea salt and white pepper. Cover loosely with foil and set aside to rest for about 15 minutes.

5. While the pork is resting, strain the cooking juices through a fine-mesh sieve into a gravy boat, pouring off the fat that rises to the top. Discard the vegetables and herbs.

6. The pork will be very soft and falling off the bone, so you may not actually be able to slice it. Rather, use a fork and spoon to tear the meat into serving pieces, and place them on warmed dinner plates or a warmed platter. Spoon the juices over the meat, and serve. Transfer any remaining juices to a gravy boat and pass at the table.

2 large bunches of fresh
   thyme sprigs

EQUIPMENT:
A large heavy casserole
   with a lid or Dutch oven.

8 TO 10 SERVINGS

Good wines with this pork include a fairly light red or a rich white: Try a good Beaujolais or a good selection from the Médoc, or a white Roussanne-Marsanne blend from the Coteaux du Languedoc Faugères house of Domaine Alquier.

Le Pré Catelan

ROUTE DE SURESNES
BOIS DE BOULOGNE
PARIS 16
TELEPHONE: 01 44 14 41 14
FAX: 01 45 24 43 25
MÉTRO: PORTE-DAUPHINE

LE MAUZAC'S HANGER STEAK

Onglet Le Mauzac

Le Mauzac is a lively lunchtime café/wine bar tucked along a romantic tree-lined street in the busy Latin Quarter. Their *onglet*—flank, or hanger, steak—is one of the best I've ever sampled. Following tradition, the quickly pan-seared meat is served with a mound of golden, delicious French fried potatoes. Although restaurants do not usually offer lemon with steak, I prefer it this way and always ask for a few wedges to squeeze over the beef. Note that in cooking the meat, I do not salt it in the beginning—only at the end. I feel that salting in the beginning draws out too many of the delicious juices we want to save. But salt at the end helps give the meat a fine, seasoned flavor.

1 tablespoon extra-virgin olive oil

1½ pounds beef hanger or flank steak, butterflied, about ½ inch thick

Freshly ground black pepper to taste

Fine sea salt

Lemon wedges, for garnish (optional)

4 SERVINGS

1. Massage a little bit of the oil into the steak, and lightly season both sides with black pepper. If your skillet is not large enough to hold the steak, cut it crosswise into two pieces and cook them one at a time.

2. Heat a large, dry nonstick skillet over high heat for about 1 minute. When the pan is very hot, sear the steak quickly on both sides, 1 to 2 minutes a side for medium-rare, longer for medium.

3. Remove the steak to a platter. Pour any pan juices over the meat. Season the meat generously with fine sea salt, and let it rest for 5 minutes (to allow the juices to retreat back into the beef). Carve the steak across the grain. Serve immediately, with a lemon wedge if desired.

Le Mauzac

7, RUE DE L'ABBE-DE-L'EPÉE
PARIS 5
TELEPHONE: 01 46 33 75 22
MÉTRO: RER LUXEMBOURG

An unusual wine worth sampling at Le Mauzac is a little-known Gaillac from France's southwest: Domaine Robert Plageoles's syrah, a young delight that goes well with the wine bar's meaty fare.

ONGLET, A BISTRO STAR:

ONGLET—FLANK, OR HANGER, STEAK—is one of the stars of bistro cooking. It's tender, beefy, and needs nothing more than salt, pepper, and a touch of lemon juice to bring out its succulent brilliance. Always cooked to medium-rare (rare is too chewy), this thin, narrow, boneless cut of meat comes from what butchers call "the hanging tender" because it literally hangs down below the ribs, an extension of the tenderloin. In France it is known as *la pièce du boucher,* "the butcher's piece," because there is only one hanging tender, weighing about 3 pounds, for each steer. Since there wasn't a lot to go around, the butcher took it home to serve to his family. The meat is prized for its chewy tenderness, silken texture, and rich meaty flavor. Butchers generally butterfly the meat, cutting it horizontally through the middle to create a large 1/2-inch-thick piece that's ideal for quick pan-searing or outdoor grilling.

LES ALLOBROGES'S BRAISED LAMB SHANKS WITH GARLIC

Souris d'Agneau Braisée à l'Ail Confit Les Allobroges

Olivier Pateyron and his wife, Annette, are an energetic pair who run a lovely small restaurant, Les Allobroges, hidden at the edge of town. Such sublime and simple fare as roasted Bresse chicken with a potato gratin, and these meaty lamb shanks flanked by whole cloves of garlic, can usually be found on the brief menu. I sampled these tender shanks on my first visit years ago, and I keep coming back for more. Chef Pateyron first roasts the shanks, then braises them in a mixture of sweet Banyuls wine from France's southwest and a touch of veal stock. The result is meat with a glistening mahogany color and a thick, voluptuously shiny dark sauce. Serve it with the chef's brilliant version of Garlic Confit (page 291).

1. Preheat the oven to 450 degrees F.

2. Rub the Quatre Epices all over the surface of the lamb shanks. Season them with sea salt and white pepper.

3. Stand the shanks, wider side down, narrow end up, in a large roasting pan. Place the pan in the center of the oven and roast, uncovered, for 1 hour.

4. Transfer the lamb to a platter and set aside. Off the heat, deglaze the pan with the wine, scraping up any cooked bits that may have stuck to the bottom. Return the

4 teaspoons Quatre Epices (page 293)

4 meaty lamb shanks (each about 1 pound; do not trim the external fat)

Sea salt to taste

Freshly ground white pepper to taste

1 cup Banyuls wine, *vin doux naturel* from Provence, or Port

1 quart Homemade Chicken Stock (page 297)

1 recipe Garlic Confit (page 291)

EQUIPMENT:
A large roasting pan with a lid.

4 SERVINGS

lamb to the pan standing on end, wider side down. Add the stock. Cover the pan and return it to the oven. Braise, without disturbing the meat, until the meat is very tender and just beginning to fall off the bone, about 1½ hours.

This simple, meaty dish calls out for one of your best reds. My first choice would be a Cairanne from winemaker Marcel Richaud or a Gigondas from winemaker Jean-Pierre Cartier at Domaine les Gouberts. Alternatively, try one of the new and up-and-coming wines from the Languedoc-Roussillon, such as a Corbières or a Minervois.

5. Remove the pan from the oven and transfer the lamb shanks to a warmed platter. Cover them with foil and let them rest for 10 minutes. Meanwhile, strain the sauce through a fine-mesh sieve into a gravy boat. Serve, passing the sauce and the Garlic Confit.

LAMB SHANKS—which the French call *souris*—are the shin portion of the legs. The fore shanks are the meatiest and the easiest to find (the rear shanks are usually sold attached to the whole leg of lamb). The shank contains a good deal of connective tissue that produces a smooth, luxurious sauce when cooked by the very slow and moist heat of a braise.

OLIVIER SAYS:

"Do not trim the fat from the lamb shanks!" The fat forms a sort of girdle, holding the lamb shanks together, and it also adds flavor, color, and body to the final sauce."

A GOOD WINE FOR COOKING: Banyuls, a sweet fortified wine from the Pyrénées in France's southwest, is a powerful wine usually made from at least 75 percent Grenache grapes and aged for 2 years. It is a distant relation of Port. The best ones bear the name Rancio and come from the Domaine la Rectoire and du Mas Blanc. In Provence, one also finds some excellent *vins doux naturels* that are great for cooking. My favorites include the 16-percent-alcohol red *vin doux naturel* from the *cave coopérative* in Rasteau, or the pure-Grenache Rasteau Rancio from Domaine Bressy-Masson.

Les Allobroges

71, RUE GRANDS-CHAMPS
PARIS 20
TELEPHONE: 01 43 73 40 00
MÉTRO: MARAÎCHERS

ERIC LECERF'S BRAISED LEG OF LAMB

Gigot d'Agneau Braisé
Eric Lecerf

Sometimes I think that lamb exists solely to be teamed up with the vibrant spices of coriander, cumin, and curry. Here Eric Lecerf—a Joël Robuchon protégé and chef at the always satisfying restaurant Astor on the Right Bank—presents one of his most popular dishes, a leg of lamb that is braised ever so slowly in the oven until it is cooked to a welcome, melting tenderness. Typical of many modern Parisian dishes, this one reveals a contemporary French love affair with a myriad of spices, as well as a return to old-fashioned dishes cooked slowly for a good, long time. I like to serve this with seasonal winter or early spring vegetables, such as a mixture of carrots, leeks, shallots, and potatoes.

1. Preheat the oven to 250 degrees F.

2. In a small bowl, combine the spices and herbs. Rub the mixture all over the surface of the lamb.

3. In a cast-iron casserole just large enough to hold the lamb, heat the oil over moderate heat until hot but not smoking. Add the lamb and brown lightly on all sides, about 5 minutes total. Do not let the spices burn. Pour the stock around the lamb. Add salt and pepper. Cover all with a piece of parchment paper. (The paper will serve as a moisture tent, to keep the meat from drying out as it cooks.)

THE SPICES AND HERBS

1 teaspoon coriander
  seeds, ground
1 teaspoon coriander seeds
3 teaspoons cumin seeds
1½ teaspoons cumin
  seeds, ground
2 teaspoons curry powder
2 teaspoons fine sea salt
1 teaspoon coarsely
  ground white pepper
4 teaspoons fresh thyme
  leaves
2 teaspoons minced fresh
  rosemary leaves
4 cloves garlic, peeled and
  finely minced

1 bone-in leg of lamb
  (about 7 pounds),
  preferably with hipbone
  removed and excess fat
  and membrane trimmed
  and reserved
4 tablespoons extra-
  virgin olive oil

4. Cover the casserole and place it in the center of the oven. Braise, basting every 30 minutes, until the meat is very tender, about 2 hours.

5. Remove the casserole from the oven. Carefully remove the lamb from the casserole, and carve it into serving pieces. Keep warm on a serving platter. Strain the sauce through a fine-mesh sieve into a saucepan. Place the pan in the refrigerator for about 30 minutes to allow the fat to rise to the top and firm up. Remove and discard the fat. Warm the sauce, and transfer it to a sauceboat. Serve the lamb, passing the sauce.

1½ cups Homemade
  Chicken Stock (page
  297)
Fine sea salt to taste
Freshly ground black
  pepper to taste

EQUIPMENT:
A cast-iron casserole with
  a lid, or a Dutch oven,
  large enough to hold the
  lamb.

6 SERVINGS

With all these spices, you need a bold red such as Michèle Laurent's velvety Côtes-du-Rhône Domaine Gramenon, *cuvée* Pascal.

L'Astor

11, RUE D'ASTORG
PARIS 8
TELEPHONE: 01 53 05 05 20
FAX: 01 53 05 05 30
MÉTRO: SAINT-AUGUSTIN

JEAN-GUY'S BASQUE-SPICED LEG OF LAMB

Gigot d'Agneau Basquaise Jean-Guy

Jean-Guy Lousteau's heartwarming bistro, Au Bascou, offers some of Paris's most unusual, hearty, and delicious regional fare. Lousteau, a Basque native, receives weekly shipments of the area's finest lamb, sausages, wines, and condiments and serves them all with flair in this tiny café-bistro. This is one of my favorite dishes on the menu there. It is prepared with the tiniest of baby lamb—weighing less than 2 pounds and so tender, so flavorful. The same dish can, of course, be prepared with a larger leg of lamb. (The average American lamb weighs about 7 pounds.)

1. Preheat the oven to 450 degrees F.

2. In a small bowl, combine the mustard, yogurt, ½ teaspoon of the ground chile pepper, and 1 teaspoon of the thyme. Stir to blend.

3. Place the lamb on a rack in a roasting pan. Brush the mustard paste all over the lamb, and then sprinkle the remaining ½ teaspoon ground chile pepper and 1 teaspoon thyme over it. Surround the lamb with the reserved bones and trimmings, the garlic, and the bay leaves and thyme. Add about ½ cup cold water (to keep the trimmings from burning as the lamb roasts).

4 tablespoons coarse-grain French Dijon mustard

4 tablespoons full-fat sheep's-milk yogurt

1 teaspoon finely ground dried red chile peppers

2 teaspoons fresh or dried thyme leaves

1 bone-in leg of lamb (7 to 8 pounds), preferably with hipbone removed and excess fat and membrane trimmed and reserved

Several plump, fresh heads garlic, halved crosswise but not peeled

Several fresh or dried bay leaves

Several springs of fresh thyme

Sea salt to taste

Freshly ground white pepper to taste

12 SERVINGS

4. Place the pan in the center of the oven and roast, turning the lamb once, until an instant-read thermometer inserted into the thickest part of the meat reads 125 degrees F for medium-rare or 140 degrees F for medium, about 1¼ to 1½ hours. (Allow 9 minutes per pound for lamb weighing under 5 pounds and 10 to 12 minutes per pound for larger legs of lamb.)

5. Remove the pan from the oven and season the lamb generously with sea salt and white pepper. Transfer the lamb to a platter, and place it on an angle against the edge of an overturned plate. Cover loosely with foil. Turn off the oven and place the platter in the oven with the door open. Let the lamb rest for a minimum of 10 minutes and up to 30 minutes. The meat will continue to cook during this resting time.

6. Meanwhile, prepare the sauce: Place the roasting pan over moderate heat, and with a spatula, scrape up any bits that cling to the bottom. Cook for 2 to 3 minutes, scraping and stirring until the liquid is almost caramelized. Do not let it burn. Spoon off and discard any excess fat. Add several tablespoons cold water to deglaze the pan (hot water will cloud the sauce). Bring to a boil. Reduce the heat to low and simmer until thickened, about 5 minutes.

7. While the sauce is cooking, carve the lamb and place the slices on a warmed platter.

8. Strain the sauce through a fine-mesh sieve into a sauceboat. Serve immediately, with the lamb.

Jean-Guy would serve this with a good Basque red, such as Domaine Brana's Irouléguy, a wine made from a blend of cabernet franc, cabernet sauvignon, and tannat grapes.

Au Bascou

38, RUE RÉAUMUR
PARIS 3
TELEPHONE: 01 42 72 69 25
FAX: 01 42 72 69 25
MÉTRO: ARTS ET MÉTIERS

VEAL FLANK STEAK BOUCHERIE DUCIEL

Bavette de Veau Boucherie Duciel

I walked into one of my neighborhood butcher shops one fall evening in search of a nice tender and juicy *onglet,* a quick-cooking cut of beef known as hanger steak or flank steak. The butcher had none, but suggested a *bavette de veau* instead, an equally muscular, fine-grained, and very thin, flat, boneless cut of veal that the butcher splits open like a book, trims, and scores. He also gave me the recipe: The meat pan-sears in a flash, and as he suggested, it's chewy but amazingly succulent, moist, fragrant, and juicy. It quickly became one of our favorite "Little Time to Cook Tonight" dinners. Although the veal cooks quickly, do not try to rush it by cooking it over high heat, or the meat will toughen.

1. Divide the butter between two skillets that are large enough to hold two steaks each, and place over moderate heat until hot. Very lightly season the veal with sea salt and black pepper. Sear the veal gently until it is cooked through but still tender, 4 to 5 minutes on each side.

2. Remove the veal to a warm platter. Add 2 tablespoons cream to each pan to deglaze it, and pour the sauce over the steaks. Season with black pepper, and let the meat rest for 5 minutes before carving across the grain and serving.

4 tablespoons unsalted butter

4 pieces veal flank, skirt, or hanger steak (each about 8 ounces), split open, trimmed, and scored (ask your butcher to do this for you)

Sea salt

Freshly ground black pepper to taste

4 tablespoons heavy cream

EQUIPMENT:
Two large skillets.

4 SERVINGS

This dish calls for a young red, such as one of my favorite *cru* Beaujolais, Moulin à Vent.

THE FRENCH BUTCHER

WHEN I FIRST MOVED TO FRANCE, I couldn't figure out why anyone would want to be a butcher. I understood one's love of dealing with sparkling fresh fish or first-of-season vegetables and fruits. But all that blood and animal parts to deal with? Well, I slowly learned the role that the butcher plays in a French woman's life. There's the way the butcher wraps a simple chicken in waxed paper, slips it into a bag, and says with a wink and a certain sense of masculine assurance, "One hour in a very hot oven. No more, no less." Women melt! I can't tell you how many times I have gone into a French butcher shop for a chicken or a rabbit and come home with two, planning to execute the recipe I had in mind *and* the one delivered to me as I scribbled on the back of an old envelope. French butchers are more than tradesmen: They are cookbook authors, seducers, philosophers, great men to have in a lady's life!

Boucherie Pascal Duciel

96, RUE DE COURCELLES
PARIS 17
TELEPHONE: 01 47 63 40 97
MÉTRO: COURCELLES

THE APPLE LADY'S APPLE CAKE

BENOÎT'S UPSIDE-DOWN CARAMELIZED APPLE TART

CARTON'S ULTRA-THIN APPLE TART

BONBONNERIE DE BUCI'S FRESH LEMON JUICE TART

FLAKY PASTRY

STRAWBERRY-ORANGE SOUP WITH CANDIED LEMON ZEST

CHERRY-ALMOND GRATIN

RUE PONCELET'S CHERRIES IN SWEET RED WINE

RASPBERRY PRIDE

FRESH RASPBERRY SAUCE

FRESH FIG AND ALMOND GRATIN

WARM FIG COMPOTE WITH LAVENDER HONEY

DESSERTS
Les Desserts

CARRÉ DES FEUILLANTS'S HONEY-POACHED PEARS IN BEAUMES-DE-VENISE

LA MAISON DU CHOCOLAT'S BITTERSWEET CHOCOLATE MOUSSE

JR'S BURNT CREAM

"THE HEART OF PARIS"

THE ASTOR'S INDIVIDUAL VANILLA CUSTARDS

BLOOD-ORANGE ICE CREAM LE JARDIN DE COURCELLES

ALMOND ICE CREAM

FROMAGERIE ALLÉOSSES FROMAGE BLANC ICE CREAM

MAISON DU MIEL'S HEATHER HONEY ICE CREAM

FRESH HONEY-ROSEMARY-GINGER ICE CREAM

FRESH TRUFFLE ICE CREAM

TRUFFLE PANNA COTTA

MINIATURE LEMON TEA CAKES

JP HÉVIN'S CHOCOLATE FINANCIERS

JEAN-LUC POUJAURAN'S SHORTBREAD COOKIES

THE APPLE LADY'S APPLE CAKE

Gâteau aux Pommes de la Reine des Pommes

Come autumn, I begin making weekly pilgrimages to the Thursday and Saturday farmer's market that rolls out along the avenue de Saxe, in the shadow of the Eiffel Tower. There, I seek out Evelyne Nochet and her stand from her family orchard, from Le Nouveau Verger, and we talk apples. What's best for the tarte Tatin? What's the best eating apple? When will the famed Saint Germain be ready for the apple cake? For months I begged her for her favorite apple recipe, and finally, one chilly day in November, her neat, handwritten apple cake recipe appeared on my doorstep. This is the sort of homey recipe that makes French home cooking so incomparable. When you make this cake, you will be surprised by the small amount of batter, the quantity of apples. In effect, this is more of a crustless pie, in that the batter is just there to hold the apples together. What I love most about this recipe is that it allows the full flavor of the apple to shine through. I prefer a more acidic cooking apple, such as Cox's Orange Pippin or the French variety of Boskoop or Reine de Reinettes. Other good varieties include McIntosh, Cortland, Gala, or Gravenstein. And if you tend toward sweeter cooking apples—Golden Delicious or Jonagold—use those. I find that this is one cake that tastes just as good the second day, should there be any left over.

Serve this with Heather Honey Ice Cream (page 267).

½ cup all-purpose flour

⅓ cup sugar

1 tablespoon baking powder

⅛ teaspoon fine sea salt

½ teaspoon pure vanilla extract

2 large eggs, lightly beaten

2 tablespoons vegetable oil

⅓ cup whole milk

4 baking apples (about 2 pounds total), cored, peeled, and cut into thin wedges

THE TOPPING

⅓ cup sugar

1 large egg, lightly beaten

3 tablespoons unsalted butter, melted

EQUIPMENT:

A 9-inch springform pan.

8 SERVINGS

1. Preheat the oven to 400 degrees F.

2. Butter a 9-inch springform pan and set it aside.

3. In a large bowl, combine the flour, sugar, baking powder, and sea salt, and stir to blend. Add the vanilla extract, eggs, oil, and milk, and stir until well blended. Add the apples and stir to thoroughly coat them with the batter.

4. Spoon the mixture into the prepared cake pan. Place the pan in the center of the oven and bake until fairly firm and golden, about 25 minutes.

5. Meanwhile, prepare the topping: In a small bowl, combine the sugar, egg, and melted butter, and stir to blend. Set it aside.

6. Remove the cake from the oven and pour the topping mixture over it. Return the cake to the oven and bake until the top is a deep golden brown and the cake feels quite firm when pressed with a fingertip, about 10 minutes.

7. Transfer the cake pan to a rack and allow to cool for 10 minutes. Then run a knife around the sides of the pan, and release and remove the springform side, leaving the cake on the pan base. Serve at room temperature, cut into thin wedges.

I adore wine with dessert, and love to serve a good German, Austrian, or Hungarian white or a lovely wine from the Loire, such as a sweet Bonnezeau, Château de Fesles.

Le Nouveau Verger
Pommes et Poires
de Touraine
Marché Breteuil

AVENUE DE SAXE, FROM AVENUE DE SÉGUR TO PLACE DE BRETEUIL
PARIS 7
9 A.M. TO NOON, THURSDAY AND SATURDAY
MÉTRO: SÉGUR

DESSERTS

231

BENOÎT'S UPSIDE-DOWN CARAMELIZED APPLE TART

Tarte Tatin Benoît

Each year in France high achievers in all of the nation's trades—from hairdressers to chefs to florists—compete for the top honor of Meilleur Ouvrier de France. When chef Benoît Guichard of Jamin competed, he placed first in the pastry category, outdistancing famous pastry chefs vying for the title. Come autumn, I make this tart every single chance I get. I love it so much that I make it for my birthday in November, in lieu of a cake! Note that the apples cook on top of the stove for one full hour before baking. This seems like a long time, but your palate will be rewarded!

1. Spread the sugar evenly over the bottom of a 9-inch tarte Tatin pan or heavy ovenproof skillet. Place the butter slices evenly over the sugar. Drizzle with the vanilla extract. Beginning at the outside edge of the pan, stand the apple halves on end on top of the butter: They should all face in one direction, with the rounded edge of the apple against the edge of the pan and the cut side toward the center. Pack the apples as close together as possible. Make a second circle of apple halves inside the first. Place one apple half in the center of the circle to fill any remaining space. (As they cook, the apples will shrink and give up their juices. They will also naturally fall in place as they

¾ cup sugar

10 tablespoons unsalted butter, cut into thin slices

1 teaspoon pure vanilla extract

3 pounds large apples (about 8), peeled, cored, and halved lengthwise (see Note)

1 recipe Flaky Pastry (page 238), prepared for tarte Tatin (page 239)

Crème fraîche or whipped heavy cream, for garnish

EQUIPMENT:
A 9-inch tarte Tatin pan or cast-iron skillet.

8 SERVINGS

shrink, with the rounded halves falling to the bottom. Try to remember that when you turn out the tart, you want to see the nice rounded halves of apple.)

2. Place the skillet over low heat and cook the apples in the butter and sugar, uncovered, until the butter/sugar mixture turns a thick, golden brown and just begins to caramelize, about 1 hour. The liquid should remain at a gentle bubble. Baste the apples from time to time to speed up the cooking and to make for evenly cooked fruit. (If the apples seem to lose their place, you can carefully nudge them back into formation.)

3. Preheat the oven to 425 degrees F.

4. Place the Tatin pan on a baking sheet. Remove the pastry from the refrigerator and place it on top of the apples,

An apple tart calls out for a sweet white, such as a honeylike and unctuous German Auslese or an intense Beerenauslese, a sweet Austrian Ausbruch, or a liquorous sweet Hungarian Tokay.

gently pushing the edges of the pastry down around the edge of the pan. Place in the oven and bake until the pastry is golden, 25 to 30 minutes. Do not be concerned if the juices bubble over—this is normal.

5. Remove the tart from the oven. Immediately invert a rimmed serving platter over the tart pan. Quickly but carefully invert the tart pan and the platter together so the pastry ends up on the platter, with the apples on top. Should any apples stick to the bottom of the pan, remove them and place them back in the tart. Serve warm or at room temperature, with dollops of *crème fraîche*.

NOTE: Recommended varieties of apples for a tarte Tatin: Cox's Orange Pippin, Fuji, Criterion, Winesap, Northern Spies, Jonagold

WHAT I LEARNED: I have made this tart dozens of times, and it took me a while to learn one thing: Find one or two apple varieties you love and stick with them—there will be fewer surprises. And only make this in season, meaning when apples are at their peak in the early fall to late winter. If you use older, softer apples, they are likely to fall apart and turn into applesauce.

Jamin

32, RUE DE LONGCHAMP
PARIS 16
TELEPHONE: 01 45 53 00 07
FAX: 01 45 53 00 15
MÉTRO: TROCADÉRO

CARTON'S ULTRA-THIN APPLE TART

Tarte Fine aux Pommes Carton

Right around the corner from my office is the excellent pastry shop Carton, on the bustling rue de Buci on the Left Bank. There are days when this very thin tart calls out to me, satisfying my need for just a gentle touch of sugar punctuated by a nice note of fruit. This is an easy tart that can be prepared in minutes if you keep prepared pastry shells on hand in the freezer.

1. Preheat the oven to 425 degrees F.

2. Trim off a very thin slice at the stem and bottom ends of each apple. (This makes the apple easier to peel and creates more uniform slices.) Peel and core the apples. Using a mandoline, an electric slicer, or a very sharp knife, slice the apples crosswise into paper-thin rings. With a cookie cutter, cut out one 1 1/2-inch disc (this will be used to decorate the center of the tart).

3. Arrange the apple slices on the tart shell: Place a single apple slice on the outside edge of the shell. Overlap with a second slice, just covering the hole in the center of the first slice with the second slice. Continue in this manner until the apple slices have formed a ring around the outside edge. Brush the ring of apples with melted butter. Continue in the same manner with a second ring of apples, inside the first one, slightly overlapping the outer

2 cooking apples

One 9-inch rimless tart shell (page 238)

4 tablespoons unsalted butter, melted

2 tablespoons granulated sugar

Confectioners' sugar, for garnish

EQUIPMENT:
An apple corer.

6 SERVINGS

ring. Brush this ring with butter. Place 2 or 3 overlapping slices in the center, again covering the hole in the center of the slices; brush with melted butter. Place the decorative circle of apple in the center; brush it with butter. Sprinkle the apples evenly with the granulated sugar.

4. Place the tart on a baking sheet. Place the baking sheet in the center of the oven and bake for 5 minutes. Remove the tart from the oven; brush it with melted butter and dust with confectioners' sugar. Return it to the oven and bake for 10 minutes. Remove the tart from the oven; brush it with melted butter and dust again with confectioners' sugar. Bake for 10 minutes more.

5. This delicate tart is best served ever so slightly warm or at room temperature. Any leftover tart may be covered with plastic wrap and refrigerated, but it will not have that just-baked flavor or freshness.

This is particularly delicious with a sweet or semi-sweet white wine such as an Anjou-Coteaux de la Loire, a young Sauternes, or a sweet German, Austrian, or Hungarian wine.

Jean-Pierre Carton

6, RUE DE BUCI
PARIS 6
TELEPHONE: 01 43 26 04 13
MÉTRO: MABILLON

BONBONNERIE DE BUCI'S FRESH LEMON JUICE TART

La Tarte au Jus Frais de Citron Pressé de la Bonbonnerie de Buci

The French love specifics, especially when it comes to food. When a pastry shop window—La Bonbonnerie de Buci on the famed market street—advertised that *their* tart was made with freshly squeezed lemon juice (as opposed the sort that comes in a bottle), I had to giggle over the precision. And I had to have one. This tart is made for those of us who love the palate-puckering acidic punch of lemon.

4 large eggs

1 cup sugar

2/3 cup freshly squeezed lemon juice (from 2 or 3 lemons)

1/2 cup *crème fraîche* or heavy cream

One prebaked 9-inch tart shell (page 238)

8 SERVINGS

1. Preheat the oven to 350 degrees F.

2. In a large mixing bowl, whisk the eggs to blend. Add the sugar and whisk until just combined. Add the lemon juice and *crème fraîche,* and whisk until just combined. Strain the mixture through a fine-mesh sieve, and pour it into the baked pastry shell.

WHAT I LEARNED: For a more refined touch, it is a good idea to strain a raw egg mixture. Eggs often contain little particles that could affect the texture and appearance of the final product.

3. Place the tart in the center of the oven and bake until the filling is set, 25 to 30 minutes. Remove it from the oven and transfer to a rack to cool. Serve at room temperature.

La Bonbonnerie de Buci

12, RUE DE BUCI

PARIS 6

TELEPHONE: 01 43 26 97 13

MÉTRO: MABILLON

237

FLAKY PASTRY

Pâte Brisée

This is my tried-and-true classic pastry recipe, the one I've been using in my Paris kitchens for more than 20 years. It is easy as—can one say it—pie. I find that once a cook is confident with pastry making, he or she is ready to attack just about anything. For great pastry, you need chilled ingredients and you must work swiftly, without hesitation. Here I offer three ways to use the pastry: As two prebaked tart shells; as flat pastry for two rimless tarts; and as pastry for a single Upside-Down Caramelized Apple Tart.

1 cup unbleached all-purpose flour
⅛ teaspoon fine sea salt
8 tablespoons unsalted butter, chilled and cut into cubes
3 tablespoons ice water

EQUIPMENT:
A food processor.

1. Place the flour and sea salt in the bowl of a food processor and process to blend. Add the butter and process until well blended, about 10 seconds. With the machine running, add the ice water and process just until the mixture begins to form a ball, about 10 seconds.

2. Transfer the dough to a clean work surface, and with a dough scraper, smear it bit by bit across the work surface until it is smooth and the flour and butter are well blended. Form into a flattened round, cover with plastic wrap, and refrigerate for at least 1 hour and up to 24 hours.

3. Roll out as required for rimless shells, prebaked shells, or tarte Tatin pastry (below).

FOR TWO PREBAKED 9-INCH SHELLS:

1. Divide the chilled dough in half. Roll one half out to form an 11-inch round. Fold the dough in half, and without stretching it, lift it up at the edges so that it naturally

EQUIPMENT:
Two 9-inch fluted tart pans with removable bottoms; two baking sheets.

falls into the rim of a tart pan. Unfold the dough. With your fingertips, very delicately coax the dough into the rim. There should be a generous 1-inch overhang: Allow it to drape naturally over the edge of the pan. Generously prick the dough lining the bottom of the tart pan. Cover loosely with aluminum foil. Repeat with the remaining half. Freeze for at least 1 hour or up to 24 hours.

2. Preheat the oven to 400 degrees F.

3. Remove the tart pans from the freezer. Unwrap and place each one on a baking sheet. Bake until lightly and evenly browned, about 25 minutes. Watch carefully: Ovens vary tremendously.

4. Remove the pans from the oven, and carefully roll a rolling pin over the tart rims to trim off the overhanging pastry and create a smooth, well-trimmed shell. Discard the overhanging pastry. Cool for at least 10 minutes (or up to several hours) before filling. Do not freeze prebaked shells.

FOR TWO 9-INCH RIMLESS TARTS

Divide the chilled dough in half. Roll one half out to form a 9-inch round. Repeat with the remaining half. Place each round on a baking sheet and freeze for at least 1 hour or up to 24 hours. (For longer freezing—up to 1 month—cover securely once the dough is thoroughly frozen.)

FOR ONE 9-INCH TARTE TATIN

Roll the dough out to form a 10-inch round. Place it on a piece of parchment or wax paper. Refrigerate for at least 1 hour and up to 24 hours. (For longer freezing—up to 1 month—cover securely once the dough is thoroughly frozen.)

EQUIPMENT:
Two baking sheets.

STRAWBERRY-ORANGE SOUP WITH CANDIED LEMON ZEST

Soupe de Fraises à l'Orange
au Zeste de Citron Confit

All it takes is an intelligent combination of fresh ingredients to create a dish with a sophisticated and pleasing dimension: The sweet, fruity flavor of strawberries reach another realm, enlivened by a touch of vinegar, sweetened with the intensity of freshly squeezed orange juice, and brought to a crescendo topped with a touch of zesty, candied lemon peel. There are just a few days in March when blood oranges are still in the market and the first strawberries of the season make their debut: That's when this dessert is at its peak. The rest of the year, make this dish with the best juice oranges you can find.

1. In a large bowl, combine the strawberries, vinegar, and sugar. Stir gently. Cover securely with plastic wrap and refrigerate for 1 hour.

2. Meanwhile, prepare the candied lemon zest: Place the zest in a medium-size saucepan, add 1 cup cold water, and bring to a rolling boil over high heat. Remove from the heat and drain the zest in a small fine-mesh sieve. Rinse with cold water, and drain.

3. In a small saucepan, combine the blanched lemon zest, the sugar, and ¼ cup water. Stir to dissolve the sugar.

1 pound fresh strawberries, rinsed, stemmed, and quartered lengthwise (or into sixths if very large)

1 tablespoon best-quality red wine vinegar, sherry vinegar, or balsamic vinegar

4 tablespoons sugar

THE CANDIED LEMON ZEST

Zest of 1 scrubbed lemon, cut into fine slivers

¼ cup sugar

1¼ cups freshly squeezed blood orange juice (about 5 oranges) or juice of top-quality juice oranges

6 SERVINGS

Bring to a simmer over very low heat and cook until the zest is transparent and just a thin veil of syrup remains, 8 to 10 minutes. Remove from the heat and let the zest cool in the liquid.

4. At serving time, add the orange juice to the strawberry mixture. Mix gently. Pour the strawberry soup into shallow individual bowls or flat-bottomed champagne glasses, known as *coupes*. Garnish with the candied lemon zest, and serve.

CHEF'S SECRET: Chef Emmanuel Leblay taught me this secret for blanching the zest of any citrus: Most recipes suggest tossing the zest into boiling water and blanching it three consecutive times, to rid it of any residue and/or bitterness. Leblay blanches it by combining the zest with cold water, bringing it just to a boil, then draining. The zest is cleaner and less bitter, and the process is much easier.

CHERRY-ALMOND GRATIN

Gratin aux Cerises et aux Amandes

I know of few greater food combinations than almonds and cherries. They love to grow side by side, and what's amazing is that in France they ripen at the very same moment, late May to early June. Of course the almonds are still raw then and need more time on the tree, but since I go by the rule that "what grows together goes together," I always add a touch of almond to any cherry dish. This gratin is simple, not too rich, and a true crowd pleaser. (If you frequently cook with cherries, it is a good idea to invest in a small gadget, a cherry pitter, which makes the job a lot easier.)

1. Preheat the oven to 375 degrees F.

2. Butter the baking dish. Set it aside.

3. In a large, heavy skillet, combine the cherries, kirsch, and sugar. Cook over low heat, stirring regularly, for 5 minutes. Transfer the cherries to the prepared baking dish and set aside.

4. Prepare the almond cream: In the bowl of a heavy-duty mixer fitted with the whisk, combine the almonds and butter. Whisk, blending until smooth. Add the eggs, cream, and confectioners' sugar and whisk until thick, smooth, and well blended. Add the kirsch, if using, and

2 pounds fresh cherries, rinsed, stemmed, and pitted

1 tablespoon kirsch (cherry eau-de-vie)

2 tablespoons sugar

THE ALMOND CREAM

1 cup finely ground almonds

8 tablespoons unsalted butter, softened

2 large eggs

2 tablespoons heavy cream

1 cup confectioners' sugar

Several drops of kirsch (cherry eau-de-vie; optional)

Several drops of almond extract

Confectioners' sugar, for dusting the gratin

the almond extract, mixing to blend. Pour the cream over the cherries in the baking dish.

5. Place the baking dish in the center of the oven and bake until the gratin is firm and a deep golden brown, 20 to 25 minutes. Remove to a wire rack to cool.

6. Dust the gratin lightly with confectioners' sugar and serve in wedges, warm or at room temperature. This dessert is best served just a few hours after it is prepared.

EQUIPMENT:
A 10½-inch round porcelain baking dish; a heavy-duty mixer.

8 SERVINGS

Ivan of Brasserie de l'Ile

RUE PONCELET'S CHERRIES IN SWEET RED WINE

Cerises au Vin Rouge Rue Poncelet

The French have a saying: "Eat peas with the rich and cherries with the poor"—meaning the best peas are the season's first (and most expensive), the sweetest cherries the season's last (and least expensive). Come May, the Paris markets are a flood of red, with mounds and mounds of sweet red fruits. I prepare this favorite dessert with a French *vin doux naturel*, usually one from the cooperative in the Provençal village of Rasteau.

1. In a flat-bottomed 6-quart saucepan, combine the wine and confectioners' sugar and stir to dissolve. Bring to a boil over high heat. Boil until reduced to 1 cup, about 10 minutes. Add the cherries and return just to a boil.

2. Remove from the heat. Cover, and set aside to infuse for about 30 minutes.

3. Serve the cherries warm or at room temperature, ladling the fruit and sauce over the ice cream. Garnish with the mint chiffonnade.

NOTE: Cherries can most easily be pitted with a small gadget, either a cherry or an olive pitter. I find that the brands from Germany work the best. Short of that, simply squeeze the cherry between your fingers to extract the pit.

1 bottle fortified red wine (*vin doux naturel*, Port, Madeira, or Banyuls)

1 cup confectioners' sugar

1 pound fresh sweet cherries, rinsed, stemmed, and pitted but left whole (see Note)

2 pints best-quality vanilla ice cream

Small handful fresh mint leaves, slivered (chiffonnade), for garnish

EQUIPMENT:
A flat-bottomed 6-quart saucepan.

6 TO 8 SERVINGS

Sweet cherries can be found at

Marché Poncelet

RUE PONCELET, BEGINNING AT AV-
ENUE DES TERNES

PARIS 17

9 A.M. TO 1 P.M. AND 4 P.M. TO 7 P.M.

TUESDAY THROUGH SATURDAY;

9 A.M. TO 1 P.M. ON SUNDAY

MÉTRO: TERNES

RASPBERRY PRIDE

Tarte aux Framboises et à la Vanille

When fresh raspberries first appear in the Paris markets in June, I find every excuse imaginable to make this dessert: Raspberries, vanilla, almonds, and thyme—what could be bad? Wait . . . Thyme, you ask? Yes, modern cooks are realizing that herbs need not be reserved for savory dishes alone. The wild herbal flavor of thyme is readily absorbed by the butter and cream, and marries beautifully with the acid/sweet flavor of the raspberry. While this very elegant dessert is a showstopper, preparing it is child's play. A simple almond cream is spread between layers of thin pastry, then baked and topped with a vanilla and thyme-flavored *crème Chantilly*. A crown of fresh raspberries adds the final touch of drama. Your guest will ask, "*You* made this?" A friend suggested I call this Raspberry Pride, and so I did.

1. Place the bowl and the whisk of a heavy-duty mixer in the freezer.

2. Preheat the oven to 425 degrees F.

3. Prepare the almond cream: In the bowl of a food processor, combine the almonds and butter and process until smooth. Add the eggs, cream, and confectioners' sugar, and process until thick, smooth, and well blended.

THE ALMOND CREAM

1 cup finely ground almonds

8 tablespoons unsalted butter, softened

2 large eggs

2 tablespoons heavy cream

1 cup confectioners' sugar

Several drops *framboise* (raspberry eau-de-vie; optional)

THE CHANTILLY CREAM

1½ cups heavy cream, well chilled

½ cup confectioners' sugar

1 teaspoon pure vanilla extract

2 teaspoons fresh thyme leaves

If desired, add the framboise, and process to blend. Transfer to a small bowl and set aside.

4. Prepare the Chantilly cream: In the chilled bowl of the heavy-duty mixer, whisk the cream at moderate speed until soft peaks form. Gradually increase to high speed, and gradually add the confectioners' sugar, vanilla extract, and thyme. Whisk until stiff peaks form. Scrape down the sides of the bowl, cover the bowl with plastic wrap, and refrigerate.

5. Prepare and bake the pastry: Butter a baking sheet. Place 1 sheet of phyllo on the baking sheet. With a pastry brush, lightly butter the dough. Dust with confectioners' sugar. Cover with a second sheet of dough. Lightly butter it and sprinkle with confectioners' sugar. Delicately spread all of the almond cream over the center of the second sheet of dough. (Do not spread the almond cream all the way to the edges, or it will ooze out in baking.) Cover with a third sheet of dough, lightly buttering and dusting with confectioners' sugar. Cover with the fourth sheet of dough, again lightly buttering and dusting with confectioners' sugar. Cover with a sheet of baking parchment. Place a baking sheet on top, to keep the pastry even and compact. Place in the center of the oven and bake for 5 minutes. Remove from the oven, remove the baking sheet and the parchment, and return to the oven. Bake until the pastry is a deep, even, golden brown, about 5 minutes. The pastry should be a deep, crispy brown: If undercooked, it will become soggy and tough. Remove the pastry from the oven and set it aside to cool on the baking sheet.

THE PASTRY

4 sheets frozen phyllo dough (each 12½ × 17 inches), thawed

4 tablespoons unsalted butter, melted

About 4 tablespoons confectioners' sugar

1 pound fresh raspberries (or substitute fresh strawberries, blueberries, or blackberries)

Confectioners' sugar, for garnish

Fresh Raspberry Sauce (recipe follows; optional)

EQUIPMENT:

A heavy-duty mixer; a food processor; baking parchment; two baking sheets.

12 SERVINGS

6. Neatly trim any ragged edges from the pastry. With a very large, sharp chef's knife, cut the pastry lengthwise into three even strips. Cut each strip into four rectangles. With a spatula, delicately spread a thin layer of the Chantilly cream over the pastry. Arrange the raspberries on top. Sprinkle with confectioners' sugar, drizzle with Fresh Raspberry Sauce if desired, and serve.

A small glass of *framboise*, or raspberry eau-de-vie.

FRESH RASPBERRY SAUCE

Coulis de Framboises

When raspberries are plentiful in Paris's outdoor markets during the summer months, I often make up a batch of this delightful sauce and freeze it for cooler days. This brilliant red sauce can be served over vanilla ice cream and is lovely with Raspberry Pride, offering diners a double hit of one of my favorite fruits.

8 ounces (about 2 cups)
  fresh raspberries
1 tablespoon
  confectioners' sugar
2 tablespoons freshly
  squeezed lemon juice

EQUIPMENT:
A food processor or
  blender.

ABOUT 1 CUP

1. In a food processor or a blender, combine the raspberries, confectioners' sugar, and lemon juice. Process to blend.

2. Strain through a fine-mesh sieve to remove the seeds. Transfer to a container and seal tightly. The sauce may be refrigerated for 2 to 3 days, or frozen for up to 1 month.

FRESH FIG AND ALMOND GRATIN

Gratin des Figues Fraîches et Amandes

I remember the first time I bought figs in Paris: I asked the vendor to select figs that were not overly ripe, because they were so delicate. He looked at me as though I were nuts. Why would anyone want an underripe fig? I learned my lesson, for underripe figs lack flavor and aroma. Ripe purple figs, dripping with their honeylike nectar, are as fragile as can be, so I always carry them gingerly, and either eat or cook them the second I get home. This is a lovely gratin that is perfect for figs or ripe summer apricots. One of the best greengrocers in Paris is Le Jardin de Courcelles.

1. Preheat the oven to 375 degrees F.

2. Butter a 10½-inch round baking dish and set it aside.

3. In a small saucepan, combine the *crème fraîche* and thyme sprigs. Heat over moderate heat, stirring from time to time, just until tiny bubbles form around the edges of the pan, 2 to 3 minutes. Remove from the heat. Cover, and let steep for 1 hour. Strain through a fine-mesh sieve, discarding the thyme. Set aside.

4. In the bowl of a heavy-duty mixer fitted with the whisk, beat the eggs, sugar, and sea salt at high speed until thick and lemon-colored, 2 to 3 minutes. Stir in the

⅔ cup *crème fraîche* or heavy cream

Several sprigs fresh thyme

4 large eggs

½ cup sugar

⅛ teaspoon fine sea salt

½ cup finely ground almonds

¼ teaspoon almond extract

2 pounds fresh figs, stemmed and an "X" cut halfway through the fig

THYME SUGAR

2 teaspoons fresh or dried thyme leaves

2 teaspoons sugar

EQUIPMENT:

A 10½-inch round porcelain baking dish; a heavy-duty mixer; a spice grinder.

8 SERVINGS

almonds, almond extract, and reserved thyme-flavored cream.

5. Pour half of the batter into the prepared baking dish. Place the dish in the center of the oven and bake just until the batter begins to set, about 10 minutes. Remove the dish from the oven.

6. Arrange the figs over the batter. Pour the remaining batter over the fruit. Return the dish to the oven and bake until the gratin is golden brown, about 30 minutes.

7. Meanwhile, prepare the thyme sugar: In a spice grinder, combine the thyme leaves and sugar and grind to a fine powder.

8. Scatter the thyme sugar over the gratin and bake for 10 minutes more, for a total baking time of 50 minutes.

9. Remove the gratin from the oven. Serve warm, cut into wedges. This dessert is best when served within an hour after it is prepared.

VARIATION: This gratin can also be prepared with apricots that have been halved and pitted and placed cut side up in the dish; or with pears that have been peeled, cored, and quartered and placed on their sides in the dish.

Le Jardin de Courcelles

96, RUE DE COURCELLES
PARIS 17
TELEPHONE: 01 47 63 70 55
MÉTRO: COURCELLES

DESSERTS

WARM FIG COMPOTE WITH LAVENDER HONEY

Figues Chaudes en Compote au Miel de Lavande

For me, this is what dessert is all about: the freshest seasonal fruit, just a touch of sugar, a tangle of memorable tastes. Really ripe figs tend to almost drip of honey, so why not combine them with a flavor—lavender—that grows side by side with the proud fig tree? Embellish, if you will, with a scoop of Heather Honey Ice Cream (page 265).

1. Prepare the fig compote: Quarter the figs lengthwise. In a large, heavy saucepan, combine them with the sugar, honey, and cinnamon. Cook over high heat, stirring regularly, until the compote is compact, about 10 minutes. Remove from the heat and set aside.

2. Prepare the remaining figs: Cut the figs to open like a flower, cutting three-quarters of the way down into quarters, leaving the stem end intact.

3. In a large skillet, melt the butter over low heat. Add the honey and bring the mixture just to a boil. Stand the figs in the skillet and cook for 4 to 5 minutes, rolling them in the butter and honey mixture. Remove the skillet from the heat and set aside. Do not discard the liquid in the pan.

THE FIG COMPOTE

1 pound (about 12) fresh black figs, stemmed and rinsed

½ cup sugar

1 tablespoon lavender honey

½ teaspoon ground cinnamon

1 pound (about 12) fresh black figs, rinsed and stemmed

3 tablespoons unsalted butter

3 tablespoons lavender honey

3 tablespoons freshly squeezed lemon juice

4 SERVINGS

4. Place the fig compote on four warmed dessert plates. Place three figs upright on top of the compote on each plate. Add the lemon juice to the skillet, and place over high heat for 1 to 2 minutes. Taste, adding additional honey or lemon juice as desired. Pour the sauce over the fig dessert, and serve immediately.

CARRÉ DES FEUILLANTS'S HONEY-POACHED PEARS IN BEAUMES-DE-VENISE

Les Poires Vigneronnes au Beaumes-de-Venise du Carré des Feuillants

Honey, pears, and sweet muscat wine make a happy triumvirate. I sampled a version of this dessert one cold wintry night at Alain Dutournier's Carré des Feuillants. With just a touch of spice and a hint of rosemary, you have a winter dessert that brings the promise of summer and the sun. The pears are delicious with Honey-Rosemary-Ginger Ice Cream (page 266).

1. In a large saucepan that will hold the pears snugly, combine all the ingredients except the ice cream. Bring just to a simmer over moderate heat, and simmer just until the pears are cooked though, 15 to 20 minutes. (Do not cover.) Using a slotted spoon, very gently turn the pears from time to time so they are evenly coated.

2. Remove the pan from the heat, and using a slotted spoon, transfer the pears to a large shallow bowl. Set it aside.

3. Strain the liquid into another saucepan; discard the rosemary, spices, and vanilla bean. Place it over high heat and reduce by half, about 10 minutes. The liquid should

4 large fresh pears, peeled, stems intact

½ cup mild honey

1½ bottles Beaumes-de-Venise or other sweet muscat-based wine

2 tablespoons freshly squeezed lemon juice

4 sprigs fresh rosemary

1 vanilla bean, split lengthwise, seeds gently scraped out

4 whole cloves

8 black peppercorns

8 allspice berries

Two 3-inch sticks cinnamon

Honey-Rosemary-Ginger Ice Cream (page 266)

4 TO 8 SERVINGS

be light and syrupy. Allow the liquid to cool slightly; then pour it over the cooled pears. Cover and refrigerate for up to 24 hours before serving.

4. To serve, cut each pear in half lengthwise and place, cut side down, on a small chilled dessert plate. Serve with Honey-Rosemary-Ginger Ice Cream, spooning the liquid over the ice cream and the pears.

Serve with a small glass of honeylike muscat wine, such as that from Beaumes-de-Venise.

> WHAT I LEARNED: When cooking with wine, always leave the pan uncovered as you cook. This allows the alcohol to burn off and results in a liquid with a rounder, firmer, fruitier flavor.

Carré des Feuillants

(ALAIN DUTOURNIER)
14, RUE DE CASTIGLIONE
PARIS 1
TELEPHONE: 01 42 86 82 82
FAX: 01 42 86 07 71
MÉTRO: CONCORDE OR TUILERIES

LA MAISON DU CHOCOLAT'S BITTER-SWEET CHOCOLATE MOUSSE

Mousse au Chocolat
La Maison du Chocolat

When I first moved to Paris in 1980, one of my biggest treats was to walk to the end of my street and wander into La Maison du Chocolat for a mid-afternoon chocolate fix. Owner Robert Linxe remains one of the city's paramount *chocolatiers*, always offering quality, creativity, and excellence. He kindly shared this exquisite chocolate mousse: It is light, rich with chocolate flavor, and as voluptuous as one could ever imagine.

1. In the top of a double boiler set over, but not touching, boiling water, heat the cream just until warm, about 1 minute. Add the chocolate pieces, and stir until the chocolate is melted. Add the butter and stir to melt and combine. Remove from the heat. One by one, whisk in the egg yolks. Transfer the mixture to a large bowl, and set it aside to cool.

2. Place the egg whites in the bowl of a heavy-duty mixer fitted with the whisk. Whisk at low speed until the whites are frothy. Gradually increase the speed to high. Slowly add the sugar, cocoa, sea salt, and vanilla extract. Whisk at high speed until stiff but not dry.

3. Stir one third of the egg white mixture into the cooled chocolate mixture, and whisk until the two are thoroughly

¼ cup heavy cream

7 ounces bittersweet or semisweet chocolate (preferably Lindt Excellence 70% or Valhrona guanaja 70%), broken into pieces (see Note)

3 tablespoons unsalted butter

2 large egg yolks

5 large egg whites

1 tablespoon sugar

1 tablespoon Dutch-process cocoa powder

⅛ teaspoon fine sea salt

½ teaspoon pure vanilla extract

EQUIPMENT:

A double boiler; a heavy-duty mixer.

8 SERVINGS

blended. (This will lighten the batter and make it easier to fold in the remaining egg white mixture.) With a large rubber spatula, gently fold in the remaining white mixture. Do this slowly and patiently. Do not overmix, but be sure that the mixture is well blended and that no streaks of white remain.

4. Pour the mousse into a large glass bowl, eight individual ramekins, or eight *pot de crème* cups. Cover with plastic wrap and store at room temperature. Serve within a few hours.

VARIATIONS:
Add about ½ vanilla bean, finely ground, to the chocolate. Do not add too much, or the vanilla will make the chocolate taste too sweet.

Add 1 small cup of very strong coffee, along with the grated zest of 1 orange or 1 lemon, to the cream when you heat it.

Add 1 teaspoon finely ground ginger to the warm cream. Let the mixture cool, then strain through a fine-mesh sieve.

NOTE: Semisweet and bittersweet chocolate can be used interchangeably, and are made of chocolate, cocoa butter, and a bit of sugar to make the chocolate more palatable. Unsweetened chocolate contains no sugar at all and is considered less palatable.

Chocolate is delicious with one of France's newly popular *vins doux naturels*, such as Boissy-Masson's Rancio, full of body with a nuttiness that pairs well with the richness of chocolate.

ROBERT LINXE SAYS:

"The amount of egg whites makes this a very light mousse."

"Don't put the mousse in the refrigerator, but in a cool spot. The cold will block the flavor of the chocolate and it will lose its smooth, creamy quality."

"For a truly rich mousse, use an extra-bitter chocolate—Van Couva from Trinidad, the best chocolate in the world."

La Maison du Chocolat

225, RUE DU FAUBOURG SAINT-HONORÉ
PARIS 8
TELEPHONE: 01 42 27 39 44
MÉTRO: TERNES

JR'S BURNT CREAM

Crème Brûlée JR

For nearly four years during the 1980s, I worked on a cookbook with chef Joël Robuchon. I spent many a day ensconced in the tiny kitchen on the rue de Longchamp, the home of the famous restaurant Jamin, where Robuchon held court. This was one of his most famous desserts, and I cannot count the number of times I sampled it as part of a multiple dessert medley. It is a dessert that holds up over time, and I have never known a guest to turn it down. The secret is in the huge amount of vanilla seeds used here, giving it an elegant, rich flavor and texture.

1. Flatten the vanilla beans and cut them in half lengthwise. With a small spoon, scrape out the seeds and place them in the bowl of a heavy-duty mixer fitted with the whisk. (The pods can be used for making Vanilla Sugar, page 301.) Add the egg yolks and sugar to the bowl and whisk at high speed for 2 minutes. Stir in the cold milk and the *crème fraîche*. Cover with plastic wrap and refrigerate for 12 hours to allow the flavors to ripen.

2. Preheat the oven to 250 degrees F.

3. Arrange six individual baking dishes on two baking sheets. Pour the mixture into the dishes. Place the baking sheets in the oven and bake until the custard is set, 40 to 45 minutes.

4 plump, moist vanilla beans

9 large egg yolks

¾ cup granulated sugar

1 cup chilled whole milk

3 cups *crème fraîche* or heavy cream

½ cup firmly packed dark brown sugar

EQUIPMENT:

Six 6-inch round porcelain baking dishes; a heavy-duty mixer; two baking sheets.

MAKES 6 SERVINGS

4. Remove from the oven and let cool to room temperature. Cover the cooled custard with plastic wrap. Refrigerate for at least 4 hours or overnight.

5. At serving time, preheat the broiler.

6. Sprinkle the brown sugar through a fine-mesh sieve over the custard. Place the baking dishes under the broiler and heat until the sugar forms a crust, watching carefully to see that it does not burn. Serve immediately.

"THE HEART OF PARIS"

Coeur à la Crème

On Valentine's Day, Paris cookery shops love to decorate their windows with charming heart-shaped white porcelain *coeur à la crème* molds. *Coeur à la crème* is a very light cheese dessert, usually prepared in molds shaped like a heart. I have a treasured collection, with molds in every size. Since I am a cheese lover, this style of dessert—with its farm-fresh lactic tang and just a touch of sweetness—speaks to me. This is an ideal dessert any time of year, delicious when served with fresh berries or homemade fruit preserves. The best *fromage blanc* I know comes from my favorite cheese shop, Alléosse.

3 large egg whites

1/4 cup sugar

2 cups fresh cheese (*fromage blanc* or yogurt cheese)

1/3 cup heavy cream

Fresh seasonal berries or fruit preserves, for garnish

EQUIPMENT:

One 2-cup heart-shaped perforated mold, or four 1/2-cup heart-shaped perforated molds; a heavy-duty mixer.

4 SERVINGS

1. At least 8 hours and up to 36 hours before serving, prepare the fresh cheese mixture: Place the egg whites in the bowl of a heavy-duty mixer fitted with the whisk. Whisk at low speed until the whites are frothy. Gradually increase the speed to high. Slowly add the sugar, whisking at high speed until stiff but not dry.

2. In another large bowl, using a hand whisk, blend the cheese and cream until smooth. Gradually fold the beaten whites into the cheese mixture.

3. Set perforated mold (or four individual molds) on a tray or pan with 2-inch sides. Spoon the mixture into the

mold, and even out the top with a spatula. Cover with plastic wrap. Place in the refrigerator to drain for at least 8 hours and up to 36 hours.

4. When ready to serve, turn the mold onto a serving plate, and garnish with fresh berries or fruit preserves.

Philippe Alléosse

Fromagerie Alléosse

13, RUE PONCELET
PARIS 17
TELEPHONE: 01 46 22 50 45
MÉTRO: TERNES

THE ASTOR'S INDIVIDUAL VANILLA CUSTARDS

Les Petits Pots de Crème à la Vanille de l'Astor

These simple, sublime traditional desserts have long been part of the repertoire of chef Joël Robuchon and his acolyte, Eric Lecerf. These delicate creams—often served in lovely antique molds or *pots de crème* molds of all colors—can be prepared up to a day in advance, allowing the flavors to mellow.

1. Preheat the oven to 325 degrees F.

2. Cut three slits in a piece of wax paper, and use it to line a baking pan that is large enough to hold eight small ramekins. Place the ramekins in the pan, on top of the paper, and set aside. (The paper will prevent the water from boiling and splashing up on the custards.)

3. In a medium-size saucepan, combine the milk and vanilla beans over high heat. Bring to a boil and remove from the heat. Cover, and set aside to infuse for 15 minutes. Once infused, remove the vanilla beans.

4. In the bowl of an electric mixer, whisk the egg yolks and sugar until thick and lemon-colored. Set aside.

5. Bring the vanilla-infused milk back to a boil, and very gradually add the hot milk to the egg yolk mixture in a thin

1⅔ cups whole milk

2 plump, moist vanilla beans, split lengthwise

4 large egg yolks

⅓ cup sugar

EQUIPMENT:
Eight ½-cup ovenproof ramekins, custard cups, or *petits pots*.

8 SERVINGS

stream, whisking constantly. Strain into a bowl through a fine-mesh sieve or a colander lined with several layers of cheesecloth. Let stand for 2 to 3 minutes; then remove any foam that has risen to the top.

6. Divide the cream evenly among the ramekins. Pour enough boiling water into the baking pan to reach about halfway up the sides of the ramekins. Cover the pan loosely with aluminum foil (to prevent a skin from forming on the custards). Place the pan in the center of the oven, and bake until the custard is just set at the edges but still trembling in the center, 30 to 35 minutes.

7. Remove the pan from the oven and carefully remove the ramekins from the water. Refrigerate, loosely covered, for at least 2 hours or up to 24 hours. Serve the *pots de crème* chilled, without unmolding.

Any good sweet regional French wine would be ideal here: Try a Loupiac, a Ste-Croix-du-Mont, or a Monbazillac—and of course one will never lose with a Sauternes.

TRUC: To prevent those moist and precious vanilla beans from drying out, place the beans in a small jar, add just enough rum to keep the tips of the beans wet, and cover securely. The beans will absorb a bit of the liquid and will not dry out with time.

Astor

11, RUE D'ASTORG
PARIS 8
TELEPHONE: 01 53 05 05 20
FAX: 01 53 05 05 30
MÉTRO: SAINT-AUGUSTIN

BLOOD-ORANGE ICE CREAM LE JARDIN DE COURCELLES

Crème Glacée aux Oranges Sanguines le Jardin de Courcelles

Blood oranges—those ruby-dappled oranges with their rich red juice—are a ray of sunshine in Paris's often gray winter. I like to keep my refrigerator stocked with citrus in the winter, and when I am in the mood for an ice cream splurge, I head over to one of the city's best fruit and vegetable shops, Le Jardin de Courcelles, for a fresh stock. If you cannot get blood oranges, top-quality juice oranges can be substituted.

1. In a small saucepan, combine $1\frac{1}{2}$ cups water with the orange zest, sugar, and orange juice. Bring to a boil over moderate heat. Boil vigorously for 2 minutes. Place a sieve over a bowl and strain the syrup through the sieve. Discard the solids. Let the syrup cool to room temperature. (To speed the cooling, place the bowl inside a larger bowl filled with ice cubes and water. Stir occasionally. The mixture should be cold to the touch. The process should take about 30 minutes.)

2. When the syrup is thoroughly cooled, stir in the cream. Transfer the mixture to an ice cream maker and freeze according to the manufacturer's instructions.

Grated zest of 4 blood oranges (or substitute juice oranges)
1 cup sugar
1 cup freshly squeezed blood orange juice (or substitute juice of juice oranges)
$1\frac{1}{2}$ cups heavy cream

EQUIPMENT:
An ice cream maker.

6 TO 8 SERVINGS

Le Jardin
de Courcelles

96, RUE DE COURCELLES
PARIS 17
TELEPHONE: 01 47 63 70 55
MÉTRO: COURCELLES

ALMOND ICE CREAM

Glace aux Amandes

I never get enough almonds in my life. This is delicious all on its own, or served with Miniature Lemon Tea Cakes (page 270) or Chocolate Financiers (page 272).

1. In a large saucepan, combine the almonds, cream, milk, and sugar. Stir to dissolve the sugar. Heat over moderate heat, stirring from time to time, just until tiny bubbles form around the edges of the pan, 2 to 3 minutes. Remove from the heat and let steep, covered, for 1 hour.

2. Strain the mixture through a fine-mesh sieve, discarding the almonds. Cover and refrigerate until thoroughly chilled.

3. Stir the almond extract into the mixture, transfer it to an ice cream maker, and freeze according to the manufacturer's instructions.

1 cup finely ground
   almonds
3 cups heavy cream
1½ cups whole milk
¾ cup sugar
Several drops almond
   extract

EQUIPMENT:
An ice cream maker.

8 TO 10 SERVINGS

FROMAGERIE ALLÉOSSE'S FROMAGE BLANC ICE CREAM

La Glace au Fromage Blanc de la Fromagerie Alléosse

Made without egg yolks, and sweetened just enough to make the ice cream only mildly tangy, this fromage blanc ice cream is always a hit. I purchase my fresh cheese—the French fromage blanc that is like yogurt in texture but has a much sharper flavor—at the city's best cheese shop, Alléosse. Philippe Alléosse and his family offer the city's finest selection of cheeses, ranging from their thick and creamy fromage blanc to an astonishing array of goat's-, sheep's-, and cow's-milk cheeses from all over France.

1. Place the egg whites in the bowl of a heavy-duty mixer fitted with the whisk. Whisk at low speed until the whites are frothy. Gradually increase the speed to high. Slowly add the sugar, whisking at high speed until stiff but not dry.

2. In another large bowl, whisk the cheese and the cream until smooth. Gradually fold the beaten egg whites into the cream mixture. Transfer to an ice cream maker and freeze according to the manufacturer's instructions.

3. At serving time, top the ice cream with berries or preserves.

3 large egg whites

⅔ cup sugar

2 cups fresh cheese (fromage blanc or full-fat yogurt cheese)

1 cup heavy cream

Fresh seasonal berries or fruit preserves, for garnish

EQUIPMENT:
A heavy-duty mixer; an ice cream maker.

6 TO 8 SERVINGS

Fromagerie Alléosse

13, RUE PONCELET

PARIS 17

TELEPHONE: 01 46 22 50 45

MÉTRO: TERNES

MAISON DU MIEL'S HEATHER HONEY ICE CREAM

La Glace au Miel de Bruyère de la Maison du Miel

La Maison du Miel—The House of Honey—is one of Paris's most traditional shops, devoted to nothing but honey and honey-related products. My favorite selection is the deep, rust-toned heather honey, *bruyère*, which is strong and pungent. I use it to make this rich honey ice cream, delicious with The Apple Lady's Apple Cake (page 230) or with crusty Miniature Lemon Tea Cakes (page 270).

2 plump, moist vanilla beans
2 cups heavy cream
1 cup whole milk
1/2 cup heather honey (or substitute another aromatic honey, such as chestnut or eucalyptus)

EQUIPMENT:
An ice cream maker.

6 TO 8 SERVINGS

1. Flatten the vanilla beans and cut them in half lengthwise. With a small spoon, scrape out the seeds. Place the seeds and pods in a large saucepan. Add the cream, milk, and honey. Stir to dissolve the honey. Heat over moderate heat, stirring from time to time, just until tiny bubbles form around the edges of the pan, 3 to 4 minutes.

2. Remove from the heat and let steep, covered, for 1 hour.

3. Cover and refrigerate until thoroughly chilled.

4. Remove the vanilla pods, and stir the mixture again to blend. Transfer it to an ice cream maker and freeze according to the manufacturer's instructions.

La Maison du Miel

24, RUE VIGNON
PARIS 8
TELEPHONE: 01 47 42 26 70
MÉTRO: MADELEINE

FRESH HONEY-ROSEMARY-GINGER ICE CREAM

Crème Glacée au Miel, Romarin, et Gingembre

Paired with Honey-Poached Pears in Beaumes-de-Venise (page 252), this is one of my favorite winter desserts, inspired by a visit to Alain Dutournier's Carré des Feuillants.

1. In a large saucepan, combine the cream, milk, honey, ginger, and rosemary. Heat over moderate heat just until tiny bubbles form around the edges of the pan, 3 to 4 minutes. Remove from the heat, cover, and let steep for 1 hour.

2. Strain through a fine-mesh sieve, discarding the rosemary and ginger. Refrigerate until thoroughly chilled. Transfer to an ice cream maker and freeze according to the manufacturer's instructions.

2 cups heavy cream
1 cup whole milk
½ cup mild honey, such as lavender
A thumb-size knob of fresh ginger, peeled
20 sprigs fresh rosemary

EQUIPMENT:
An ice cream maker.

8 SERVINGS

WHAT I LEARNED: When you want to infuse a liquid with the flavor of an herb or a spice, heat the liquid with the flavoring and then set the pan aside, covered. Sealed in this manner, the herb or spice will have an opportunity to transfer its oils and flavors, permeating the liquid.

Carré des Feuillants

(ALAIN DUTOURNIER)
14, RUE DE CASTIGLIONE
PARIS 1
TELEPHONE: 01 42 86 82 82
FAX: 01 42 86 07 71
MÉTRO: CONCORDE OR TUILERIES

FRESH TRUFFLE ICE CREAM

Glace aux Truffes Fraîches

I know, the first time you hear the words "Truffle Ice Cream," you make a face and say, "It can't be true. It can't taste good." I used to be totally against mixing sweet and savory, sort of like polka dots and plaid all at once. But I've changed my tune. This dessert is always on the menu when a truffle feast is in order.

3 cups Truffle Cream
(page 287)
1½ cups whole milk
1 cup sugar
About 2 tablespoons
minced fresh black
truffle

EQUIPMENT:
An ice cream maker.

8 TO 10 SERVINGS

1. In a large saucepan, combine the cream, milk, and sugar. Stir to dissolve the sugar. Heat over moderate heat, stirring from time to time, just until tiny bubbles form around the edges of the pan. Remove from the heat, add 1 tablespoon and 1 teaspoon of the truffles, and let steep, covered, for 1 hour.

2. Cover and refrigerate until thoroughly chilled. Just before churning the ice cream, stir in the remaining 2 teaspoons minced truffles. Transfer the mixture to an ice cream maker, and freeze according to the manufacturer's instructions.

TRUFFLE PANNA COTTA

Panna Cotta de Truffes

I have decided that truffles are nature's way of saying "February is OK!" In France, the precious black truffle is in season from late November to the first of March, giving us reason to indulge when truffle season is at its peak. Minced truffles and cream make a great combination, for the fat of the cream seems to virtually inhale the fragrance and flavor of the truffle. What's more, with fresh truffles, there are always little bits that can be set aside for mincing, and with canned truffles, the sliced or minced version is generally less expensive. While the name—*panna cotta*, or cooked cream, in Italian—implies that the mixture is cooked, it is only brought to a boil then mixed with gelatin, which helps it set. Without truffles, the recipe is also delicious and serves as a recipe for the traditional dessert of Italy's Piedmont. This is a dish I created to keep smiles on our faces until the first blossoms of spring appear.

2 teaspoons (1 package) unflavored gelatin

2 cups whole milk

1 cup confectioners' sugar

2 cups Truffle Cream (page 287)

2 tablespoons minced truffles

EQUIPMENT:
Eight ½-cup ramekins.

8 SERVINGS

1. Place eight individual ramekins on a tray. Set it aside.

2. In a small bowl, sprinkle the gelatin over ¼ cup of the milk and stir to blend. Set aside until the gelatin has completely absorbed the milk, 2 to 3 minutes.

3. In a large saucepan, combine the remaining 1¾ cups milk, the confectioners' sugar, and the truffle cream. Bring to a boil over moderate heat, whisking to dissolve the sugar. Remove from the heat.

4. Stir in the gelatin mixture, and then strain through a fine-mesh sieve set over a large measuring cup with a pouring spout. Pour the strained mixture into the ramekins. Cover with plastic wrap and refrigerate until set, about 4 hours. (The panna cotta can be prepared up to 1 day in advance. Refrigerate until serving time.)

5. Run a sharp knife around the inside edge of each ramekin to help loosen the custard. Dip the bottom of each ramekin into a bowl of hot water, shaking to completely loosen the custard. Invert them onto chilled dessert plates. Sprinkle with the minced truffle shavings, and serve.

MINIATURE LEMON TEA CAKES

Mini-Madeleines au Citron

Ever since I moved to Paris in 1980, *madeleines*—tiny scallop-shaped sweets that look like a cookie but taste like a miniature cake—have been one of my greatest treats. When working on *The Food Lover's Guide to Paris* in the early 1980s, I was obsessed with these tiny cakes: I couldn't pass a pastry shop without examining the golden sweets. When I deemed the shop's *madeleines* potentially worthy, I'd purchase one and decide whether or not this pastry chef made the cut. Today my preference is for the miniature version, which has more crust and crunch than the traditional ones twice the size.

2 large eggs

½ cup sugar

Grated zest of 1 lemon

¾ cup all-purpose flour

⅛ teaspoon fine sea salt

6 tablespoons unsalted butter, melted and cooled

EQUIPMENT:
Madeleine tins for 60 mini-*madeleines*; a heavy-duty mixer.

60 1½-INCH
MADELEINES

1. Butter the *madeleine* tins and place them in the freezer.

2. Place the eggs and sugar in the bowl of a heavy-duty mixer fitted with the whisk. Beat at high speed until thick and lemon-colored, 2 to 3 minutes. By hand, stir in the zest. Stir in the flour and sea salt. Stir in the butter. Cover and refrigerate for at least 1 hour and up to 24 hours.

3. Preheat the oven to 375 degrees F.

4. Remove the *madeleine* tins from the freezer. Spoon the batter into the prepared molds, filling nearly to the top. Tap the molds gently against a flat surface to evenly distribute the batter. Place the tins in the center of the oven

and bake until the *madeleines* are golden brown, 10 to 12 minutes. Remove to a rack to cool. Remove the *madeleines* from their tins as soon as they are cool. The *madeleines* are best eaten immediately. They may, however, be stored for several days in an airtight container.

TRUC: As soon as you remove the *madeleines*, wash the tins with a stiff brush and hot water but no detergent, so they retain their seasoning.

Miniature madeleine molds
can be found at

Geneviève Lethu

95, RUE DE RENNES
PARIS 6
TELEPHONE: 01 45 44 40 35
FAX: 01 44 39 27 51
MÉTRO: RENNES

JP HÉVIN'S CHOCOLATE FINANCIERS

Financiers au Chocolat JP Hévin

Jean-Paul Hévin is one of Paris's finest chocolate makers. His Left Bank shop offers no fewer than 28 different dark chocolate confections. I admit to a serious weakness for these shiny, rich *financiers*—pure, hedonistic chocolate. *Financiers* are small rectangular cakes, most often made with almonds. They are so called because a *financier* is a banker and the rectangles resemble a gold brick. While one finds *financiers* in all sorts of "fantasy" shapes—round, square, even made in *madeleine* pans—I am a purist and insist on the authentic traditional shape.

1. Butter the *financier* molds. Place them side by side on a baking sheet, and place the baking sheet in the freezer.

2. Preheat the oven to 350 degrees F.

3. In a small saucepan, heat the cream to a gentle simmer over moderate heat. Add the chocolate and mix until melted. Set aside to cool.

4. In a large bowl, stir together the confectioners' sugar, flour, almonds, baking powder, and sea salt. Set aside.

5. In a small saucepan, heat the butter over moderate heat until it is golden and gives off a nutty aroma. Immediately remove the pan from the heat and transfer the butter to a small bowl to prevent it from burning. Set aside to cool.

2/3 cup heavy cream

5 ounces bittersweet chocolate (preferably Lindt Excellence 70% or Valhrona guanaja 70%), broken into pieces

1/2 cup confectioners' sugar

1/4 cup all-purpose flour

1/2 cup finely ground almonds

1/2 teaspoon baking powder

1/4 teaspoon fine sea salt

4 tablespoons unsalted butter

3 egg whites, lightly beaten

1/2 teaspoon pure vanilla extract

EQUIPMENT:

21 rectangular *financier* molds, measuring 2 × 4 inches.

MAKES 21 *FINANCIERS*

6. Add the egg whites to the sugar/flour mixture, and stir until thoroughly blended. Add the cooled butter and stir until thoroughly blended. Add the chocolate mixture and stir that until thoroughly blended. Finally, add the vanilla extract, and stir until thoroughly blended.

7. Remove the *financier* molds from the freezer. Spoon the batter into the prepared molds, filling nearly to the top. Tap each mold gently against a flat surface to evenly distribute the batter. Place the baking sheet in the center of the oven and bake until the *financiers* are firm and springy, 20 to 25 minutes.

8. Remove the molds from the oven, transfer them to a wire rack, and allow to cool for 5 minutes before unmolding.

Jean-Paul Hévin

3, RUE VAVIN
PARIS 6
TELEPHONE: 01 43 54 09 85
MÉTRO: VAVIN OR NOTRE-DAME
DES CHAMPS

DESSERTS

273

JEAN-LUC POUJAURAN'S SHORTBREAD COOKIES

Les Sablés aux Amandes
de Jean-Luc Poujauran

These delicate cookies come from one of my favorite bakers in Paris, the outgoing and talented Jean-Luc Poujauran. This recipe is dedicated to Susan Marcus, one of my students, who begged that these be put on the menu for the Paris cooking class. So here they are!

1. Place the almonds and confectioners' sugar in the bowl of a food processor and process to blend. Add the flour and sea salt and process to blend. Add the butter and process until the mixture resembles coarse crumbs, about 10 seconds. Add the egg and lemon zest and pulse until the dough begins to hold together, about 10 times. Do not overprocess. The dough should not form a ball.

2. Transfer the dough to a clean work surface, and using a dough scraper, smear it bit by bit across the work surface until the butter is thoroughly incorporated. Form into a flattened round, cover with plastic wrap, and refrigerate for at least 1 hour and up to 48 hours.

3. Divide the chilled dough into four equal parts. Refrigerate three of the parts and place the fourth on a lightly floured surface. Roll out the dough until it is ⅛ inch thick. Use flour sparingly and touch the dough as little as possi-

2 tablespoons finely ground blanched almonds

½ cup confectioners' sugar

1 cup bleached all-purpose flour

⅛ teaspoon fine sea salt

5 tablespoons unsalted butter, cubed and chilled

1 large egg, at room temperature

Grated zest of 1 lemon

EQUIPMENT:
A food processor.

ABOUT 30 COOKIES

ble while rolling. After each few strokes of the rolling pin, gently unstick the dough from the surface and spread a bit more flour underneath if necessary. Once the dough is rolled to the desired thickness, use a pastry brush to dust off any flour that sticks to either side of the dough.

4. Using a 1½-inch round or fluted biscuit cutter, cut out rounds of dough and place them about 1 inch apart on a parchment paper–lined baking sheet. Refrigerate until firm, about 20 minutes and up to 1 hour. Repeat with the remaining portions of the dough.

5. Meanwhile, preheat the oven to 350 degrees F.

6. Place the baking sheet in the center of the oven and bake for 20 to 25 minutes. The cookies should color only slightly, but they must be cooked through. Cool completely on wire racks.

Jean-Luc
Poujauran

20, RUE JEAN-NICOT
PARIS 7
TELEPHONE: 01 47 05 80 88
MÉTRO: LA TOUR-MAUBOURG

DESSERTS

CLASSIC VINAIGRETTE

LE GRAND VÉFOUR'S VINAIGRETTE

NIÇOISE VINAIGRETTE

MUSTARD VINAIGRETTE

MUSTARD MAYONNAISE

BLACK TRUFFLE MAYONNAISE

TRUFFLE BUTTER

TRUFFLE CREAM

THAI CURRY PASTE

THE PANTRY
Au Garde-Manger

HOMEMADE CURRY POWDER

LEDOYEN'S FRESH GARLIC AND LEMON PURÉE

LES ALLOBROGES'S GARLIC CONFIT

FOUR-SPICE BLEND

CHERRY JAM

SORREL SAUCE

HOMEMADE CHICKEN STOCK

OVEN-ROASTED TOMATOES

SUN-DRIED TOMATO PASTE

TOMATO SAUCE

VANILLA SUGAR

Chef Guy Martin of Le Grand Véfour

CLASSIC VINAIGRETTE

Vinaigrette Classique

This is the simple, classic vinaigrette always found on my kitchen counter, along with the salt and pepper mills. I insist upon two vinegars—a top-quality red wine vinegar and a Spanish sherry vinegar—to give greater depth of flavor to my salad dressing. I keep the mixture corked in a small wine bottle, so I always have a vinaigrette on hand when I'm in the mood for a salad. Since the mixture contains only vinegars, oil, and salt, there is no fear of spoilage.

2 tablespoons best-
    quality sherry vinegar
2 tablespoons best-
    quality red wine vinegar
Fine sea salt to taste
1 cup extra-virgin olive oil

ABOUT 1 ¼ CUPS

Combine both vinegars and the sea salt in a bottle. Cover, and shake to dissolve the salt. Add the oil and shake to blend. Taste for seasoning. The vinaigrette can be stored at room temperature or in the refrigerator for several weeks. Shake again at serving time to create a thick emulsion.

LE GRAND VÉFOUR'S VINAIGRETTE

La Vinaigrette du Grand Véfour

This brilliant, unusual creation of Grand Véfour chef Guy Martin quickly became a staple in my home. I love the complex blend of hazelnut, walnut, and olive oils, enriched by a bit of homemade chicken stock, then given that proper bite with just a touch of sherry vinegar. Use it to dress any green salad or blanched fresh vegetables. This easy-to-prepare vinaigrette is typical of Guy Martin's style: modern, classic, and thoughtful all in one.

In a small covered jar, combine the vinegar and sea salt. Shake to blend. Add the remaining ingredients. Shake to blend. Taste for seasoning. The vinaigrette can be stored in the refrigerator for up to 2 days. For longer keeping, omit the chicken stock and add it when ready to serve the vinaigrette.

1 tablespoon best-quality sherry vinegar
Sea salt to taste
4 tablespoons extra-virgin olive oil
2 tablespoons hazelnut oil
1 tablespoon walnut oil
3 tablespoons Homemade Chicken Stock (page 297)

ABOUT ¾ CUP

Le Grand Véfour

17, RUE DE BEAUJOLAIS
PARIS 1
TELEPHONE: 01 42 96 56 27
FAX: 01 42 86 80 71
MÉTRO: PALAIS ROYAL—MUSÉE DU LOUVRE

LE GRAND VÉFOUR IS ONE OF PARIS'S MOST
ALLURING RESTAURANTS. There are few greater
gastronomic pleasures than sitting in the sparkling
eighteenth-century dining room, a former café set at the
edge of the historic Palais Royal gardens. The restaurant
always makes me feel just a bit like a princess, or maybe a
queen, sitting at the table once shared by Colette, or Victor
Hugo, or even Napoléon. The restaurant's decorative
painted-glass panels and ceilings, the *trompe l'oeil* painted
chimney in the private dining room upstairs, its red velvet
banquettes and swirling red, white, and black carpet, are all
there to be admired as one dines in pampered splendor on
chef Guy Martin's inventive food that is very much of today.

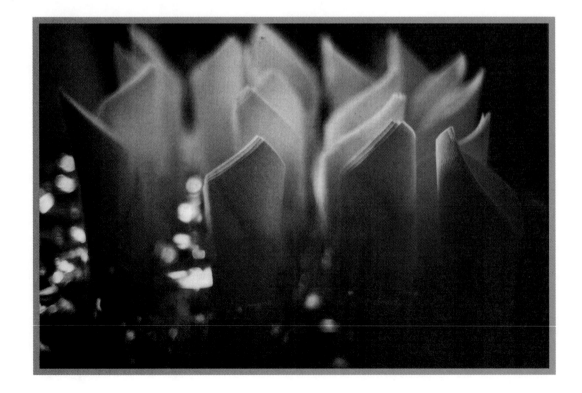

NIÇOISE VINAIGRETTE

Vinaigrette Niçoise

This zesty vinaigrette can turn a dish of simple grilled vegetables into a satisfying meal all on its own: My favorite version is with grilled baby asparagus or leeks.

Combine all the ingredients in a small bowl. Taste for seasoning. Pour over warm or room-temperature vegetables.

Grated zest of 1 lemon

1 tablespoon freshly squeezed lemon juice

3 tablespoons extra-virgin olive oil

2 teaspoons capers, rinsed and drained

12 top-quality black olives (such as Nyons)

4 tablespoons finely chopped fresh parsley leaves

4 anchovy fillets, preferably salt-cured, minced

4 TO 6 SERVINGS

MUSTARD VINAIGRETTE

Vinaigrette à la Moutarde

The addition of walnut oil adds that perfect, slightly mysterious touch to a rather classic dressing. If you want to experiment, try substituting hazelnut or grilled peanut oil.

Place the mustard, vinegar, and sea salt in a bottle. Cover and shake to blend. Add the oils and shake to blend. Taste for seasoning. The vinaigrette can be stored at room temperature or in the refrigerator for several weeks. Shake again at serving time to create a thick emulsion.

3 tablespoons French
   Dijon mustard
1 tablespoon best-quality
   red wine vinegar
Fine sea salt to taste
2/3 cup extra-virgin olive
   oil
1/3 cup French walnut oil

ABOUT 1 CUP

MUSTARD MAYONNAISE

Mayonnaise à la Moutarde

When I want a bit of tang in a dressing, this is the mayonnaise I use.

BY HAND:

1. In a small bowl, combine the lemon juice, sea salt, and mustard, and whisk to blend.

2. Place the oil in a measuring cup with a pouring spout.

3. In a medium-size bowl, whisk the egg yolks until light and thick. Add the lemon juice mixture and whisk until thick and smooth. Continuing to whisk, gradually add just a few drops of the oil. Whisk until thoroughly incorporated. Do not add too much oil at the beginning, or the mixture will not emulsify. As soon as the mixture begins to thicken, add the remaining oil in a slow, steady stream, whisking constantly. Taste for seasoning. The mayonnaise can be stored, covered and refrigerated, for up to 3 days.

IN A FOOD PROCESSOR:

In the bowl of a food processor, combine the lemon juice, sea salt, mustard, and egg yolks. Pulse until well blended. With the motor running, very slowly add several tablespoons of the oil, processing until the mixture thickens. With the motor still running, gradually add the remaining oil in a slow, steady stream. Taste for seasoning. Transfer to a bowl. The mayonnaise can be stored, covered and refrigerated, for up to 3 days.

2 teaspoons freshly squeezed lemon juice, or to taste

½ teaspoon fine sea salt, or to taste

1 tablespoon French Dijon mustard

2 large egg yolks, at room temperature

1 cup grapeseed oil

ABOUT 1 CUP

BLACK TRUFFLE MAYONNAISE

Mayonnaise aux Truffes Noires

This is unquestionably one of the best and most full-flavored uses of fresh black truffles. The mayonnaise is delicious on just about everything, from warm sautéed potatoes, to cold chicken, to cubed chicken brochettes. Try it also as the dressing for a fresh Celery Root Remoulade (page 24).

1 cup grapeseed oil (or substitute canola, peanut, or safflower oil)

2 large egg yolks, at room temperature (preferably eggs that have been enclosed in a glass jar with the truffles for 1 day)

1 teaspoon freshly squeezed lemon juice, or to taste

1 teaspoon French Dijon mustard

¼ teaspoon fine sea salt, or to taste

3 tablespoons finely minced fresh truffle

ABOUT 1 ½ CUPS

BY HAND:

1. Place the oil in a glass measuring cup with a pouring spout.

2. In a medium-size bowl, whisk the egg yolks, lemon juice, mustard, and sea salt until light and thick. Continuing to whisk, gradually add just a few drops of the oil. Whisk until thoroughly incorporated. Do not add too much oil at the beginning, or the mixture will not emulsify. As soon as the mixture begins to thicken, add the remaining oil in a slow, steady stream, whisking constantly. Stir in the minced truffles. Taste for seasoning. Cover, and refrigerate for up to 3 days.

IN A FOOD PROCESSOR:

In the bowl of a food processor, combine the eggs, lemon juice, mustard, and sea salt. Pulse until well blended. With the motor running, very slowly add several tablespoons of the oil, processing until the mixture thickens. With the motor still running, gradually add the remaining oil in a slow, steady stream. Taste for seasoning. Transfer to a small bowl and stir in the minced truffles. Cover and refrigerate for up to 3 days.

TRUFFLE BUTTER

Beurre aux Truffes

This incredible butter becomes an essential ingredient during the dreary winter months! Use it wherever you would use butter in a recipe: Everything from omelets to cooked lentils to macaroni to cannelloni profits from this rich and intensely flavored concoction. And of course there's nothing to stop you from simply spreading it on toast!

4 tablespoons unsalted
   butter, softened
2 tablespoons minced
   truffle peelings
$\frac{1}{2}$ teaspoon coarse sea
   salt

4 TABLESPOONS

On a small plate, mash the softened butter with a fork. Sprinkle with the truffles and coarse sea salt, distributing them as evenly as possible. Transfer the butter to a ramekin and cover securely. Refrigerate for up to 3 days or freeze for up to 1 month. Serve at room temperature.

TRUFFLE CREAM

Crème de Truffes

During the truffle season, I always keep some of the truffle cream on hand, for seasoning everything from soups to desserts with the fragrant richness of truffle essence.

5 tablespoons minced truffle

2 cups cream

2 CUPS

Combine the minced truffles and cream. Refrigerate at least 2 days before using.

THAI CURRY PASTE

Pâte de Curry Thaïlandaise

This is a curry paste to knock your head off. The explosion of flavors is wild, so fasten your seat belt with this one! Use it to baste Flora Mikula's roasted spareribs (page 210) or a simple pork roast.

During the past decade Asian food has become more popular in France. So much so that ingredients that were not a part of classic French cuisine—from Japanese wasabi to Indian spices—are now looked upon as commonplace. But don't get me wrong: French chefs rarely stray far from the center and tend to use foreign ingredients with a great deal of forethought.

1. In a small dry skillet, combine the coriander, cumin, fennel, and peppercorns. Place over medium heat and toast, shaking the pan often to prevent burning, 2 to 3 minutes. Remove from the heat and let cool to room temperature. In a spice grinder or a clean coffee mill, grind to a fine powder. Transfer to a small bowl.

2. In a blender or food processor, combine the cilantro, ginger, lemongrass, ground chile pepper, shallots, garlic, lime zest, shrimp paste (if using), sea salt, and nutmeg. Process until very finely chopped. Add the ground toasted spices. With the machine running, slowly pour in the peanut oil. Cover and refrigerate until ready to use. The paste will keep, covered and refrigerated, for up to 1 week.

2 teaspoons coriander seeds

1 teaspoon cumin seeds

1 teaspoon fennel seeds

1 teaspoon black peppercorns

1/2 cup tightly packed fresh cilantro leaves

Two 1/4-inch slices fresh ginger, peeled

1 stalk lemongrass, bottom third only, chopped

1 tablespoon finely ground dried red chile peppers

2 shallots, peeled and chopped

4 plump, fresh cloves garlic, peeled and chopped

Grated zest of 1 lime

1 teaspoon shrimp paste (optional)

1 1/2 teaspoons fine sea salt

1 teaspoon freshly grated nutmeg

1/3 cup peanut oil

EQUIPMENT:

A spice grinder or coffee mill.

1 CUP

HOMEMADE CURRY POWDER

Curry en Poudre Maison

While excellent commercial versions of curry powder exist on the market, I prefer to make my own. Here is a recipe I have been using for years. In truth, my husband, Walter, teased me back into making my own after he found a commercial jar in my spice drawer. His response was "I remember when you used to make your own curry powder," as though my standards had slipped drastically. Well, he teased me enough. From now on, it's homemade curry powder or none at all. Although one may not instantly associate curry powder with French cuisine, the French actually use it quite often, more as a delicate seasoning to nudge flavors a bit than as a huge hit of spice. When I worked with chef Joël Robuchon in the 1980s, curry powder became a joke between us. As he dictated recipes, he often ended with "and at the end, add just a little speck of curry powder."

2 whole, small dried red chile peppers
2 tablespoons coriander seeds
1 tablespoon cumin seeds
1/2 teaspoon black mustard seeds
1 teaspoon black peppercorns
1 teaspoon fenugreek seeds
1/2 teaspoon ground ginger
1/2 teaspoon ground turmeric

EQUIPMENT:
A spice grinder or coffee mill.

5 TABLESPOONS

1. In a small dry skillet, combine the chile peppers; coriander, cumin, and mustard seeds; and peppercorns. Place over medium heat and toast, shaking the pan often to prevent burning, 2 to 3 minutes. Remove from the heat, transfer to a bowl, and let cool to room temperature.

2. Transfer the cooled spice mixture to a spice grinder or coffee mill. Add the fenugreek seeds and grind to a fine powder. Transfer to a small container. Stir in the ground ginger and turmeric. Store in an airtight container in a cool place for up to 3 months.

LEDOYEN'S FRESH GARLIC AND LEMON PURÉE

Purée d'Ail et de Citron Ledoyen

When I spend time in restaurant kitchens I like to sleuth about, sticking my nose in pots and asking questions. How else is one to learn? When I was spending a morning with chef Christian Le Squer at Ledoyen on a spring day, I asked about the whole cloves of garlic simmering away on the stove. Le Squer explained that the garlic was to be cooked in milk until tender, then peeled and puréed with cubes of lemon. The purée serves as a condiment for slices of seared fresh foie gras. I also love it as a condiment for roasted meats and poultry.

4 plump, fresh heads garlic, separated into cloves but not peeled
1 quart whole milk
1 lemon, preferably organic, rinsed, sliced, and cut into small dice
Fine sea salt to taste

¾ CUP

1. Place the garlic in a small saucepan and cover with about 2 cups of the milk. Bring just to a simmer over moderate heat. Then pour the garlic and milk through a fine-mesh sieve, draining and discarding the milk. The garlic cloves will be whole but soft. Return the garlic to the pan, cover with the remaining 2 cups milk, and simmer, uncovered, over low heat until the garlic has softened and a small knife inserted into a clove meets no resistance, about 20 minutes. Remove from the heat and let cool in the milk.

2. Gently press the garlic cloves between your fingers, removing and discarding the peels. Transfer the garlic to the bowl of a food processor and purée. Add the diced lemon and pulse just to blend. Add sea salt to taste. The purée can be stored, covered and refrigerated, for up to 2 days.

Ledoyen

CARRÉ CHAMPS-ELYSÉES
PARIS 8
TELEPHONE: 01 47 42 35 98
FAX: 01 47 42 55 01
MÉTRO: CHAMPS ELYSÉES—
CLÉMENCEAU

LES ALLOBROGES'S GARLIC CONFIT

Confit d'Ail Les Allobroges

Garlic-lover's delight! This is the simplest and purest way to enjoy whole cloves of garlic: popping them out of their skins and into your mouth like candy. No more burnt garlic at the bottom of the roasting pan. These tender cloves are cooked to what the French call a *confit*, a melting tenderness. Serve this with roast chicken or lamb, or Allobroges chef Olivier Pateyron's Braised Lamb Shanks (page 220).

4 plump, fresh heads garlic, separated into cloves but not peeled

1 cup extra-virgin olive oil

1½ CUPS

Place the garlic in a small saucepan, and cover with the oil. Cook, uncovered, at the barest simmer over the lowest possible heat until the garlic is soft and a small knife inserted into a clove meets no resistance, 45 minutes to 1 hour. (Watch carefully to avoid burning the garlic. You may need to place the saucepan on a flame tamer.) The garlic can be served immediately or allowed to cool in the oil. Reheat at serving time. Allow guests to pop the cloves of garlic out of their skins. The oil can be used in cooking or for preparing a vinaigrette.

Les Allobroges

71, RUE GRANDS-CHAMPS
PARIS 20
TELEPHONE: 01 43 73 40 00
MÉTRO: MARAÎCHERS

WHAT IS A CONFIT?

The word *confit* comes from *confire*, meaning to conserve or preserve an ingredient—by enrobing it in fat (such as a *confit* of pork, duck, or goose), by enrobing it in a sugar syrup (such as candied fruits), by putting it in a jar with alcohol (such as cherries or plums in *eau de vie*), by submerging it in vinegar (capers, pickles), or by cooking it in a sweet-and-sour preparation (such as a chutney). Today the word is used quite liberally in French cuisine and applies to just about any method of conserving an ingredient in a liquid, such as lemon *confit* (preserved in lemon juice, salt, and sometimes oil) or garlic *confit* (preserved in oil).

FOUR-SPICE BLEND

Quatre Épices

Quatre épices, literally "four spices," is a classic, evenly flavored French seasoning used to flavor meats, terrines, and beef or chicken stock, as well as dried vegetables, tomato sauces, marinades, wine sauces, and gingerbread. I prepare the mixture in small amounts, grinding the spices in a spice mill.

One by one, grind the allspice and cloves in a spice grinder. Combine the spices in a small bowl, add the freshly grated nutmeg and ground cinnamon, and use immediately.

1 teaspoon allspice
  berries
1 teaspoon whole cloves
1 teaspoon freshly grated
  nutmeg
1 teaspoon cinnamon

EQUIPMENT:
A spice grinder or coffee
  mill.

4 TEASPOONS

CHERRY JAM

Confiture de Cerises

Cherries have always held a fascination for me. During my childhood in Wisconsin, we had cherry trees in the backyard. At that time I thought cherry trees were the best climbing trees in the world, for they were tough and sturdy and not too high. Today, in Provence, we are blessed with half a dozen giant trees, which in fact I never climb. Rather I stand on tiptoe to reach the best and ripest red fruit and leave the ladder for others to manipulate.

Over the past few years I have adopted the wonderful Basque habit of serving a few spoonfuls of cherry jam with *fromage de brebis*, the rich sheep's-milk cheese of the region. The jam, of course, can be used in more traditional ways—spread on toast at breakfast time or spooned over vanilla ice cream. This simple, straightforward recipe is embellished with a touch of kirsch and a bit of almond extract to bring out the almond flavor of the fruit.

The task of pitting cherries can be eased if you have a cherry pitter handy, a utensil found at most kitchen shops. I prefer the German brand Westmark.

5 pounds fresh cherries

3 pounds sugar

3 tablespoons kirsch (cherry liqueur)

1 teaspoon almond extract

ABOUT 7 PINTS

1. Rinse and drain the cherries. Stem and pit them. Place the cherries and the sugar in a large copper jam pot or heavy-duty Dutch oven and stir to blend. Bring to a boil over moderately high heat, stirring regularly, about 7

minutes from the time it comes to a boil. Place a large sieve over a large bowl. Pour the cherries into the sieve to separate the cherries and the juice. Return the juice to the jam pot, bring to a boil, and boil until it is thick and syrupy (240 degrees F on a jelly thermometer, or when it is at the "soft ball" stage), about 6 minutes. Carefully skim off the foam that rises to the top. (There will be a lot of foam. Skim carefully, or the jelly will be cloudy and the foam will rise to the top in the jar.)

2. Return the cherries to the jam pot and bring to a boil over high heat, skimming all the time. Boil for 2 minutes. Remove the pot from the heat and let rest for 2 minutes. Repeat this two more times, for a total cooking time of 6 minutes. Examine the syrup: It should be clear and about as thick as maple syrup. Off the heat, stir in the kirsch and the almond extract.

3. Carefully pour the jam into sterilized jars and seal according to the manufacturer's instructions.

SORREL SAUCE

Sauce à l'Oseille

This is my classic sauce to serve with the elegantly simple Slow-Roasted Salmon (page 182). It is also delicious with roast or broiled chicken, in place of mayonnaise in a chicken salad, or as a sandwich spread. Alongside, I often serve a chiffonnade of sorrel—sorrel leaves cut into fine strips and tossed with Classic Vinaigrette (page 278).

In the bowl of a food processor, combine the sorrel, egg yolks, lemon juice, and sea salt. Pulse until well blended. With the motor running, very slowly add several tablespoons of the oil, processing until the mixture thickens. With the motor still running, add the remaining oil in a slow, steady stream. Taste for seasoning. Transfer to a small bowl. The sauce can be stored, covered and refrigerated, for up to 3 days.

3 ounces fresh sorrel
  leaves, trimmed and
  stemmed
2 large egg yolks, at room
  temperature
2 teaspoons freshly
  squeezed lemon juice,
  or to taste
1/2 teaspoon fine sea salt,
  or to taste
1 cup grapeseed or canola
  oil

1 CUP

HOMEMADE CHICKEN STOCK

Fond de Volaille Maison

If you ask me what ingredient I could not be without in the kitchen, I would say a good homemade chicken stock. Many a day in Paris, when I know that I will be working in my office all day long, I buy a batch of chicken wings and make this, inhaling the healthy aroma of the simmering stock through the afternoon.

1. Place the chicken pieces in a heavy stockpot and cover with cold water by at least 2 inches. Bring to a gentle simmer over medium heat. Skim to remove the scum that rises to the surface. Add more cold water to replace the water removed, and continue skimming until the broth is clear.

2. Add the salt, the vegetables, and the bouquet garni. Return the liquid to a gentle simmer, and simmer gently for 2 hours. Skim and degrease as necessary.

3. Line a large colander with a double layer of dampened cheesecloth and place the colander over a large bowl. Ladle—do not pour—the broth into the colander; discard the solids.

4. Refrigerate the stock. When it is chilled, spoon off all traces of fat that rise to the surface. The stock may be refrigerated for 3 or 4 days, or can be frozen for up to 6 months.

4 pounds raw chicken
   parts, or raw or cooked
   carcasses
Pinch of sea salt
4 carrots, scrubbed and
   halved
2 large onions, peeled, 1
   stuck with 2 cloves
4 ribs celery, with leaves
1 head garlic, halved but
   not peeled
1 leek, white and tender
   green portions, halved
   lengthwise and rinsed
1 bouquet garni: parsley
   leaves, bay leaves, and
   celery leaves tied
   together with string

2 QUARTS

OVEN-ROASTED TOMATOES

Tomates Confites au Four

Use this in salads, on sandwiches, for pasta, or anywhere you want a rich, pure, tomato flavor.

1. Preheat the oven to the lowest possible setting, about 200 degrees F.

2. Arrange the tomato quarters side by side on a rimmed baking sheet. Sprinkle each side lightly with sea salt, pepper, and confectioners' sugar. Scatter the thyme leaves over the tomatoes and place a garlic sliver on top of each quarter. Drizzle with the olive oil. Place in the oven and cook until the tomatoes are very soft, about 1 hour.

3. Turn the tomatoes, baste with the juices, and cook until meltingly tender and reduced to about half their size, about 1 hour, for a total of 2 hours. Check the tomatoes from time to time: They should remain moist and soft. Remove from the oven and allow to cool thoroughly.

4. Transfer the tomatoes to a clean jar, cover with the cooking juices and oil, cover securely, and refrigerate for up to 1 week.

2 pounds fresh plum tomatoes, peeled, cored, seeded, and quartered lengthwise

Fine sea salt to taste

Freshly ground black pepper to taste

A pinch of confectioners' sugar

2 sprigs fresh thyme, stemmed

4 plump, fresh cloves garlic, peeled and slivered

2 tablespoons extra-virgin olive oil

2 CUPS

SUN-DRIED TOMATO PASTE

Pâte de Tomates Séchées

This delicious herb-flecked paste is a versatile condiment. It's an integral part of Taillevent Goat Cheese and Dried Tomato Appetizer (page 7) and can also be used as a sauce for your favorite pasta.

In the bowl of a food processor, combine all the ingredients and process until the paste is lightly emulsified but still quite coarse and almost chunky. (You do not want a smooth paste.) The paste can be stored in a jar in the refrigerator for up to 1 month. If you do so, first cover the paste with a film of olive oil. When using the paste, stir to incorporate the oil.

10 sun-dried tomatoes

1 plump, fresh clove garlic, green germ discarded, minced

½ teaspoon crushed red pepper flakes, or to taste

6 tablespoons extra-virgin olive oil

2 teaspoons minced fresh thyme leaves

2 teaspoons minced fresh rosemary leaves

½ CUP

TOMATO SAUCE

Sauce Tomate

This simple, classic tomato sauce can always be found next to the homemade chicken stock in my freezer. I depend on both of these staples for so many dishes. People are always surprised to learn that most homemade tomato sauce is made from canned tomatoes. But good-quality canned tomatoes offer excellent flavor and deep color, something that fresh tomatoes generally do not.

In a large skillet, heat the oil, onions, garlic, and salt over moderate heat. Cook just until the onions are soft and translucent, 3 to 4 minutes. Place a food mill over the skillet and purée the tomatoes directly into the pan. Add the bouquet garni and stir to blend. Simmer, uncovered, until the sauce is thickened, about 15 minutes. Taste for seasoning. Remove and discard the bouquet garni. The sauce may be used immediately, stored in the refrigerator for up to 2 days, or frozen for up to 3 months.

4 tablespoons extra-virgin olive oil

1 small onion, peeled and sliced

2 plump, fresh cloves garlic, peeled and minced

Sea salt to taste

Two 28-ounce cans peeled tomatoes in their juice

1 bouquet garni: several sprigs of fresh parsley, several bay leaves, and several celery leaves, tied in a bundle with cotton string

ABOUT 3 CUPS

VANILLA SUGAR

Sucre Vanillé

While tiny packets of vanilla sugar are a staple found in French supermarkets, I find it just as easy and economical to make my own, either using fresh or leftover vanilla beans.

8 cups (3½ pounds) sugar

2 fresh vanilla beans, or 4 used vanilla beans

8 CUPS (3½ POUNDS) SUGAR

Pour the sugar into an airtight container. Push the vanilla beans down into the sugar. Cover securely and let ripen for at least one week. Replenish the sugar as you use it, removing the sugar that is already flavored, adding new sugar to the container, and topping it off with the flavored sugar. Replace the vanilla beans every two months.

GENERAL BONAPARTE

MENUS

AN EASTER FEAST

Chez Benoît's Spring Salad

Jean-Guy's Basque-Spiced Leg of Lamb

L'Ambroisie's White Beans with Mustard and Sage

Eight-Grain Parisian Bread and Brie

Benoît's Upside-Down Caramelized Apple Tart

IT'S APRIL IN PARIS

Asparagus Velouté

Slow-Roasted Salmon with Sorrel Sauce

Noirmoutier Potatoes with Fleur de Sel

Parmesan Bread and Goat Cheese from the Loire

Strawberry-Orange Soup with Candied Lemon Zest

Miniature Lemon Tea Cakes

MAKE IT BISTRO

Hors d'Oeuvres Variés: Beets, Carrots, and Celery Root Remoulade

Le Mauzac's Hanger Steak

David Van Laer's Potatoes Anna

Chocolate Financiers

The Astor's Vanilla Custard Tarts

LEFT BANK MADNESS
Lamb's Lettuce and Beets
Chez Henri's Sautéed Potatoes
Benoît's Fricassee of Chicken with Morels
Carton's Ultra-Thin Apple Tart

WINTER IN THE CITY
Gallopin's Green Bean, Mushroom, and Hazelnut Salad
Place Monge Market Guinea Hen with Sauerkraut and Sausages
Bonbonnerie de Buci's Fresh Lemon Juice Tart

A SPRINGTIME PARISIAN PARTY
Boulevard Raspail Cream of Mushroom Soup
Asparagus, Morels, and Asparagus Cream
Manu's Grilled and Roasted Squab
JR's Herb Salad
Rue Poncelet Cherries in Sweet Red Wine
Alléosse Fromage Blanc Ice Cream

SUMMER ON THE SEINE
The Market Gardener's Zucchini and Curry Soup
The Bistrot du Dôme's Clams with Fresh Thyme
Rye Water Crackers and Camembert
Raspberry Pride

END-OF-SUMMER VEGETABLE FESTIVAL
Gazpacho
Domaine Saint Luc's Cake aux Olives and Tomato Sauce
Zucchini Stuffed with Goat Cheese and Mint
Eggplant, Tomato, and Parmesan Gratin
Fresh Fig and Almond Gratin

HALLOWEEN, PARIS-STYLE
Toasty Salted Almonds
JR's Parmesan Chips
Pumpkin Soup for Halloween
Parisian Roasted Turkey
Jerusalem Artichoke Purée
Benoît's Carrots with Cumin and Orange
Alain Passard's Turnip Gratin
The Apple Lady's Apple Cake
Maison du Miel Heather Honey Ice Cream

RIB-STICKING FARE
Flora's Polenta Fries
Flora's Spicy Spareribs
Blood Orange Ice Cream, Le Jardin de Courcelles
Jean-Luc Poujauran's Shortbread Cookies

MAKE MINE BISTRO

Mollard's Ham and Goat Cheese Wraps

Fricassee of Chicken with Two Vinegars

Sautéed Potatoes La Fontaine de Mars

Cherry-Almond Gratin

A SEAFOOD CELEBRATION

Spicy Langoustine Broth

La Cagouille's Sea Scallops with Warm Vinaigrette

Le Dôme's Sole Meunière

JR's Burnt Cream

A SPECIAL WINTER FEAST

Arpège Eggs with Maple Syrup

Taillevent's Cream of Watercress Soup with Caviar

Memories of Brittany Lobster with Cream

La Maison du Chocolat's Bittersweet Chocolate Mousse

A NEW YEAR'S CELEBRATION

Taillevent Goat Cheese and Tomato Appetizer

Le Duc's Hot Curried Oysters

Scrambled Eggs with Truffles

Jean-Luc Poujauran's Shortbread Cookies

Fresh Truffle Ice Cream

INDEX